Th

The Whole Truth, and Nothing but the Truth, so Help Me…

Peter E. Saunders

Fortis
Publishing Services

First Edition 2023

ISBN-13: 978-1-913822-37-8

This is a true story. All the major events happened.

Dedication

For Verity

Verity Elson passed away at the beginning of October 2021. She was a beautiful person and the last time I met with her, and her husband was in the early summer of that year. Verity was battling cancer, but she still welcomed my wife and me into her garden and even made a delicious cake for us.

As we sat in her garden, she asked me how I was progressing with my book. I admitted that I was struggling with it because I kept remembering things and wondering whether they should go in the book or not. Again, this goes back to my own self-doubt about whether I should be writing a book at all.

How I met Verity was interesting. She had seen me interviewed on TV and then agreed to take part in a documentary fronted by the well-known broadcaster and journalist Julie Etchingham. The documentary was mostly about the late Clement Freud and the abuse he had been accused of perpetrating. But Verity's story was told too, and shortly after the public screening she got in touch and we met for lunch. That was also the first time I had met Julie Etchingham when she came to the National Association for People Abused in Childhood (NAPAC) office to interview me for the documentary. Julie was very supportive of our work, and it was lovely to spend some time with her.

Verity urged me to finish my book because she wanted to read it before she died. I am so sorry that I didn't do that for her but because of her support and encouragement, at last I have achieved what I set out to do.

I dedicate this book to her memory.

Acknowledgements

I could probably fill a whole book with the names of people who, over the years, have helped me in a variety of ways. I start with my wife, Tricia. I can't begin to thank her enough for the love and support which she has given for nearly three decades, including at times when I have deserved neither. Tricia and I met when I was setting up NAPAC and from those earliest days she was my source of strength, determination and direction. NAPAC would not have happened without her. I thank our five precious children. From the earliest of days, they contributed to helping me and Tricia set the charity up and from those early days we had the support of so many other kind and generous people.

The early Trustees and supporters of NAPAC include Katie John - who I mention in the book -, Chris and Veronica Shellam, Debbie Keane, Gill Thomas, Delma Hughes, Fred Fever, Peter McParlin, Anita Scidoris, Jean Renvoize, Lee Moore, Hilton Dawson, Clive Brock, Clare Woodward, Jayne Larnie, Paul Hurford, Karen Nock, Laura Gordon, Debbie Allen and Josie Collins. There's Jim Harding too. He is the former director and chief executive of the NSPCC and was a supporter from the start and remains a great friend.

Doctor Valerie Sinason will never know just what an inspiration she is to me, as is my former therapist and life saver, Susie Orbach. Later Trustees include John Griffiths who not only became a Trustee but also raised money for the charity. We were also privileged to have the support of

Brian Douieb and Liz Davies. Liz is a professor of Social Work and for several years she invited me to give a lecture to her students. Brian, her partner, was briefly a greatly valued Trustee.

NAPAC had many wonderful volunteers, too. People like Maureen Floyd, Jean Gee, Anne Beard, Morven Fyfe and Diane Brown. If I tried to name them all I would inevitably miss some out, so I will just say they all know who they are, and I will be forever grateful for all they did.

The former chief executive of ChildLine Valerie (now Baroness) Howarth was incredibly kind and supportive. The late Claire Rayner OBE and many other agony aunts and uncles encouraged me. Deirdre Sanders was perhaps my greatest encourager in those early days.

Bob Borzello the founder of Camden Press was very generous and helpful. David Watson is a creative guy who did a lot to raise the image of the charity. And he did quite a lot free of charge. Thank you, David.

It's impossible to overstate just how much I and NAPAC owe to Ken Newell and his very supportive wife Lynne. At one point Ken seemed to be Chair, Treasurer and Secretary all rolled in to one. I met barrister James Badenoch KC whilst working for AVMA and he was also very supportive as I left that organisation and began to work full time for NAPAC.

I received encouragement from a great many people in the media. At the BBC there were Tom Symonds and Daniel De Simone. Martine Croxall was someone else at the BBC who was always good to talk to and always very supportive of the cause. At Sky News I received great encouragement from Martin Brunt and I took part in a number of documentaries where again I met some wonderful people, Julie Etchingham and Jane McSorley to name but two. Then there was Neal at LBC. I never met this chap but he used to ring me regularly and I was a speaker on many of their radio programmes. There was James O'Brien, Sheila Fogarty, Nick Ferrari, Eddie Mayer and Ian Dale. They all gave me a lot of airtime and I am grateful.

Jeremy Vine and Nicky Campbell at the BBC were also very supportive and Nicky recently revealed the abuse he suffered at his school in Edinburgh. Colin Campbell at BBC News South East also did a great deal of work uncovering abuse scandals, particularly in religious institutions, and he always got in touch with me for comment when relevant. I would also like to thank Tara Brown, Gareth Harvey and the team at *60 Minutes, Australia.* They were incredibly kind and flew me and my wife to Rome for a very important interview. Later on they flew me to Australia for another interview. This was all in connection with the scandal surrounding the late Cardinal George Pell, the former head of the Vatican's economic department.

Peter Spindler is a retired police officer with the London Metropolitan Police. I mention him in my book, but he also deserves a special mention here because he supported the charity outside of his official duties. He brought his wife and teenage children to our fundraising comedy night at the Bloomsbury Theatre, as did Martin Brunt.

Although I never had the pleasure of meeting her, I was encouraged in my pontifical commission role by Mary McAleese, the former president of the Republic of Ireland. We exchanged a few pleasant emails and we had planned to meet up one day, but it didn't happen.

I thank my dear friend Miguel Hurtado, a Spanish survivor and activist and fellow scribe, who was one of the first people to encourage me to write this book.

Valerie Jay supported me from the earliest days and did a fantastic job responding to the many letters from survivors which NAPAC received every day. We were fortunate to have some amazing and dedicated staff. Helen Munt joined NAPAC virtually straight from university, and what an asset she was to the charity. Likewise, Julie Brock was an inspirational colleague. Other staff who were to prove so vital to the charity's success include Jon Bird, Sarah Kelly, Heather Brook, Rob Jones, Jackie Duffy and Lorraine and Jo Hawkins. We also benefitted from having a couple of volunteer interns, Josh Henry and Luke Newell. Each was only with us a short time, but their contributions were very helpful to the organisation.

Other supporters like Julien Whiting and Geoff Reed came up with some great fundraising ideas and are loyal friends. Noel Chardon and Margaret Kennedy are two people who deserve medals for the work they did in challenging the Catholic Church and its appalling record on child abuse. Some, who couldn't give their time, gave us financial support instead. These included Pete Townshend (yes! he of The Who) and John Newton. Two remarkable men. Another early and greatly valued supporter was Tricia Kreitman.

My good friends in Seattle, Tim and Chris Law, George and Cheryl Mead and Sheila and Charlie Wyckoff-Dickey have all been incredibly kind and generous to me and NAPAC. They were also instrumental in setting up the organisation Ending Clergy Abuse (ECA).

Others involved in setting up ECA include Francesco and Simone in Italy, Matthias Katsch in Germany, Alberto

Athie in Mexico, Sara in Ecuador, Francois and Nadia in France, Evelyn in Canada, and a whole host of wonderful people from Chile and Peru. I am privileged to have supportive friends as far afield as New Zealand. Campaigning activist Murray Peter Heasley and his wife Analyn live there, as does Dame Justice Lowell Goddard, the former chair of the Independent Inquiry into Child Sexual Abuse. It's been good to keep in touch with her. Someone else who I will always be grateful to is another former inquiry staff member. Her name is Ella O'Brien. She is a very special lady because in the dark days of the summer of 2019, she really was able to help me put the unpleasant goings on into perspective. She remains a much-loved friend. I've met with many good and kind people as I have battled with the Church establishment. I mention Tom Doyle in the book. What an amazing man. Jason Berry is another author who shone a light on the corruption within the Church as well as Lieve Halsberghe, a Belgian woman, who has done so much to challenge the Church and support survivors.

From long ago I remember the kindness of Stacey Watts and Rita Harrison. The people who used to run the Body Shop Foundation were so kind, too. Such a shame that this wonderful organisation disappeared when the business was taken over by another corporation.

I remember my friends in the legal profession who were kind to both me and NAPAC. Tracey Storey at Irwin Mitchell Solicitors stands out, as do the folk at Leigh Day, Slater Gordon and Gary Walker at Enable Law in Devon. Peter Garsden at Simpson Millar in Manchester was also a great friend. Keith Porteous Wood at the British Secular Society has also been a constant supporter and friend. I will leave aside the names of the celebrities who have supported NAPAC. As one A-lister said to me many years ago, he doesn't want the *Daily Mail* knocking on his door wanting all the salacious detail. But they all know who they are.

And to my friends in my cycling club, especially Jon Bentley, Mike Robson, Hugh Webb, Mike Casey, Neil Morgan, Andy Ivy, Bill Mantz, Neil Morgan, Debbie Curran, Karen Jones and Steve Fagan. You have all helped me more than I can say. And Panagua Bike Shop in Hayes, Bromley deserves a mention. Dave and the team there were always helpful and willing to have a NAPAC collecting tin in their beautiful shop. A very special thanks to my cycling friend Andrew Burbridge. Andrew was a champion cyclist in his younger days (something I aspired to) but more importantly he has always been a good friend. And like the saying says, friends are like stars, you don't have to see them to know they are there'. While on the sporting theme, I must mention my great and inspirational friend, Oliver Dudley. Oli was part of a crew that broke the trans-Atlantic rowing record in 2008. In doing so he raised thousands of pounds for the charity and it was when I went to Barbados to welcome their boat that I met footballing legend John Barnes, who I mention a little later.

I must also thank Mike Rezendez, Sacha Pfieffer and Marty Baron, the Pulitzer Prize winning team at the Boston Globe, for their support and a very special thanks to Tom McCarthy, the director of the Oscar winning film *Spotlight* who kindly mentioned me live on TV at the BAFTAs in 2016.

And finally … thank you to my dear friends at Fortis Publishing. I spent a month with Ken Scott near his home in Spain, on this, the final draft. I was also lucky enough to catch up with Reinette Visser, one of the directors, who treated me and my wife like royalty! It was a difficult time writing this and I visited many dark places, and without Ken Scott's encouragement and determination to get this story out, and at times his not so gentle persuasion, this book may never have been completed. Thank you for your patience, amigo!

'Good is something you do, not something you talk about. Some medals are pinned to your soul, not to your jacket.'
Gino Bartali - Tour de France winner, 1938, 1948.

I thank you for buying my book and ask that you kindly write a review on Amazon.

If you would like to contact me, I am available on Facebook, X, Instagram, and LinkedIn

With thanks,
Peter E Saunders

Part One

Chapter 1

July 2014. As I exited the arrivals hall at Rome's Leonardo da Vinci airport, I spotted a man with a sign bearing my name. He had been sent from the Vatican to pick me up. It wasn't quite the big limousine I was half expecting but it bore a papal flag and as it whisked me and my travelling companion in the direction of Vatican City, I sensed something very special was happening. I was on my way to meet Pope Francis.

If you weren't raised Catholic it is quite hard to describe the lasting impact this experience has on you. Other religions are sometimes accused of brainwashing or radicalising their members but I don't think there is an institution that achieves this more successfully than the Roman Catholic Church.

My faith meant everything to me as a boy and as a young adult. I liked the idea of being a priest, to be able to change bread and wine into the body and blood of Jesus was very appealing. I knew priests were supposed to be celibate, but I liked the idea of an adoring church full of young women swooning over my every word and flocking to me for spiritual guidance.

To Catholics, a priest is the conduit to God and the pope his representative on earth. All this was reinforced by my Catholic education, firstly at the Sacred Heart Primary School then later at the Jesuit run Wimbledon College. I have more to say about these institutions a little later.

The historic meeting with the pope was in no small part due to the amazing, unique organisation I had set up in the UK. It is called NAPAC, The National Association for People Abused in Childhood. It was also due in part, no doubt, because I had been an outspoken critic of the Catholic Church on matters of abuse for many years.

I was speaking from experience. I was abused throughout my early life, firstly by a teacher at my primary school and then by a non-blood relative. Two Jesuit priests at the aforementioned Wimbledon College also abused me, a place where my brother Mike was also abused and it seems, countless others.

When, for a number of reasons which I will elaborate on later, my life seemed to be falling apart and as I was approaching 40 years of age, I discovered that there was virtually no help out there for people like me – for adults who had suffered childhood abuse. There seemed to be no one I could talk to about it, nobody who would understand.

The strange thing is, at that point I didn't realise just how many people in this world had suffered abuse in their childhood. Little did I know then that it is an evil pandemic.

However, the scariest thing of all is that it is a pandemic that exists and thrives in plain sight. The outrage about the late Sir Jimmy Savile is a case in point. His history of abusing was virtually an open secret, but nobody did anything about it. Even in the face of his own boasts about abusing young girls no one tried to stop him.

He counted Prime Minister Thatcher and members of the royal family among his friends. In some ways it seemed the more outrageous and boastful Savile was the more he got away with. The TV programme that exposed his life of offending, ITV's Exposure, aired in the autumn of 2012 and it was to bring NAPAC and me the sort of media coverage that corporations would pay millions for.

Every day for many, many weeks I was sitting in a TV or radio studio talking about Savile. And it wasn't just in the UK. It was a scandal that was picked up in many other parts of the world, doubtless because he was so closely associated with the BBC, a media corporation that certainly up to that point was seen as the global leader in broadcasting.

Other scandals or events that helped to put NAPAC firmly on the map included, no surprise here, those around the Catholic Church. When Pope Benedict was to visit Britain in 2010, NAPAC received a delegation of people from the National Catholic Safeguarding body. Whilst at first I hoped they were coming along to throw their weight behind our work supporting survivors of abuse, it seemed their real intention was to dissuade us from saying or doing anything negative during the pope's forthcoming visit.

Pope Benedict's own brother (another priest) had been accused of abuse cover-ups but this didn't overshadow his visit to Britain. But many other churches' abuse scandals certainly did. And I make no apologies for my constant references to the Catholic Church. It is an institution that had me in its grip from the day I was born. Catholics will understand this and it has taken me a long, long time to grasp the benign nature of its power and to finally break free. Jesus, the man, had a simple message that said love one another for which he was crucified by religious zealots.

For thousands of years, that simple message of love has been turned and twisted by the religious zealots to suit their own agenda and purpose. For example, take a look at this historical religious oath.

> *I furthermore promise and declare that I will, when opportunity presents, make and wage relentless war, secretly or openly, against all heretics, Protestants and Liberals, as I am directed to do, to extirpate and exterminate them from the face of the whole earth; and that I will spare neither age, sex or condition; and that I will hang, waste, boil, flay, strangle and bury alive these infamous heretics, rip up the stomachs and wombs of their women and crush their infants' heads against the walls, in order to annihilate forever their execrable race. That when the same cannot be done openly, I will secretly use the poisoned cup, the strangulating cord, the steel of the poniard or the leaden bullet, regardless of the honour, rank, dignity, or authority of the person or persons, whatever may be their condition in life, either public or private, as I at any time may be directed so to do by any agent of the pope or Superior of the Brotherhood of the Holy Faith, of the Society of Jesus.*

You could be forgiven for thinking that they may have been the words of some crazed Nazi, or the Mongols who slaughtered a large percentage of the world's population during their reign of terror. But no, I'm quoting the Catholic brotherhood of the Jesuits, the oath that all Jesuits used to take and the pope I was going to meet was a proud Jesuit.

Today the Jesuits take three simple vows of poverty, chastity and obedience to the superior of their Order and the pope.

Jorge Mario Bergoglio became Pope Francis a year before my visit, and I had high hopes that he was going to do something about the abuse that was gripping our Church. I was on my way to meet a man who one could argue was the most powerful person on the planet, a man who led a congregation of more than a billion people, a man who thus far seemed to have achieved universal praise, and not just from Catholics.

To this very day and doubtless to his passing, Jorge Bergoglio seems to have the 'Teflon' gift. Whatever he does, or doesn't do, it really does not seem to affect his favourable ratings. He comes across as an affable grandfatherly figure, always smiling, always willing to kiss a baby. He has the air of someone who sometimes looks a little uncomfortable in his role.

Yes, Pope Francis remains popular but on the issue of child abuse he has done absolutely nothing concrete to stamp it out in the Church. In fact his affable personality and great public relations skills have potentially made him a more dangerous individual than his predecessors. Never forget, even evil dictators of the 20th century were kind to children and animals. Or so it appeared.

As our car swept through the gates of the Vatican, Swiss Guards saluted and when we stopped by the door of the Domus Sanctae Marthae, the residence where the pope lives, we were greeted by more saluting Swiss Guards. There was not a hint of security, no checking of bags.

Nothing, but I had the strongest feeling that not just anyone could walk in there as easily as I had.

After checking in at a large reception desk staffed by two young women, I was given keys to my room and a key fob that would allow me entry and exit to the Vatican. My room, which as I recall was on the second floor, was large but sparsely furnished. There was no TV and no minibar! It seemed very appropriate accommodation. There was the obligatory large crucifix above the bed.

I unpacked my bag, pinched myself that this was really happening, had a shower and went downstairs. It was dinnertime so I headed for the refectory. Already seated was my travelling companion, Danny Sullivan, and a man in a brown monk's outfit who turned out to be cardinal archbishop of Boston, Sean O'Malley. A more affable looking chap you couldn't wish to meet. Sean O'Malley is a member of the pope's inner circle, he is also the President of the pope's recently formed Pontifical Commission for the Protection of Minors.

As I sat down I was pleased to see there was wine to drink. I wondered how tortuous the evening might become without a little alcohol, sitting in a room with a bunch of clerics being served by nuns.

Dinner was served buffet style and I made sure I poured myself a large glass of wine. Halfway through the meal I noticed the door open and in walked the pope. He was on his own, he glanced across in my direction and presumably was thinking, 'Who are those people, I haven't seen them before.' He went to the buffet bar, served himself some food then sat down. It really did seem a little surreal, sitting in a canteen with the pope.

The conversation with Cardinal O'Malley was convivial. My darling wife had long challenged me to not be overawed or intimidated by "celebrity", they are just people like us, she said, they fart just like the rest of us. Typical of her line of thinking!

Cardinal O'Malley was talking to me and he suggested that it could be quite an overwhelming experience, perhaps even anticlimactic, when I meet the pope the following day.

I responded, 'If the Holy Father has such an experience I am sure he will soon get over it.' Everybody laughed. Well, not everybody. There were a few sour-faced people sitting round the table who looked rather disgusted at my wise crack. If you want to experience sour-faced people look no further than a Catholic community of clerics.

The pope stood up and made his way to the door. I looked straight at him and caught his eye. I waved and beckoned him over. Amazingly, he came.

I turned to O'Malley. 'The pope is coming over.'

'He won't want you to stand up for him,' he said.

I stood up. Pope or no pope it is polite to stand when you meet someone for the first time. The cardinal introduced him to the people sitting round the table and then he got to me.

I was introduced as 'Peter Saunders, the man who set up NAPAC in the UK.' The pope clearly knew who I was and we exchanged a warm handshake. I asked him if he would be watching the football later because Argentina was to play Germany in the World Cup. (The pope is Argentinian and most Argentinians are football crazy.) He smiled and laughed with me and in that moment I realised that my wife was right. He was just a man in a posh white outfit.

After dinner I snuck out of the Vatican and headed for the nearest bar. One can only take so much clericalism and pomp. But I didn't stay out late. I had to be up early in the morning because the pope would be saying Mass and I had a front row seat. Mass took place in the pope's private chapel. It was small, intimate and nicely furnished. After Mass we had breakfast then was told that we would each be seeing the pope on our own and there would be no time restriction.

This seemed to me to be getting better and better. There were a few other survivors of clergy abuse from different European countries, including Germany and Ireland. I think there were six or seven of us, so the pope was looking at a potentially long morning of discussions.

Of course he was not on his own, Cardinal O'Malley was with him, ostensibly to simply interpret, but I know that senior clerics such as the pope would always have someone with them to make sure he doesn't say the wrong thing, to make sure he sticks to the party line.

I am reminded of my meeting with Cardinal Basil Hume, the archbishop of Westminster many years earlier, whom I met, just the two of us in his office. He was full of promises and offers of help, he even promised to help me set up NAPAC. Needless to say his offers of help never materialised, they died in that room on that day.

It's a bit like meeting government ministers. I've done it a few times and they always have officials and advisors watching over them. A bit like the popular TV comedy, *Yes Minister*, I suppose.

Having met Pope Francis the previous evening I felt very comfortable going into the small room where he and O'Malley were sitting. We each sat in comfortable armchairs. It didn't have the feel of an interview and I didn't feel intimidated at all.

I would be a liar if I said I could remember everything I said to the pope, once again it all felt rather surreal but I genuinely thought I was a part of history-making. I had high hopes, I really thought things in the Church would change. I was fully prepared and open for Pope Francis to prove to me that he wanted to be part of history too, to bring in a new dawn, an era of openness and one in which he would embrace us survivors. I wanted him to be so different from his predecessors.

The Jimmy Savile scandal really put NAPAC on the map but the charity had already received a lot of media attention in the past, especially around Pope Benedict's visit to the UK four years earlier in 2010. That was the year when I strongly re-connected (if that is the right expression) with the Catholic Church.

In the run up to Benedict's visit, as mentioned above, NAPAC received a delegation from the Catholic National Safeguarding Commission. In a way I suppose these interactions with Church officials was to be the basis on which I would later be invited to meet Pope Francis. Little did any of us know at this time that Pope Benedict would end up resigning from the Papacy and would be succeeded by a much friendlier, much more PR savvy Jorge Mario Bergoglio.

The Catholic delegation clearly wanted me and NAPAC to keep a low profile during Pope Benedict's visit, but that was never going to happen.

Around this time I had made contact with an American organisation called SNAP, the Survivors Network of those Abused by Priests. Another amazing community of survivors. They were to send a delegation over to the UK to stand alongside survivors and protest at the pope's inaction.

Barbara Blaine, the founder of SNAP, a woman of true vision and inspiration, arrived from Chicago just before Pope Benedict's trip. Barbara became a great friend. One of the delegation, a former policewoman from New York, stayed at our home during the visit. She was a lovely lady but her story was heart-breaking. As a young girl she had been held down by nuns whilst a priest raped her. This had been a regular occurrence in her childhood and the effect it had on her was profound and painful. How could it not be? To be held down by "women of God" and raped by a "man of God" is almost beyond belief. Pure evil. And again, not uncommon. I have heard similar accounts of abuse from other survivors over the years.

Benedict had joined a long line of popes for whom the abuse scandal in the Church was a major nuisance and who took no real action to tackle it. Pope Benedict, as well as failing to tackle abuse in the Church, also had a brother named Father Georg Ratzinger (another priest), who was heavily implicated in an abuse scandal. More than 200 children in a choir had alleged they had been beaten and sexually abused over almost four decades in Germany. Although there was no suggestion that Georg Ratzinger was involved in the alleged crimes, many of the allegations came at a time when the choir-linked boarding school was under his directorship. Franz Wittenbrink, a composer who had been at the school, said 'a sophisticated sadistic system of punishment in connection with sexual lust had been installed in the Regensburger Domspatzen boys choir.' He said that it was inexplicable that the pope's brother knew nothing about it.

In response, a Vatican spokesman at the time stated, 'The allegations of sexual abuse in the Regensburger case was a campaign aimed against the pope and the Catholic Church comparable to Nazi propaganda.'!

The allegations were nevertheless investigated. Ulrich Weber, a lawyer leading the probe commissioned by the Catholic Diocese of Regensburger, said that 231 alleged victims included 50 who had made "plausible" claims of sexual abuse between 1953 and 1992. More than 140 people were interviewed as part of his 8-month investigation which concluded that almost a third of all pupils at the school suffered some form of abuse, including sexual assault ranging from touching to rape. A report in 2017 faulted Ratzinger for "looking away" and "failing to intervene", but he was never implicated in any of the accusations. By then the figure of boys "plausibly physically or sexually abused", stood at a staggering 547.

Ratzinger had a long and distinguished career in the Catholic Church. In his later years he was awarded the Austrian Cross of Honour for Science and Art (2004), The Honorary Citizenship of Castel Gandolfo (2008), The Order of Merit of the Italian Republic (2009) and awarded Pontifical Vespers of the Bishop of Regensburger Cathedral (2009).

Pope Francis had also come in for his fair share of criticism when it came to a controversy in Chile about abuse that had occurred and been overlooked by successive popes. But Pope Francis took the controversy to a whole new level when he promoted to bishop a man who had been seriously implicated in one of the biggest abuse scandals in South America.

Father Juan Barros had been present when the infamous priest Father Karadima had abused dozens of boys and young men and failed to report it.

To promote Father Barros to Bishop of Osorno was as big a slap in the face to survivors as there could be. Even when I was still part of the papal commission, the previous summer, I and a number of other commission members had flown to Rome to speak with the pope about this grave error he was making. We weren't allowed to speak to him and instead was fobbed off with an archbishop who said, 'Osorno is just a tiny blip on a map and not a great part of the pope's thinking'. I pointed out to the archbishop that children and their protection was as important in this little outpost of Osorno as it was anywhere else in the world. He reluctantly agreed.

That response shocked me and to add fuel to the fire, when some Chileans had protested in Rome about the Barros appointment, the pope made some quite disparaging remarks about the people of Osorno. He said the Osorno community is suffering as, 'It's dumb, because it has let its head be filled with what politicians say, judging a bishop without any proof. Don't be led by the nose by the leftists who orchestrated all of this,' he said.

So bearing in mind the anger and dismay I felt at Pope Benedict's inaction, I made it plain to Pope Francis that I didn't want to be part of a public relations exercise. I wanted strong and immediate action and in the moment I thought I was talking to a man who was going to do just that. I was wrong, but I didn't know that at the time.

At the end of the conversation - by the way, Pope Francis certainly knew some English - , I gave him a Big Foot Cycling Club racing hat and pointed out that on this very day of meeting him, the Tour de France had a stage finish in London and that it had been a toss-up as to whether I stayed for that or I came to Rome to meet him. Once again he laughed, once again I realised that he was just a man like me. We shook hands and then I asked Cardinal O'Malley if he wouldn't mind taking a photo of me with the Holy Father.

Francis even offered to place the racing cap on his head but I thought that might be a slightly humiliating thing for him to do, though looking back I wish I'd let him!

The resulting photo of me with my arm round the pope is, in the words of one of my cycling club pals, a professional photographer himself, the best photo he has ever seen.

I spoke to the pope a few more times during my few days at the Vatican. I really thought we had made some sort of connection. We agreed to pray for each other and I told him if he ever visited the UK he could come to our house for a roast dinner. My wife's is the best! He laughed and nodded and I even asked him to write a message on a postcard to my dear friend Kathy, which he did.

That's when I realised that his English was better than had been made out. He asked me how to phrase something as he wrote. Yes, the pope understands my language!

Although we (the survivors who met Francis) were offered the opportunity to speak with the world's press, this was something I turned down. I wanted to wait and see if the pope was a man of his word, to see if he was really serious about this issue.

I only gave one interview and that was to a young freelancer who was writing for *The Boston Globe*. I told her I was impressed with the pope, that he had listened and taken me seriously. I told her I was confident he would take positive steps to protect our children.

I wasn't sure I would ever visit Rome again. This was my first visit, so I thought I would take in and absorb as much as I could in the brief time I was there. I didn't venture far from the Vatican but I noticed how affluent and how ostentatious some of the Vatican's employees were. It wasn't just the Swiss Guards in their colourful outfits. I saw cardinals and bishops wandering around in outfits that must have cost a fortune, some even carried swords. Yes, men of God carrying swords in 2014!

I went out the next evening and had dinner with Danny. He is a good man. He was previously the head of the Catholic Safeguarding Body in England and Wales. But again, I noticed the sheer number of clerics who were dining out in splendour. I'm not saying priests and other clerics aren't entitled to the occasional treat but this just didn't feel right. It was quite seductive in some ways, seeing how these people lived, but by this time I was already having serious doubts about the whole religious thing. I had long realised that it would not have been a life for me. I used to think that being a Christian was about loving one another and loving God, but the atmosphere surrounding the headquarters of the biggest church on the planet, felt false and wrong.

When I look back on my visit I realised that all I really got from it was a rosary from the pope and a constant pleading from him to, 'Pray for me.'

Chapter 2

Being a "good boy" as opposed to the "naughty boy" I was frequently referred to, seemed more important to my parents than having fun. My parents rarely played or interacted with me and I was always conscious that I was something of a nuisance to them. My mother frequently said I would be 'the death of her,' not a good burden to place on a child.

I still remember crying myself to sleep believing that Mum was going to die and it would be my fault. What a horrible thing to say to a child and it's a story I've heard repeated.

My parents' expectations of their children were not particularly high and in many ways we (five of us) all lived up to their assessment. By this I mean my mother used to say she always wanted a son to be a priest. None of her three boys became priests, though I seriously considered it as a teenager but knew I could never be celibate.

The fact that one of her girls became a nun didn't seem to count.

My parents met during the early days of World War II. Dad was in the Royal Air Force and Mum was in the

Woman's Auxiliary Air Force, the "WAAFs". They married in uniform in November 1940 whilst Dad was on weekend leave. I still have the telegram my dad sent to my mum that November, stating that he had a weekend leave pass and would return so that they could get married, which they did at the local Catholic Church.

By the end of the war they had three children: Anthony, Mary and Pauline. They lived in a one bedroom flat in Wimbledon. None of my siblings was evacuated during the conflict. Mum wanted them to stay together, which they did throughout most of the war. I remember her telling me how my eldest brother Tony would run his rattle up and down the bars of the bomb "cage" they all got into during the bombing and Mum would shout, 'Stop it, I can't hear the bombs.' The place they lived in was not far from a railway marshalling yard so bombing was a regular occurrence.

I was born in 1957 during the same week that my eldest brother Tony left school. He was 15. I found out many years later that Tony had been offered a place at an independent boarding school but the cost would run to about a pound a week. Whilst that may have caused some financial hardship for my parents it was not insurmountable.

What was insurmountable was my mother's determination not to let him go. She had an almost obsessive sense of possession around her precious boys and we all suffered from this in different ways. So, Tony missed out on a potentially better education though from what we now know about many boarding schools he may have had a lucky escape. Tony, I was told, was a "naughty boy" and got up to all sorts of mischief. Consequently he received regular beatings from Dad.

I remember one of my sisters telling me that Tony was caught trying to give the household cat a bath in the kitchen sink. That didn't go down well with either the cat or Dad, who then gave Tony a thrashing for his efforts.

All my grandparents predeceased me. My mum's dad was killed in action during World War I and her mum died when Mum was a teenager. Mum had a brother, a sister and a half-sister.

Mum was born and raised in a mining community in north-east England, Seaham in County Durham, but when her mum died she moved to London where she went into service. This would have been in the 1920s. I am aware that Mum had a stepfather (following the death of her dad) but all she ever said about him was he was a horrible man and that she didn't want to talk about him. I also remember her referring to some very cruel nuns at the school she attended. Where have I heard that before?

My dad's parents also died before I was born. My grandad died in 1955 and my grandmother died the year before I was born. All our family have brown eyes except me. Mine are blue and I was told I got them from my grandmother.

Ours was a devout Roman Catholic family. I was the baby, or the mistake, as my sister used to call me. Pauline, who was 13 when I was born became my primary caregiver. My other sister, who was 14 years older than me, left home at 17 and entered a convent. My eldest brother was 15 when I was born and the sibling closest to me in age was Michael who was six years older than me.

I slept in a cot in my parents' room until I was three or four then shared a room with my two brothers. I slept in the lower bunk bed with Mike above, but I always aspired to sleep up there instead. I didn't have to wait too long. By the time I was about 12, Mike had pretty much moved out. He went travelling. He hitchhiked to India. We used to get postcards from all over the world, not enough to keep my mum happy, just the occasional message.

My father was an accountant and my mother a housewife. Corporal punishment was routine at home and at school. I was a lonely child and was never encouraged to have friends around to play. Every night we all knelt down to say the rosary. Many Catholic families will doubtless be able to identify with that and the first thing my dad would do the moment he got up in the morning was go downstairs, light the coal fire and say his prayers, on his knees. He did that pretty well until the days leading up to his death.

At age five I went to the Sacred Heart Primary School in New Malden. As a child not used to mixing with other children, I found the whole experience daunting. I also found out quite quickly that some of the teachers there were not good news for children. Some clearly did not like us. I often wonder why on earth some of them went into teaching.

The head teacher, Mr O'Brien, was a serial child abuser. Years later I found out that some of the mothers of the children at the school had reported him to the local bishop. Some of their children had come home and told them that Mr O'Brien had regularly abused them in his office and to use their exact words, 'Made us do things to each other'.

It doesn't take a great deal of imagination to work out what this sick individual was making the children do.

What he did to me still traumatises me to this day because I was small and physically unable to resist or repel his advances. I was still in the infants school when he first made me drop my trousers and underpants for a reason that was so trivial I can't even recall what it was. He then made me lie across his lap and spanked me hard for three or four minutes. It bloody hurt, it was so painful but even at that age, it wasn't the pain that disturbed me the most but the manner in which it was carried out, behind a locked door.

I found out what he did to other children many years later in 1995. This was the year my father died. Dad's death was the trigger that set me on the long path of healing and the setting up of NAPAC.

For as long as I can remember I was brought up to feel worthless and guilty. Being born into a strict Catholic family, the teachings of God and the Church were drummed into me from a very early age. That said, there were parts of the Church and Christ's teachings that I adored. As a child and teenager I served Mass at our church on a regular basis and my dad was a reader at Sunday Mass, the nine o'clock edition. He never missed it. He also served Mass every Friday evening where he taught youngsters how to serve.

My dad really loved the Church and spent many hours at meetings of Catholic organisations, like the Knights of Saint Columba and the Sodality of Our Lady. He was also involved in the local interdenominational movement but being a good Catholic always regarded "our" Church as the only real one.

Dad was also an ardent supporter of the anti-abortion movement and an active member of ACTU , the Association of Catholic Trade Unionists. Looking back I wonder how much of Dad's church activities were down to him actually wanting to get away from Mum. She gave us all a hard time and Dad was not excluded from that.

The extrovert in me used to enjoy Mass. It was a lot less boring than sitting in the pews and you got a great view from the sanctuary. What's more, lighting and blowing out the candles was fun and there was something strangely hypnotic about being in the sacristy both before and after Mass. I think it was the strong smell of incense and, of course, at Benediction (another regular serving opportunity), you occasionally got to carry and swing the thurible - the vessel into which the priest poured incense over hot coals and which subsequently stunk the church out.

One of the other benefits of being a regular Mass server was the opportunity to serve at weddings and funerals and these tended to bring in a hefty financial bonus. I sometimes got the equivalent of a weeks' pocket money for one wedding service.

And yet it somehow all came back to worthlessness and guilt.

As a Roman Catholic child I was introduced to the idea of mortal sin and the stain of original sin. From an early age I felt I was up against it.

I had strong feelings that I was stained with sin. I was told by a priest that I had been born with the stain of original sin. I felt dirty even before I had been abused. I remember thinking about how to scrub clean this dirty soul of mine. I had a very strong belief in God but I suspected I was always going to have problems living up to expectations.

A mortal sin cannot happen by accident. A person who commits a mortal sin is one who knows that their sin is wrong, but still deliberately commits it anyway. It's a rejection of God's law and love. That's fine, I thought, as long I knew what they were. We had a list of sins handed to us on a pamphlet. The first few… no problem: magic, sorcery, sacrilege, atheism, murder, blasphemy, perjury. Simple, I could avoid all of those. Next, failure to attend Mass. I loved Mass, but even so, even as a small child I thought it a bit harsh. Missing Mass was a mortal sin which would ultimately end with me going to hell?

I read on. Scandal, drug abuse, gluttony, alcohol abuse. My brother was abusing alcohol frequently at this point. Oh, dear. Extreme anger, hatred, pornography, prostitution, rape, homosexual acts, incest, masturbation, theft, cheating, unfair rages, taking advantage of the poor, false witness, adulation, lying, lust, envy, doubt of faith, heresy, despair in hope, presumption, indifference, ingratitude, lukewarmness. Was there no end to this list?

Now I was seriously worried because even at that young impressionable age, I knew that I had committed at least half a dozen of these "mortal sins", and therefore I would surely be condemned to an early death and end up in hell. And Hell was no holiday camp, it was a terrifying concept, a place of torment, everlasting punishment for the wicked, the land of darkness and deep shadow, anguish and burning flames.

I now know only too well what was happening in my early Catholic Church education. I was being indoctrinated and fed a diet of guilt. The Jesuits believed that if they could teach the child what they needed to teach them from an early age, they would belong to them forever. As they wrote way back in the 15th Century, 'For thus could the mind, reason and imagination of innumerable young people, from their first inclination towards independent thought and emotion up to full maturity, be permanently and systematically influenced in the best and most effective manner.’

From the priests and the nuns to the lay teachers, and even my own parents, my indoctrination was well and truly under way.

Chapter 3

From the age of eight until I was 14 my brother-in-law sexually and psychologically abused me. In common with many other survivors of abuse I cannot say how often it occurred. I remember the first time it happened. He sneaked into my bedroom when I stayed over at his house and climbed into bed with me. He lay on top of me, he was so heavy. I couldn't move an inch and was finding it difficult to breath.

To my utmost horror he shoved his hand down into my pyjama bottoms and grabbed my genitalia. He wouldn't let go and he was rubbing and pulling me, saying things that seemed to make no sense. I was crying and telling him to stop, I closed my eyes and started to pray to God, 'Please Lord, please make him stop.' The tears were running down my cheeks and I was begging him to leave me alone but he wouldn't and nor did God come to rescue me.

"C'mon Peter, I'll make you come, let me make you come."

I had no idea what on earth he was on about. Eventually after what seemed like an eternity, he left, snorting as he sneaked quietly out of the bedroom.

I didn't sleep that night. I lay in bed terrified, shaking like a leaf wondering what had happened and, more importantly, why this man who I looked up to had done what he had done. I watched as the rays of the sun crept into my bedroom and dared to hope that what had happened was a bad nightmare.

I wished it had been a bad nightmare and yet who was I kidding, I knew it had happened.

I heard the sounds of the breakfast table being set, my sister talking to George and realised that I had to go downstairs. I pulled on my clothes and reluctantly walked down the stairs, wondering what George's reaction would be when he saw me. He acted as if nothing had happened and asked me if I wanted some cornflakes or something cooked. I looked at my sister who stood by the kitchen bench making coffee.

'Sleep well, Peter?' she asked.

I mumbled, 'Yes', sat down at the table and we ate breakfast.

George was 22 years older than me and died a few years ago at age 82. He was separated from my sister many years before his death. His assaults and humiliations of her became too much for her to bear and she made him move out. By this time they had four children. I adored them all and I was pretty much the permanent babysitter. Why, you might ask, was I a regular babysitter when part of that scenario was to suffer abuse? All I can say is that I was a child. He came into my life when I was seven and he held great power over me and, needless to say, I adored my sister with whom this man was living and fathering their four children. If you ask an adult domestic abuse victim why they didn't just leave, you will struggle to understand the answer.

Think about how a small child feels. Confused is an understatement.

I am unable to recall how many times the sexual assaults took place. Like many other survivors I blocked out as much painful memory as I could and even as I write now, decades later, some memories are coming back. One thing is for certain and that is that I got absolutely no pleasure from what this man did to me. It was painful and he said things to me which at the time meant nothing and only as an adult do I understand what he was saying.

At that time I was also being abused at primary school by Mr O'Brien. I hated it. Some of the teachers were also very vicious in their treatment of us. One in particular used to shake me so violently that I felt as though my head would fall off.

Another teacher, I'll call him Mr Scott, used the cane so viciously that at times we thought he was going to burst a blood vessel or have a heart attack. His reddened, contorted face was a most scary sight for us as young children. Nobody wanted the cane from Scott, how he didn't break anyone's wrist I'll never know.

I got the cane several times from Scott in class, always in class. I think if anyone had seen him publicly being so violent towards young boys he would have probably ended up on a grievous bodily harm charge.

I was in the school dining room one day, we were having fish and chips, and Mr Scott was the teacher on dining room duties, wandering around the tables, making sure we ate our lunch and didn't misbehave. I remember the fish was bloody awful and I made a comment to the boys on my table that the piece in my mouth was so bad it must have been the bum hole of the fish. They all laughed, and I laughed along with them, but when Mr Scott took hold of my right ear and twisted hard, the smile was quickly wiped from my face.

He pulled my ear, forcing me to stand and marched me to Mr Hawkins' office. He was the head teacher at the time. I was going to be caned. Scott told Hawkins that I had said a rude word in the dining hall and, of course, I couldn't deny it.

Scott left and Mr Hawkins dished out two strokes of the cane. It hurt like hell but I remember walking out of his office thanking God that it hadn't been Mr Scott who had caned me, such was the ferocity of his beatings.

I lived in fear of being hurt at that school and still remember vividly the abuse I went through as a young boy.

Many years later, after doing a lot of media (during the popes' visit to the UK in 2010), I was contacted by a woman who had been at primary school with me. We had been in the same class. We had a long chat on the phone and it stuck in my head how she said she noticed that as a child at school I usually looked lonely and sad. Funny how another child spotted that, but not the many adults around me. The reason she rang was to thank me for speaking out. A kind and lovely call. Thank you, Loretta.

I took and failed my 11+ exam. I have no recollection of taking the exam but I must have failed because I was offered a place at the Richard Challoner Secondary Modern school in Malden Manor. I was quite happy at this school though my brother-in-law, who was abusing me frequently, mentioned to my parents that it was not a good school and that I would be better off at Wimbledon College where he was a teacher.

Well, he was quite wrong about it being a second rate school. It would probably have suited me perfectly to stay there, but lo and behold, a couple of years later, when his school became a comprehensive, he persuaded my parents to have me swap schools. Although I had already suffered abuse at the hands of my brother-in-law, I still thought I was moving to his school for the best of reasons, namely my education. As a young boy I still rather naively thought that my brother-in-law loved and cared for me.

Far from it. I was now even more under his power and control (which is what most abuse is really about) and furthermore, I was now to fall victim to teachers at the college who I had previously known as friends of George's, and who I had met socially at my sister's house when I was a young child.

I had been born and raised in a Jesuit parish, went to a Jesuit church and now I was in a Jesuit school.

As a child, I knew nothing about the Jesuit belief that if they could teach a child from an early age they would have us forever, but as a young adult and now as an older man, I realise we were indoctrinated at that school. It was as simple as that. It wasn't a case of being taught how to think, more a case of what to think.

Mark Twain summed it up perfectly when he said, 'When even the brightest mind in our world has been trained from childhood in superstition of any kind, it will never be possible for that mind, in its maturity, to examine sincerely, dispassionately, and conscientiously any evidence or any circumstance which shall seem to cast a doubt upon the validity of that superstition.'

When I was a youth, I never really made a point of finding out what the Jesuits were all about. I believed and trusted them. What I have experienced and found out since makes my skin crawl.

My brother-in-law was not the only abuser on the staff at Wimbledon College. During my time there, I know for a fact that two of the priests were abusers, as both of them assaulted me and one of those had abused my brother, Mike, who had passed his 11+ exam and attended the school six years before me when it was still a grammar school. A recent article in *The Guardian* newspaper talked about another abusing priest at Wimbledon College. His name was Father Peter Orr SJ. Orr would have been there at the same time as my brother. I will never know if Mike was one of Orr's victims too.

It was in between our dad's death and Mike being sent to prison (for drink-related offences, he was an alcoholic), that he told me that he had been one of Father Battersby's "little favourites". Mike was most reluctant to talk about it, downplayed the abuse and once said that far worse things happened to some of the other boys who were taken down to the cellars. I dread to think.

When I did a bit of digging into my old school's archives, specifically the Old Boys section of a website, I saw a reference to the late Father Battersby SJ and how it was well known that he used to like touching the boys. You have to look back and wonder why in God's name did no one stop this kind of behaviour?

As a young boy I naively walked into Father Battersby's office one day. My brother Mike had told me about him but not that he was an abuser. Mike used a schoolboy nickname and referred to him as "Batts". I strolled in and introduced myself as Mike Saunders' brother. Oh dear, what a mistake. Battersby's face lit up as he invited me to sit down and almost immediately, he was standing over me, his hands already wandering.

His sweaty face and perverted grin is still etched into the deep recesses of my mind.

I was feeling decidedly uncomfortable as he stroked my thigh and my stomach. As he lingered over me for some minutes, his hand inevitably found its way to my groin and as soon as it did, I jumped up and announced that I was late for class. I recall Battersby looking disappointed, but I wasn't going to hang around.

How did these people, these priests, get away with so much? And how many lives did they ruin along the way? We should have a law of mandatory reporting of abuse in what are known as places of state or local regulation, the best example being a school. I have lost count of how many times I have heard of known abusers working in schools or care homes and nothing is done about it. It's ridiculous that some of the UK's biggest so-called child protection charities oppose the introduction of mandatory reporting. I have yet to meet a victim/survivor who opposes such a move.

The other abuser that I was aware of at Wimbledon College was the headmaster, Father Robert Carty SJ. His "touching" of me was something I will never forget. If anyone touched my children the way Father Carty touched me (and like Father Battersby did) I would waste little time in addressing their perverted behaviour. And that reminds me of something a senior police officer said to me many years ago. He said if his children had been abused he would not report it to the police. He would deal with it himself.

I think I knew what he meant and I have to say that a number of other fine officers I've met over the years indicated a similar intention about what they would like to do to people who rape and abuse our little ones. Fortunately for the abusers, we live in a reasonably civilised society where we don't generally take the law into our own hands.

Chapter 4

Once I enrolled at the Jesuit-run Wimbledon College it quickly became apparent that having George as my brother-in-law was not to bring me any perks or privileges. It did the opposite. I was picked on by some of the teachers and attracted ridicule from some of the bullying students in my year. But I was trapped. I had nowhere to go.

I spent a lot of time at my sister's looking after my nieces and nephews and at school I was near to George and the bullying and violence that went with that. One teacher in particular, I will call him Mr Violent, was really vicious towards me. As a young child I had seen him drinking at my sister's house. He had been kind to me at the time but at school he was a monster. He was our line master and if he happened to be standing outside his room as I walked past he would grab me by my hair or ear, drag me into his room for no reason, hit and humiliate me just for the hell of it and then tell me to get to class.

He's one individual I wouldn't mind bumping into now.

I was also being bullied by some fellow pupils at this time and I made the mistake of reporting the bullies to him. He wasn't one to shirk a little violence, so I thought he'd sort the bullies out.

Big mistake. He called me to his office and then, to my horror, summoned three or four of the nastiest bullies and told them that I had reported them. They all denied everything and he did nothing to them. He wouldn't, he was a coward too. Most bullies are.

Before we even left the room the bullies were mouthing, 'Snitch, grass', shaking their fists at me. When the line master turned away one of them spat in my face, another drew his finger across his throat and pointed at me, whispered that I was 'for it'.

The bullying continued but I wasn't the only victim, it was rife and the school did nothing about it. Even some of the teachers were targeted.

There was a lovely chap, a science teacher, who always arrived at class in a nice white lab coat. By the end of the lesson it was covered in a combination of spit and ink. In those days we had to use ink pens and the thugs of the class took great delight in flicking it all over his back as he walked through the class. I still remember the teacher's name and I remember he was a very powerfully built chap. He could probably have taken on the entire cohort of thugs and dealt with them but he was just too nice and dedicated a teacher to do that. I felt desperately sorry for him.

I can still remember the names of some of those boys. They will be etched in my memory forever.

One of the reasons I became a teacher, (I did it for 10 years) was to do a better job than some of those I had encountered in my own schooling and also because I wanted to prove to George that I was as clever as him. Dumb reasons I suppose, but I was a very confused young man back then. Today I am a confused older man.

Realising that my bullying was going to continue, that our line master was not going to do anything about it, I decided to take matters into my own hands. I knew I had no other option but to stand up to them. A few days later as one of these thugs had a go at me I found some courage from somewhere and challenged him to a fight.

At the end of the school day we found an empty classroom, one that was well away from the staff rooms and admin offices. We cleared the room, pushing all the desks and chairs to one side. A couple of my friends were present and the kid I challenged had most of his fellow thugs around him. But thankfully, for once they didn't get involved, this was just about him and me.

We went for each other quickly and wrestled for a second or two before separating and before he could get near me again I punched him twice in the face, which really shocked him. I had the upper hand. I was bigger than him and I hit him again, and as he spun around I jumped on his back and got him on the ground. I hit him a few times and felt the fight in him leaving. I wasn't finished, I pulled him up by his shirt collar, banged his head against a desk and then jammed his head in one of the desks, using the lid to crack his head several times. All of my anger and frustration spilled out that day.

Eventually I knew that he was spent and defeated as he lay in a crumpled heap on the floor, blood running from a head wound and his nose.

'Do you want to continue?' I asked.

'No.'

I lifted him from the floor and we shook hands. We didn't become friends but neither he nor his mates ever bothered me again. That would have been the last time I was in a fight, more than 50 years ago.

My brother Mike was six years older than me and understandably wasn't particularly interested in his little "brat" of a brother. Corporal punishment was "normal" in our household and when Dad hit me it hurt. It could be his slipper, hand or, worst of all, a cane which he kept above the living room window.

The words, "God help you when your father gets home," struck terror into my young heart. Mum was not averse to hitting me too but I tended to be able to outrun her. I still remember her running around the kitchen table, wooden spoon in hand, trying to catch me to give me a hiding.

But there was no escaping Dad. I would make sure I was upstairs in my bedroom if Mum had uttered those terrible words.

Then it would happen. I would hear the front door open. Dad was home. A period of silence would follow then I'd hear, 'Peter, come down here now.' A beating would almost inevitably follow although it tended to be preceded by some sort of trial or interrogation.

There was no getting out of it. I'm pretty sure I always cried when the punishment was inflicted. I didn't hate my dad for what he did. I figured I must have done something bad to deserve the beatings but it meant I was always scared of him and hence unable to really talk to him about anything serious.

I remember him smacking me across my face and it really hurt. I couldn't begin to imagine doing that to my own children or grandchildren but those were different times. If a child is hit at school today likely a parent or parents would march to the school and demand an explanation. In my day if I was punished at school I wouldn't have dared tell my parents for fear that Dad would inflict further punishment!

A couple of other events around physical punishment stick in my mind. One I remember quite clearly; my brother Mike and a couple of his schoolfriends had skipped school and were planning to go abroad, attempting to escape from Wimbledon College and all the crap it threw at them. I'm guessing they were about 14 or 15. I remember Mike being brought home by someone from the school and it was all quite serious. My father was livid and he struck a deal with the person who had brought Mike back. He then offered Mike the choice of a beating from his father, or a beating from the school. It was all quite bizarre looking back and Mike opted for Dad.

Dad didn't hold back that day and, as I watched, Mike was viciously caned countless times. It was terrible to witness and reminded me that as I grew older and inevitably stepped out of line occasionally, I would not be immune from a beating either.

The other, much more vague memory is of my dad putting Mum over his knees and spanking her. I'm 99% sure this happened but I cannot for the life of me remember what Mum had done to deserve this humiliation. It's just too long ago to remember with any sort of clarity.

Apart from that one time I never saw my dad raise a hand, or even his voice, to my mother. Indeed, I think he was totally devoted to her throughout their many years together. But I really think Dad wanted a quiet life and that seemed to mean always giving in to Mum.

Another incident I remember quite clearly was when I had stolen some money from my dad's tallboy drawer. I discovered that he kept some coins there. Mostly shillings and half-crowns which to me was a lot of money. The reason behind this theft was that I wanted to buy sweets to share with some children at school whom I felt sorry for. I know this must sound strange but I went through a period of stealing, which coincided with when I was first being abused. Imagine my guilt at that time, I was fully aware that stealing was a mortal sin and I was fully aware that I had been stealing of my own volition, so in the eyes of my Church I was going straight to hell!

But somehow trying to make other children feel better made me feel better. It was a very early experience of trying to be a rescuer and a people pleaser. Classic traits of those who have been abused.

Well, Dad knew exactly how much money he had in his drawer and now that some was missing he decided to find out who took it. He asked Mum, 'Did you take the money?'

'No, dear,' Mum replied.

'Michael, did you take the money?'

'No, Dad.'

Then he turned to me. 'Peter did you take the money out my drawer?'

'N … n … n … no, Dad.'

I could feel my face going red with fear and embarrassment but Dad accepted the denial. Another mortal sin, lying. Strangely enough, that was the end of the matter and Dad never said another word.

But I knew that they all knew it had to be me. I was the thief. And it hadn't been the first time I had stolen from that little pot of money. But it never happened again and if I'm honest, the embarrassment, burning red face and feelings of guilt I experienced was worse than the beating I would have received from Dad had I admitted my crime. One reason I know why hitting kids just doesn't work!

I also went through a period of stealing from other children at school. I can't really explain why I did this given that I wanted to buy sweets to make other kids feel better. I guess that by this time in my life I was a pretty confused and messed up young boy.

There was a time at primary school when, as well as buying sweets for some of the girls I felt sorry for, I was unkind to one or two boys. I won't go into detail suffice to say that it wasn't of a particularly serious nature though on one occasion I did knowingly inflict grievous bodily harm on one of my peers.

My brother Mike, who I used to pester incessantly to fight with me, would generally do his best to ignore me but sometimes he wouldn't. I wanted to fight because I really wanted my brother's attention. I was lonely. I still remember him saying that if we fight I would end up getting hurt. I wanted to play flight. I didn't want to get hurt!

I ended up getting hurt and crying and, naturally, I got no sympathy from my mum. On one occasion Mike initiated the conflict by asking me if I had ever seen a match burn twice.

'Of course not,' I replied, whereupon he struck a match, blew it out and stuck the hot end on my bare skin. I screamed the house down. Once again, Mum had no sympathy because if I played such silly games someone was always going to get hurt and in Mum's eyes Mike could do no wrong. He was always the favourite.

Years later I remember when he and I would go drinking together (Mike was already a fully-fledged alcoholic, I was working on it). We would come home and

Mike would decide to drink whatever spirits were in the house.

There was nothing I could do to stop him (try keeping alcohol from a determined alcoholic?), and the next morning I would be the one who was blamed for Mike's boozing session and the theft of Dad's whiskey!

The grievous bodily harm of the match-burning incident was repeated a few days later. This time I did it to a school friend. I can still remember the scream it evoked in my victim and I pleaded with him not to tell. To his amazing credit he didn't. I dread to think what the punishment would have been for something like that.

Decades later I was able to apologise to some of these poor souls who suffered at my hands more than 50 years ago and to my eternal relief and gratitude, I was forgiven.

A couple of other incidents spring to mind. The one and only time I was allowed to have a birthday party was when I turned 11. It was my last year at primary school. Unusually, I was allowed a few friends around and we played in the garden. One of my friends (I can still remember who it was!) brought me a football (amazingly I had never possessed one before) and it got kicked into the garden behind our house. I called over and asked the neighbour to throw it back. He refused. It's a long time ago but I remember this individual was not a particularly pleasant person.

A few nights later, while Mum and Dad were out, I sneaked into their bedroom and took my dad's air rifle out of the bottom of their wardrobe. It was wrapped in brown waxed paper. I can't remember when I had first discovered that Dad had it. It was very old and it nestled in the wardrobe alongside a bayonet and a fencing foil.

Apparently fencing had been one of my dad's hobbies before the war. That, and cycling.

I turned the lights off in the back bedroom, opened the window, loaded the rifle with a pellet and prepared for action. I fired the gun through the trees and hedges at the end of the garden and heard the pellet crack loudly against the neighbour's window. I remained still in the dark and reloaded. There was no reaction. It was dark, I could barely see the back of this man's house but I let off another round and it slammed into his kitchen window.

Then I saw a light come on, heard a door open and a voice shouted, 'You are hitting my bloody windows!'

I momentarily felt sorry for this chap but I also smiled. Did he deserve to have his windows air pelleted? Oh yes, he did. He had stolen my new ball. Did he know who was firing at him? Obviously not, thank God, because he never came knocking on our door but he also never threw my ball back, so my child's logic figured that he got what he deserved.

Chapter 5

There is no question that I was a lonely child. I always felt that and as I grew up I did quite a lot of things on my own.

I took up cycling at 14. An old cycling club friend of my dad's bought me a brand new Holdsworth racing bike. This was the summer of 1971. Dad had been a keen rider in his youth and was a racer before World War II. He had belonged to St Christopher's Catholic Cycling Club and he and the friend who bought me the bike were still old members who met regularly to talk about "the good old days".

I mention this love of cycling because it was another aspect of my youth and early adulthood that was severely affected by the influence of my brother-in-law. George, as mentioned before, was a Physical Education teacher at my school. He had been a gifted rugby and cricket player and was a keen golfer. I even remember carrying the golf clubs for him and his father as they played on Wimbledon Common. I especially remember being hit by a golf ball in my face which dislodged a tooth. I was about 14 at the time. What followed was one of the worst experiences of my life in a dentist's chair where my teeth were drilled for nearly two hours without any anaesthetic. I was in so much pain I don't know how I managed to get out of the dentist's chair and I did not visit another dentist for another four years. And all this for half a crown and a shandy in the golf clubhouse. I never caddied again! And, as a footnote to this, I was told that not long after this torture I had endured the dentist was "struck off". Too late for me though. He had instilled in me a lifelong fear of dentists.

As an aside, a couple of years later my sister Mary and Tony got married. This was in the summer of 1973. Father Bill McCurtain SJ was officiating at the ceremony. Although we didn't know it at the time, this priest was an abuser too. William Segodisho says he suffered sexual abuse at the hands of a Catholic priest, known as Father Bill, who took William under his wing when he was a teenager.

Bill McCurtain was a member of the British Province of the Society of Jesus and went to South Africa to work for a limited period of time before returning to his home province. McCurtain returned to the United Kingdom over ten years before the allegations were made known to the Jesuits in 2002. The Jesuits said they were not aware of the abuse until they received an allegation from Mr Segodisho.

McCurtain was then immediately removed from ministry and an investigation initiated; as part of this, Mr Segodisho saw a psychologist. A legal process led to a grant of financial assistance to Mr Segodisho so that he could receive some counselling and further education.

I'm not aware of any charges, or any court case relating to the abuse by Father McCurtain, but he acknowledged that Mr Segudisho was telling the truth and issued a full apology. He said, "I recognise that my behaviour towards Mr Segudisho in the 1980s violated the trust he had put in me as a Catholic priest. I deeply regret the pain that I have caused Mr Segodisho and would wish to apologise to him unreservedly. I realise, though, that such an apology cannot right the wrongs done to him at that time, or the suffering that he has endured since." McCurtain has never been allowed to minster again.

And while we are on the subject of priests who featured strongly in my childhood years, Father Tony Laundy, my scout chaplain (Sacred Heart 9th Wimbledon Troop), also turned out to be an abuser. While I was never one of his victims, Father Laundy was charged, convicted and sent to prison. But even when he died there was much controversy attached to the Catholic Church and a charity called the HCPT, who organised trips abroad to places such as Lourdes. A mother whose son was abused by Laundy, was horrified when she read about donations to the charity made in the name and the memory of Tony Laundy.

She said, 'It is beyond comprehension that a priest who was convicted of sexual abuse and served a prison sentence and who was subsequently defrocked by the Catholic Church is still revered by members of the parish where he was a priest'.

I'm not sure Laundy was ever defrocked. Few abusers within the Catholic ranks are taken out of priesthood, even those convicted. Generally, they are simply moved elsewhere.

One of the donations on the charity's Justgiving page reads: "In memory of Anthony Laundy and his much-valued time at St Winefride's, Kew. May he rest in peace."

The HCPT's chief executive, Phil Sparke, when contacted by *The Wimbledon Guardian* newspaper, said the donations were made around the time of the funeral and confirmed that they were made in memory of Father

Laundy. Mr Sparke said, 'We reserve the right to decide which funds we accept' but disclosed that they would be returning all donations that had been made in Laundy's name.

The victim's mother added: 'I would like to talk to the person who made this donation in the name of Anthony Laundy and give them a clear understanding of the sentence he gave to those he abused.'

I couldn't have put it better myself.

She continued, 'I assume that they disregard the court judgements in relation to Rolf Harris, Stuart Hall and Max Clifford as well.'

The charity spokesman said they had been unaware of the donation until *The Wimbledon Guardian* had got in touch. 'The Pilgrim Trust abhors all forms of abuse of children and vulnerable adults. We are therefore in the process of refunding the donations received.'

Dare I be cynical and suggest that the money would have remained with the charity had *The Wimbledon Guardian* not intervened? Just my opinion, but the charity must have known all about Laundy prior to his death.

As a Physical Education teacher George had many opportunities to come and stare at naked boys because after any of the Physical Education sessions we were always made to shower in the nude in the communal showers. I can still remember him standing in the doorway of the showers staring at my private parts. It's hard to describe the humiliation particularly as he was not averse to making comments about me to the rest of the boys.

He would say, 'You'll not interest many girls with that,' as he glared at my penis. I was hardly into puberty at that time and certainly hadn't even grown pubic hair by then. As always, it was about power, control and humiliation and I knew all about humiliation.

George knew that I was very interested in cycling and I will never forget him telling me that I would never win a bike race. He said I had no aptitude for ball games and at Wimbledon College the boys who represented the school at rugby and cricket were the revered ones, (including one or two of those bullies I mentioned earlier), and I simply didn't have the temperament to be a winner. So the loser mentality seeds of worthlessness had been firmly planted in my psyche, especially by George, over and over again. Sadly, I believed him; his power over me was overwhelming.

However, he had always taken more interest in me than my parents had. I thought it was because he loved me but now I know it was all part of his grooming and he knew exactly how to hurt me, how to humiliate and control me.

At the start of the racing season a couple of years later in 1975, after some good winter training, I entered a road race. It was just for junior and 3rd category senior riders. I was still a junior at the time.

I felt good for once, I was fit and had cycled hundreds of miles in training. I think the race was about 40 miles and by halfway the riders had split into two distinct groups. To my surprise I was in the leading peloton, perhaps around 30 riders strong, and as we entered the last five miles the group split yet again, leaving around a dozen cyclists in the leading pack, of which I was one. For as long as I could remember I was loving every second of life. I was at one with nature, breathing fresh country air and the feel good chemicals coursing round my body was making me feel alive.

I followed behind the previous year's schoolboy national road race champion, figuring that if I could get anywhere near him at the finish line it would be a huge achievement. We left the remaining riders as we hit the mile marker. There were now just four of us and I stuck to my gut instinct, sitting behind the schoolboy champion. I could now see the finishing line and there was a gap opening up as two riders hit the front as they duelled for the gold medal. My head was telling me that there was no way could I compete with these adults and I expected the gap to widen. 500 yards to go now and the gap was no more than 30 yards and I was still just six inches off the wheel of the schoolboy champion.

I climbed from the saddle and went for it, still doubting myself, still doubting that I could get past the champion. After all, he was a champion and I was a loser. But I sailed past him without any real effort and before I knew it I was on the back wheel of the leading two riders. But the line came up too fast and I couldn't get to them. I finished third.

With better positioning before the final sprint, I knew I could have won the race, but I had doubted myself yet again. There were a few people applauding and congratulating me and initially I felt great elation; it was a decent opener to the racing season. But by the time I had packed my bike up and made it home I was back to normal, a dark depressing cloud hanging over me. I knew I could have won the race but I didn't win the race and that confirmed everything that George had told me: I was a born loser.

I didn't get much in the way of praise from either of my parents but it was another cycling pal, John Cunningham in St Christopher's Catholic Cycling Club, who had seen my name in the results page of the weekly *Cycling* magazine. He wrote to me, congratulating me on a great start to the season and a fantastic placing. But even his warm and generous encouragement couldn't make up for the fact that I had "lost" the race.

It was typical of John, he always did his best to build people up and was always first to defend the underdog in any situation. I was so very sad when I heard that he had died during the summer of 2020 but I was privileged to be asked to attend his celebration Mass and funeral at a time when COVID-19 restrictions limited numbers who could attend such events. Very sad.

The following week I took part in another race, this time a national race with some of the best riders from around the country. The evening before I had stayed over at my brother Tony's house in Windsor. The following morning I cycled to the start of the race, and unknown to me, a few hours later, Tony had driven to see the finish. I got dropped by the leading riders quite early on and at one point was some 15 minutes behind the leading peloton. But nevertheless I kept on going and finished 10th. I felt as if my racing career was virtually over before it began.

I spotted Tony near the finish and pushed my bike over to him. I was inconsolable, totally dejected.

Tony said, 'At least you didn't give up like half the others'. He explained that there was only around half of the competitors who had actually finished the race, the pace had been far too quick for them and they had given up. He said that 10th place in such a national event was more than respectable.

His words of encouragement fell on deaf ears.

I continued to compete for the next couple of years but never came close to realising my potential, even though many cycling friends couldn't understand why I wasn't winning races. At times it was almost as if there were a

brick wall in front of me, stoppi
knew I could beat. Little did they

One friend in particular, an e
Mick Coward, said he could not
winning races. He had seen me tr
couple of my other training par
races on a regular basis. Mick s
waiting. He said that if I put my mind to it I could even challenge for the world track pursuit title.

He joked that my problem started when I put a number on my back.

He was right, my problem was psychological, my mind very much elsewhere. I was already a generally depressed individual with zero self-esteem and was firmly under the psychological control of my brother-in-law. I was still only 17.

Another incident I remember clearly was when I shared with George and my sister my desire to become a priest. I can't be precise about what age I was but it was certainly when I was still a teenager. I will never forget the torrent of abuse that came out of George's mouth about this suggestion. I recall him saying that I was too stupid to become a priest and besides, 'There is no fucking God.'

This incident devastated me because George was a "good church-going Catholic", and despite everything he did to me, he appeared to the outside world to be a good pious man. I believed he was good at heart. While I looked up to him, I now realise it was just his orchestrated and carefully managed control. His heart was far from good.

He had convinced me on more than one occasion that I was too stupid to become a priest. I knew that, but his denial of my faith was beyond painful. I remember leaving their house that night and crying all the way home.

[illegible]r of Pauline and George's boys, Simon, was [illegible]h a serious heart problem. At the age of around [illegible] and a half he had to undergo open-heart surgery. [illegible]ior to his operation I went up to the hospital every day to be with him. My sister had recently given birth to their third child and was still breastfeeding so I volunteered to spend each afternoon with Simon on the ward. It was the amazing Great Ormond Street Hospital in London.

George, because he was a teacher at my school, was able to free me up every day after lunch so that I could go and sit with Simon.

Crazy, when I look back on the schooling I missed, but at the time I was delighted. I hated school and adored being with my little nephew.

The day of Simon's big operation came. My sister and I stayed with him until he was wheeled off to the operating theatre. I still remember his bravery as a big needle was put into his little body. Fighting back tears and tightly hugging his teddy, he was taken away. I remember seeing my sister upset. Seeing your little boy like that must have been very hard.

I stayed at the hospital to be near my little nephew until George arrived a few hours later. He said to me that Simon was not in a good way which I thought was strange because I had been the first person George had seen when he arrived at the hospital and Simon wasn't even out of theatre.

He looked glum. 'You do realise he isn't very good.'

'He's fine, he's in theatre,' I replied.

George shook his head. 'He will probably die you know.'

It was a horrible thing to hear. He knew I adored my nephew and I began to get upset. George clearly enjoyed seeing me distressed.

I remember going home that night and being distressed at the prospect of Simon dying. My sister Mary had left the convent by now and was living back at home. I remember her trying to comfort me as I told her what George had said and how the little boy might die.

Of course George was wrong, Simon's operation went well and he was fine. Back then, I couldn't work out why his dad had been so pessimistic but a few years later a similar situation developed and George was exactly the same.

Their eldest child, my niece Mary, became unwell during the summer of her thirteenth year. From being an energetic, school-loving, soccer playing tomboy she became very quiet and tired. She took to wrapping herself in a scarf even though it was warm weather. The doctor was called but on at least two occasions the suggestion was that she probably just didn't want to go to school. I knew that nothing could be further from the truth with Mary.

A family member, a doctor was called, and he told us that she urgently needed a blood test. The next visit by a GP included a blood test and within twenty-four hours Mary had been admitted to hospital with suspected leukaemia. The diagnosis was confirmed.

I was heartbroken by this tragic turn of events, but she was in the Royal Marsden, one of the finest cancer-treating hospitals in the world, so we had hope. Well, most of us did. When George and I were alone he was taunting me yet again. 'You do know she will probably die, don't you?'

What kind of a man talks like that about his own daughter?

Mary bravely battled the disease for five years until just one week after her 17th birthday, when she could battle no more. I remember with tears in my eyes the conversation she had had with her mother a few months earlier where she had said, 'Why doesn't God take me?'

She had endured so much pain during her short life. She died on 19 April 1983, and her funeral was a week later - on my birthday.

The homily or "eulogy" for Mary was spoken by one of the nuns who had taught her. It was beautiful and touching. She ended by saying thank you to God for lending Mary to us but now it was time to give her back.

I still have that eulogy script and read it once in a while. It makes me cry but it also gives me hope. And we all need that, don't we?

But even then, not long after Mary's funeral, my brother-in-law was up to his old mind games. Although I wasn't present on that particular occasion, one of my relatives had overheard a conversation he'd had with his other daughter. He told her that he wished it had been her, Mary's sister, who died instead of Mary.

It's hard to believe but true, and it told me everything I needed to know about this sick, twisted, individual. Only a very corrupt mind could utter such heinous words.

Chapter 6

In 1974 I took an overnight train from London to Plymouth to watch a stage of The Tour de France. It was *Le Tour*'s first ever visit to the UK.

A drunk man got into the compartment with me. In those days compartments were separate and each would sit six to eight people but there were just the two of us in this one. Each had a sliding door with blinds and curtains. In the middle of the night, I woke to find this man lying on top of me kissing me and trying to touch my genitals. I fought him off and punched him as hard as I could and shouted, 'Fuck off!'. To my relief he left the compartment.

I curled up in a corner and tried to sleep, wondering why in God's name he had attacked me. I never saw him again and I remained silent about this assault for decades to come. I mention this because it led me to believe that I must have had something tattooed on my forehead that said, 'Abuse me', and in the last twenty odd years I've heard many other survivors say exactly the same thing.

I have learned over the years that many abusers have the knack of spotting a vulnerable child. It's the same with rapists. Some seem to know who they can target and who they can't, a victim that they can perhaps assault and get away with it.

It reminds me of how my mother would ridicule me over my chosen sport, cycling. I would come back from a long training ride, perhaps to Brighton and back. I would be covered in grime and sweat and absolutely shattered (we all were!). Mum would look at me and say, 'Oh Peter, you're not tough like the other boys, are you?' Once again, she reinforced my low self-esteem, exactly the same way George had, the teachers at the school had and even the priests had. It seemed that the entire adult world was telling me that no matter how hard I tried, I'd never be much good at anything.

How I wish I had not taken all these comments and insults to heart but as a vulnerable child, I did. If you tell a child or a young adult often enough that they are worthless and keep repeating it, they will eventually come to believe it.

When people you love hurt you it is very hard to recover, particularly when you are a child.

There were other aspects of my childhood which were a little out of the ordinary. From a very early age I used to go and visit my cousins who lived at different ends of the country. One lived in Bristol and a whole big bunch of them lived (and many still do) in Seaham, County Durham. As a toddler I would go to see them and stay over with my mum. Dad never made those journeys.

When I got a bit older, when I was still just a child, I would go on my own. I dread to think what Social Services would say today about a primary school child being allowed to travel hundreds of miles on his own but that is what used to happen. And I loved every minute of that independence, being on my own, nobody telling me what to do or how unworthy I was. They were moments of loneliness but happy loneliness!

Because my dad was quite senior in the Railways we got free first class travel, so going to Bristol or Durham was no great hardship. I do remember one journey when a posh-looking businessman got into my first class compartment and muttered something like, 'You shouldn't be in here, sonny.'

I ignored him and when the ticket inspector came along he just glanced at my freebie pass and smiled at me before thoroughly examining and clicking the ticket of the man in his fancy suit sitting opposite me.

When I was just 14, I went youth hostelling on my own. I travelled to my cousins in Seaham for a few days then headed north to Edinburgh then on to Inverness and the beautiful Isle of Skye. I always managed to meet lovely people on these journeys and most of them used to say how amazing it was that such a young lad was travelling around on his own.

I had left school at the end of 1973. For a short time I worked in Ely's department store in Wimbledon then tried my hand as a cycle frame builder at Geoffrey Butler Cycles in Croydon. I wanted a job that had some connection with my sport. George had convinced me I would never make a good cyclist but perhaps there was another way, perhaps I could build bespoke bicycles?

That didn't last long. I had absolutely no aptitude for metalworking and after a short time I transferred from the back workshop to the shop itself. I much preferred that. Selling bikes was easier, cleaner and a lot more satisfying than trying to build them. However, under some pressure from my dad to "get a proper job" I applied to British Railways for an admin position and ended up working indirectly for my father in Southern House, Croydon. I started there in the winter of 1974. Dad had worked for the Railways throughout his life, interrupted only by his National Service during the Second World War. His father, my grandfather, had also worked on the Railways.

I cringe when I look back at my time at that office in Croydon. Many lovely people worked there but the things that stick in my memory were how the place was constantly under a pall of tobacco smoke and how sexist the behaviour of many men was towards the women who worked there. Pinching bottoms and lewd comments were commonplace. At the Christmas parties some of the senior management, all of whom were men, would turn into drunken groping sex pest individuals.

I think the Me Too movement was way overdue!

But not all the men were bad news. Most of them were decent, hard-working individuals and I learnt a great deal from many of them. My boss and another close colleague had both served in the army during World War II. Both had seen action in North Africa and they had some amazing stories to tell. My dad had also served in the armed forces during the war but he rarely spoke of it and I guess it may have had something to do with the fact that his brother, my uncle, had been killed in the last months of that dreadful conflict. The only time I ever saw a tear in my dad's eye was one Remembrance Sunday, when I was a very small child. We had come home from Mass and I can remember Dad wiping a tear away as we heard the Remembrance Day guns being fired at 11 o'clock on Wimbledon Common. I didn't really understand why he was crying. I was too young to understand but having lost both my brothers now, I can feel for him. Looking back, I understand.

My aspirations about a possible vocation to the priesthood may have reached the ears of some of the Jesuits in our parish because after morning Mass one Sunday in 1976 a visiting Jesuit priest, speaking on behalf of Jesuit Missions, asked whether I would be interested in going to a Mission Station in Zimbabwe, or Rhodesia as it was then called.

I said I would be very interested, not really thinking about the implications, but hey, it would mean getting away from home. I was told to start saving towards my fare.

It might seem odd to some, that I toyed with the idea of the priesthood and welcomed this opportunity to travel to a Jesuit Mission given the abuse I had experienced at the hands of the two Jesuits (Carty and Battersby). But I didn't make the connection between their actions and my forthcoming adventure to Zimbabwe (Rhodesia) with Jesuit Missions.

I think I wanted to be a priest because I saw it as a way of helping others to heal and at that point I had no idea that the whole God thing was just a huge distraction because I didn't need any of that religious stuff to care about other people.

Another chap who had quite an influence on me was a super athlete called Andy Kerr. Andy was the British super heavyweight lifting champion and represented Great Britain in international events. In fact, he won a silver medal at the Commonwealth Games in New Zealand in 1974, not long after I joined the railways. We became good friends and actually worked together for a while in a small office near Clapham Junction. Andy was a very bright man and he respected me because I was a fellow sportsman - albeit in a slightly different league to him.

We chatted away about all sorts and I once asked him how he came to be a weightlifter. He told me that a family member used to taunt him when he was a child because he was so skinny. Andy's response was to prove this person wrong, and so he became a champion lifter. I suppose there was some parallel with me wanting to become a teacher - to prove my abusers wrong. But if I'm honest I wish I had done what Andy had done with his sport and become a champion racing cyclist. Looking back, I know I had the physical ability but I never believed in myself. I still castigate myself for that and curse those who implanted those negative thoughts long, long ago. Thoughts that, as I write, are very much with me. I still can never comprehend being a winner.

When I was offered the opportunity to go to Rhodesia I applied for a years' unpaid leave. I was turned down. Unknown to me at the time, my dad wrote to our Member of Parliament. Our MP replied that he thought it was unfair that I should be denied such an opportunity and said he would have a word with the chairman of British Rail, Sir Peter Parker. Michael Havers MP, KC evidently kindly did this and word came from the top to give this brave lad his leave.

Something else happened between the offer of going to Rhodesia and actually leaving. I fell in love. I had been at a Boxing Day party at the home of my good friends Tony and Barbara Mills. It went on until the early hours and I met a beautiful young woman, Helena, who I ended up sleeping with that night. We were inseparable after that, I spent every single minute I could with her. It had not escaped me that I was leaving for Rhodesia on 6 January and I wanted to cool the relationship but thought about her constantly. My head and heart were turning summersaults, the timing could not have been worse, what was the "Architect of the Universe, God, thinking? After two or three days, I had serious concerns about going to Africa.

I had so many episodes in my life, that I relive, over and over again, moments where I could have taken different decisions that would have meant my life would have moved in a totally different direction.

It reminds me of the movie with Gwyneth Paltrow, *Sliding Doors*. She misses the train by a split second, the sliding doors closing before she can squeeze through. The movie cleverly focuses on the two different directions her life could have taken, the narrator asking, "Have you ever wondered what might have happened - if?".

My life has had many "sliding door moments", most of my decisions shaped by those who put me down and made me feel like nothing.

And so it happened all over again. She was very beautiful but I felt inferior to her, that I was not good enough for her. I have beat myself up many times over the years about this and now know that my insecurity was mostly down to George.

I had a big decision to make. Do I cancel my trip to Africa so that I could carry on this new relationship or did I go, hoping that she would wait for me and be there when I returned in a year's time? Who was I kidding? What could I possibly offer a beautiful young woman, it was only a matter of time before she would dump me.

We discussed it. I told her that I was willing to give it all up for her. She said it was an incredible opportunity and begged me not to give it up. She said she would wait for me and we could write to each other.

Even though it broke my heart I made my decision and had to go.

She came with me to the airport, which made it a hundred times worse. But it gave me a glimmer of hope that she would still be there when I returned.

The doubts set in as soon as I sat down in the plane, especially when I realised I didn't have her address. Best to forget her, before the plane crossed into African airspace there would be another man knocking at her door.

Another thing of significance that happened during those months before leaving for Jesuit Missions, was I had a long conversation with the editor of *Cycling* magazine, Ken Evans. He had seen some of the pieces I had written about cycling for my local newspaper, *The Wimbledon News.* He had also printed one or two of the letters I had sent into the magazine. He said I had a talent for writing and asked whether I was interested in becoming a trainee journalist at his magazine?

'Of course."

He said there were no immediate positions and urged me to watch out for a forthcoming advert.

Not long after I left for Rhodesia, the advertisement was published but because I didn't get a copy of the magazine (sent by my dad) for several weeks after the closing date, I was overlooked for the traineeship. Ironically, the person who took up the position eventually became editor of the magazine. I can smile about it now, but my life has been a series of big decisions and more often than not I managed to make the wrong moves.

Chapter 7

I set off for the Southern Hemisphere on a cold winter's day, 6 January 1977. Rhodesia was still a rogue state, had been ejected from the Commonwealth of Nations and was subject to international sanctions. The prime minister of Rhodesia, Ian Smith, had made an illegal Unilateral Declaration of Independence (UDI) in 1965.

The reason that Rhodesia was deemed a rogue state was because its majority black population was not entitled to vote. The minority population of whites, or Europeans as some of them liked to call themselves, were. So, in some respects it was a regime not dissimilar to neighbouring South Africa, and that country also had international sanctions imposed on it. The big difference with Rhodesia was that it's discrimination was somewhat more subtle. In South Africa you would see poor whites, but not in Rhodesia. To be white was to be politically and economically superior to the majority black population. There was a smattering of well-off black people but they were very few in number.

I remember that when I flew to Rhodesia one of the stopovers to refuel was in the Canary Islands, and the second stop was Salisbury (current day Harare), but it was not announced because officially the plane was not stopping there. I was one of only a handful of people who actually left the plane in Rhodesia, most passengers were flying on to Johannesburg in South Africa.

One thing I remember about that flight was that I sat next to the only black face on the plane, a humble man, and I was dismayed at how the white cabin crew treated him, like a second class citizen. They threw him glances that seemed to say, 'What are you doing on this flight?' Sad but true.

I remember flying low towards Salisbury and noticed how dry the land was. As the plane touched down and taxied towards the small terminal, I spotted a row of black men in white coveralls digging some land. It looked like a scene from an American movie based in the deep south at the time of slavery.

It made me feel distinctly uneasy.

The plane was met by quite a crowd. This was a weekly event so people came to watch, even if they weren't actually meeting anyone. I was greeted by a small group of clerics, all as keen to greet me as they were to receive the gifts I had brought with me, namely duty free alcohol and a new typewriter!

I was driven to Salisbury where I went straight to the Jesuit house near to the Catholic cathedral.

This was to be my first meal in a religious community and interesting it was, too. The food was cooked and served by nuns and we all sat at long tables similar to school dining halls. I remember the chat I had with one of the priests, Father Martin Thomas, who was British but had lived out there for some years. He was warm and welcoming, I took to him immediately.

After lunch it was back into an old pick-up truck and an 80-mile drive to what I thought was going to be my home for the next 12 months. We picked up some supplies from a general store in the city then headed south.

The first 60 miles were on smooth roads and after passing through the small town of Beatrice we turned right on to a dirt road which shook my bones to pieces for the next 20.

Arriving at this remote spot, I looked around and wondered what would happen next.

This was St Michael's Mission, Mhondoro. I had already been introduced to my fellow volunteer, he had arrived a few weeks earlier and was one of those who met me at the airport. I was shown around the mission station. There was a small hospital, a slightly larger maternity unit and various other buildings such as the refectory, a convent, kitchen, washing block, toilet and shower block, all run from a single generator and some rudimentary solar energy panels. In the carpenter's block the main item of production was coffins!

My new home was a perfectly round hut built with home-made bricks, a floor made of crushed animal dung (highly polished), and a thatched roof. The hut was placed near a couple of high trees. Many people die from lightning strikes in that part of Africa, as I was to sadly find out a few days later.

In my hut was a bed, a side table and a table, nowhere to hang clothes and no electricity. There were a couple of small windows and the walls were covered in spiders.

One of the first things I did was to borrow a broom and sweep all the spiders down from the walls and out into the dusty yard. Lo and behold, the next day they were all back. I dumbly asked one of the lovely sisters what I should do about them. She laughed and said they were my protection from more harmful creatures, like mosquitos.

There were separate school buildings, dormitories, classrooms and the church; the biggest building of all but no pews and no pulpit. There were no thrills of the usual variety in the church, no gaudy statues or pictures, no grand show of opulence. It was a church as it should be - for its people.

After a tour of the mission it was time to walk to a village nearby where a funeral was taking place. One of the Jesuit brothers was conducting the service, which took place outside in the blazing heat near a tree where the old fellow who had died was to be buried, his favourite spot.

The sermon, all in the local language, Shona, seemed to go on for ever and I wondered how long I could stay upright. I had been on a plane all night with no sleep, driven deep into the bush in a vehicle in need of new suspension, and now I was standing in the heat of the day listening to a sermon I didn't understand, about an old man I had never met.

Still, it was an experience I would never forget. I remember as they carried the coffin towards the freshly dug grave, the pallbearers stopped and spun the coffin round a couple of times. This was my first experience of how the ancient traditions of Mashona culture mixed with a Christian burial. Apparently the spinning around of the coffin was to confuse the evil spirits as to where the dead man's soul would be.

A couple of days later more tragedy struck in another nearby village. Two little children, sisters I recall, had been struck by lightning and were killed. I visited the hut where it had happened. They were cuddled up together during one of the many electrical storms and died in each other's arms. I was beginning to see why the mission carpenter was kept so busy.

It was not long after my arrival that I witnessed one of these electrical storms. It was spectacular and, after the events of a few days earlier, quite scary. Knowing that the two little girls had died inside their mud hut I was keen to point out that my roof was also made of thatch. Brother Andrew, a Lithuanian Jesuit and the handyman of the mission, pointed out that the two tall trees near my hut were the perfect lightning conductors and I would be safe. I prayed he was right!

Another thing I remember vividly from those first weeks was the fact that both girls and boys would come up and hold hands with me. This was normal in Mashona culture. There was nothing vaguely sexual about it but it took a bit of getting used to.

Quite why I was allowed to go to Rhodesia (at not inconsiderable expense), I will never know because they sent me to a bush mission secondary school to teach. I had left school with two O Levels. I was not qualified to teach anything.

I sometimes wonder whether being given the opportunity to serve in Rhodesia was a sort of reward for my dad for his incredible and longstanding service to the Church. I will never know.

The short time I spent on Mhondoro Mission certainly changed my perspective on life. If nothing else, it taught me that we should be grateful for all we have in the UK. For example, the variety of foods we were able to put on the table back home. In the mission the children ate a staple of boiled maize, occasionally mixed with crushed beetle for protein. The students slept on the floor in big dormitories and textbooks didn't exist.

But when I walked into the crowded classrooms, packed with up to 60 children, you could hear a pin drop, such was their hunger to learn and their incredible sense of respect for their teacher. I still have some of the amazing letters these youngsters sent me months after I was forced to leave the country.

I had arrived in Rhodesia with a British passport and so the Rhodesian army came looking for me to conscript me into their forces. I only discovered that this had happened sometime after my return to the UK. There is no way I could have joined their illegal army because the struggle for freedom by the majority black population was a struggle I closely allied myself with. Apparently an army Jeep had turned up at the mission looking for me. No one told them where I was. At the time I was actually in the capital.

What was interesting and a little reassuring for me was that the children at the mission (I say children but some were barely younger than me) said that if the Zimbabwean freedom fighters were to visit our mission I would not be harmed. They could not say the same for my Glaswegian volunteer colleague because he had expressed some overt racist views during his time there.

Although my time at Mhondoro was brief it left many happy memories. I had taken certain items of clothing with me, shirts and ties, and I gave these to the young students who would proudly wear them on Sunday mornings for Mass. I also took a cassette player and some tapes. The Bob Marley tape was the favourite and I had numerous people offering to buy it off me! You simply could not purchase that sort of thing in white Rhodesia.

Sunday Mass was also quite an event. People would walk through the night to get to church and the women's singing was sublime. The men, on the other hand, would mostly sit around outside church smoking cigarettes and putting the world to rights. Mass lasted a long time, far longer than here in the UK and that was because the sermons tended to be lengthy. Because the services were generally conducted in Shona I rarely knew what was being said. What I do remember was that the women took every opportunity to burst into song and sometimes the priests, most of whom I remember with great affection, would have to shut them up.

Chapter 8

A month after I arrived in Mhondoro we heard some terrible news about Father Martin Thomas and the Musami Mission, news I could hardly comprehend. On 7 February 1977 a group of men arrived at the mission. They rounded up the white staff, including Father Martin Thomas, two other Jesuits, a Jesuit Brother and three European nuns.

The group was taken a short distance from the mission by the men, who were said to be Selous Scouts, which was part of the Smith regime whose tactic was to pretend to be guerrillas. An eyewitness report from one of the other priests, Father Myerscough, who I met up with a few days after the massacre, said he had managed to get away as the armed group began to argue and one of them started shooting.

Father Myerscough was lucky to survive, he had thrown himself to the ground and pretended to be dead. He told me that God didn't want him to die that day. I wanted to ask him why God had deserted his six brothers and sisters. I bit my tongue and didn't ask him why he thought they were not so fortunate. They were all defenceless, murdered in cold blood.

I went along to see the poor brothers and sisters in their open coffins. I wish I hadn't. Some of them had been shot in the face. These are images that will never leave me as long as I live.

Soon after I read The Rhodesian Herald ,which ran a story blaming Mugabe's terrorists (freedom fighters). Yet, it was commonly known in the streets and villages that this was a tactic that Smith had used on more than one occasion.

It is quite hard to describe the sheer terror I experienced after hearing of this terrible attack. Only weeks before I'd been having lunch with Martin Thomas, now he was dead. I lay in my bed gripped with fear. I was waiting to hear footsteps and the cocking of rifles. I felt sure that my life may be coming to an end soon. I was only 19. The reassurances I got from the students were one thing but they were only speaking of who they termed the freedom fighters. I was safe from them, but not from the Selous Scouts. Nevertheless, I and the other volunteer were evacuated to the city.

After our evacuation from the mission, the other volunteer and I lived at a Jesuit school in Salisbury. It was called St George's College and was one of the best public boys schools in Rhodesia. The other volunteer taught the older boys at the main campus and I was made a housemaster at the boarding prep school, Hartmann House, that was next door. The children were mostly white Rhodesians with a smattering of black kids.

I was in charge of getting them up in the morning, making sure they were ready for their classes and took them for Physical Education. This included rugby, a game I hated as I associated it closely with my past experiences of abuse. George and his family and many teachers at Wimbledon College were all massive rugby fans and because Rhodesia was a former British colony, rugby was the big game there too.

To this day I find it hard to watch a rugby match on TV without it triggering unpleasant memories, because watching rugby at my brother in law's house was accompanied by lots of drinking alcohol and often led to abuse.

My last duty of the day was to see that the children would all be tucked up in bed, preceded by prayers of course, and then I would put the dormitory lights out. They were lovely children and we had some great laughs together. I remember them and the young people of the mission station with great fondness. Having a Brit as their housemaster was certainly a novelty and they delighted in my casual approach, one which I employed years later with great success in my teaching career.

A teaching career? The reason I went into teaching, as I mentioned earlier, was because of what George had said to me about not being particularly clever. As a young adult I returned to education to prove him wrong. Not the right motivation, I know, but to my young and confused mind it seemed the right thing to do and after experiencing so many horrible teachers in the past I just knew I could do a better job.

As the weeks at Hartmann House turned into months, it became clear the civil war was not going to ease up and I was unlikely to ever go back to Mhondoro for anything other than a social visit, which I did once or twice. On one of those social visits on a Saturday evening I took the bus out to the mission. Bus rides were always interesting. For one thing, I was the only white person on the bus and this drew some funny looks. In a way the apartheid was worse in Rhodesia because your colour absolutely defined your economic status. Little wonder the whites didn't want to give all that up.

One of the things I remember from that bus ride was that it started to rain during the journey. The luggage on the bus's roof rack was going to get wet. However, instead of pulling over to strap the tarpaulin to protect it, a couple of the passengers climbed out of the windows and secured the tarpaulin whilst the bus was belting down the road. Health and safety was a phrase yet to be invented in that part of the world.

I got off the bus at the stop nearest to the mission and as I walked through the gate the man in charge, Father Ray Armstrong, was coming towards me on his motorbike. He stopped and said he on his way to another part of the bush to say Mass first thing the following morning. I wished him luck on his long ride and mentioned that I had a bottle of gin in my backpack.

As I continued to walk towards the recreation room Father Ray turned his trail bike around and announced that he would leave early the following morning. It was the gin!

By now I was receiving regular mail from Dad, but I hadn't received one single correspondence from Helena. It was to be expected I told myself, someone as gorgeous as her would have no shortage of male suitors. I knew there was a problem with the post and I had also been evacuated from Mhondoro Mission, but Dad's mail had eventually caught up with me, so why not Helena's?

I tried not to beat myself up too badly, I hadn't written to her either. Not that I could do this without her address!

One afternoon, a few months after arriving in Hartmann House, I was summoned to see the superior of the Jesuits in Rhodesia. He said I couldn't go back to the mission because of the civil war and asked what qualifications I had. In other words, could he put me to work at the main school? I remember feelings of humiliation as I replied, 'Two O Levels, Father.'

'Not very good, is it?'

'No, Father.'

He had no idea what I had been going through as a boy and how that still affected me when I sat my exams, but I wasn't about to tell him. How dare you, I wanted to shout at him, just who do you think you are? Have you seen the good work I actually did at the mission school? He hadn't. He hadn't visited at all while I was there. Father, haven't you noticed the smiles on the children's faces, how they are progressing, haven't you noticed how respected I am and how much they love me?

But I said nothing and sat in silence while he berated me. Berating me for failing at a Jesuit school, where abuse was rife and I had been a victim.

He sent me to see another Jesuit known as Brother Fitz, who would arrange my flights home.

Although disappointed I believed God had a plan for me and perhaps returning home would enable me to rekindle my relationship with Helena.

Whilst in Salisbury I made friends with a few families who showed great kindness to me. One was the McNally family. Nick, the father, was a human rights lawyer and after Independence went on to become a judge of the Zimbabwe Supreme Court. I remember chatting to him and how he said the British government had let the people of Rhodesia/Zimbabwe down when they didn't send in troops to arrest Ian Smith when he declared the illegal Unilateral Declaration of Independence in 1965.

‘They could have sent in a couple of helicopters with troops to arrest him,’ he said, ‘there would have been no bloodshed. But what followed was years of civil war and unrest with all the citizens of this beautiful country suffering the consequences of international sanctions.’

I often wonder what happened to all my friends in the new Zimbabwe, a country destined for many problems. A few of the children had relatives who were being held in Rhodesian detention camps. One such detainee was a chap called Canaan Banana. He, along with many other alleged freedom fighters was being held in a place called Wha Wha detention centre. One of the few useful things I did when I returned to Britain was to contact Amnesty International and help close that particular place down.

I had quite a bit of correspondence with Amnesty International and was so pleased that they took up the case. Wha Wha was just one of many camps around Rhodesia where Africans who dared to question the regime were held, mostly without trial.

Canaan Banana was the first president of the newly independent Zimbabwe. I received an invitation to the independence celebration in Harare in 1980, where he became president of Zimbabwe and the Jesuit-educated Robert Mugabe became the first black prime minister. Unfortunately I was unable to attend.

I warmed to Canaan, we wrote to each other a few times after my return to the UK. I was very distressed to read, in 1999, that he had been jailed for sex offences. He was a former Methodist minister, a man of God. Not another one, I thought to myself.

Banana insisted that he was not a homosexual and said the accusations against him were part of a malicious vendetta. I knew that in a country such as Rhodesia that was highly likely, but I read testimony from Banana's trial, which included details of sex with gardeners, cooks and one bodyguard who detailed a lurid testimony of how Banana drugged and raped him on a carpet at State House in the 1980s.

Banana's trial was an embarrassment to Robert Mugabe when it became patently obvious that he knew all about Banana's sexual misconduct and did nothing to stop it. Where had I heard that before?

The other volunteer I was with in Rhodesia was a chap who had a hugely inflated opinion of himself and was already planning what clerical suits he was going to buy himself in Rome on his way back to the UK. He was Scottish, from Glasgow as I recall. We were living in a big school in Salisbury, where he stayed in the main school and I stayed in the prep school annexe. We didn't see a great deal of each other, which I have to say suited me as he had a knack of making me feel inferior, but we tended to meet for meals which were taken in the main school building.

We also went drinking together on a few occasions in the city centre. On one occasion, when walking home after some drinks, this man who planned on becoming a priest attacked me. He grabbed me and attempted to touch my genitals.

'Just let me have a feel,' he snorted in my ear as I fought him off.

This was another incident I will never forget, try as I might.

Even after we returned to the UK he wrote to me. I hope he never became a priest. But what seems a little bizarre is that I wrote back to this chap, not to chastise him for his assault but simply to see how he was doing. Once again, I was ignoring the abuse. Somehow, and for a reason difficult for me to understand, I blocked it out and did my best to believe it had never really happened. At the time, writing to him as if nothing had happened seemed the best way to "forget about it".

I had a conversation on BBC Radio 5 Live some years ago with Mark Lawrenson, the former Liverpool soccer star. We were discussing the case of a chap called Patrick Raggett, who had successfully sued the Jesuits because of the abuse he suffered at the hands of one of their priests at the school he attended in Preston, Lancashire.

Patrick won his case. The judge accepted that he had been abused by Father Michael Spencer SJ, and he was awarded around fifty thousand pounds in damages. Mark Lawrenson, who was at the same school in Preston, pointed out that Father Spencer had officiated at Patrick's wedding years after the abuse, his implication being why would a person ask the man who abused him to officiate at his wedding.

Mark couldn't get his head around that, but I knew exactly why. Many abused people bury the sexual and physical assaults and don't fully understand the nature of the abuse and its consequences until many years later.

Chapter 9

The trip home from Rhodesia was memorable. I had gone out to Mhondoro to say a final farewell to the lovely people who were still there and told them that I hoped we could all meet up again one day, in peaceful times.

I travelled back via Victoria Falls, South Africa, Kenya and Israel. I only spent two days at the falls but it was one of the most exhilarating experiences of my life. I am generally hesitant to say, 'You must visit such and such a place', but Victoria Falls is a sight to behold and I would highly recommend it to anyone wanting to see a truly awesome, and very wet, wonder of nature. I visited Victoria Falls as a tourist many years later and it was as impressive as I remembered it from back in 1977.

After Victoria Falls I flew to Johannesburg to pick up a northbound flight to Nairobi. I then spent a week in Nairobi, including a couple of days with friends of the white folk I had met in Salisbury. They ran a pineapple plantation near a beautiful spot known as Thika, a small town in central Kenya immortalised in a book called *The Flame Trees of Thika* by Elspeth Huxley.

I stayed in a very basic, no-frills hotel called Brunners, and every night around teatime a man would bash on the door and shout 'DTT!' He would then come into the room and spray the place for pests. It was a wonderful few days and again I was fascinated at how different life was there but also how there were similarities to good old Blighty, the love of a drink or two for example.

I had gone into one or two bars in Nairobi and on each occasion had been greeted like a long lost brother and these were black bars, not white ones. I also remember watching a tall, black shepherd herding his sheep and goats through Nairobi city centre. It was fantastic.

When I left Kenya I flew to Tel Aviv. I wanted to visit the Holy Land and having read a book called, *In the steps of the Lord*, I was keen to witness the place of Christ's birth and short life. This book had been written in the days before the state of Israel had been established in 1948. Prior to 1948 the country I was about to visit was known as Palestine. I was now heading to a very different place, to a relatively new state, Israel.

I had been told by Brother Fitz back in Salisbury, that I could go to a special place where I would be welcomed and given a bed. He gave me the address in Jerusalem with the assurance I would be warmly welcomed.

Even the journey from Nairobi to Tel Aviv was an adventure. It was my first time on an El Al (Israeli Airlines) flight. When I arrived at the airport I noticed a group of soldiers sitting in a bar drinking, their guns stacked up in the corner. "Laid back" is an understatement.

When I checked in they discovered that my bag was too heavy and suggested I put some heavy items in my hand luggage. I had bought quite a bit of soapstone and this was heavy. I pulled my case off the counter, laid it on the floor and started to unzip it. I suddenly noticed several pairs of heavily booted feet next to me. As I looked up I realised that Israeli secret service agents had surrounded me and I'm assuming they thought I was about to pull out a bomb or a gun. It was momentarily scary but also quite reassuring to know that security was very tight. It was only one year or so since an Air France passenger jet, with many Israelis on board, had been hijacked by Arab fighters and flown to Entebbe in neighbouring Uganda.

Kenya had allowed the Israeli defence forces' planes to re-fuel after their raid on Entebbe and I'm guessing the Israelis were not taking any chances with their own aircraft, albeit at a friendly airport.

Every bit of my hand luggage was carefully scrutinised even down to squeezing my toothpaste up and down to make sure it had nothing sinister concealed. I must say I felt pretty safe as I boarded the plane.

As the embarking passengers were driven out to the aircraft (which was stopping over *en route* from Johannesburg), our bus was flanked by military Jeeps and on reaching the plane I could see it was encircled by armed Kenyan troops under strong floodlights.

I remember two things about that flight, the first being the ferocious storm we encountered over Addis Ababa. As the Boeing 747 shook violently, a TV projector fell from the ceiling of the main cabin, injuring one of the passengers. The other thing I remember was the singing from the passengers as the plane made its final approach and landing. It seemed they were overjoyed to have reached the Promised Land in one piece.

When I exited the main terminal at Tel Aviv airport I noticed that all the buses had departed for the night. Being very short of money there was no way I could afford a taxi for the journey to Jerusalem so I decided to settle down and spend the night in the terminal. Not that there was anywhere comfortable to sit. A few taxi drivers kept coming up to me but I insisted I could not afford the fare.

Amazingly, after about an hour one of the drivers, having made several attempts to persuade me to use his services approached me and once again I said no thanks.

'Come on, I drive you to Jerusalem for free.' He was going home anyway.

It was a lovely ride and we chatted all the way. I told him of the place Brother Fitz had recommended, the Casa Nova, and he knew it.

It was a spectacular sight as we approached Jerusalem. The walled city and the lights had a medieval feel and, being the early hours of the morning, there was hardly a soul anywhere. This was my first experience of the Holy Land and it certainly felt different. The narrow cobbled streets, the white flat-roofed buildings, it was not that hard to imagine Jesus walking these streets,

We stopped near the Casa Nova and the taxi driver kindly knocked on the door, just to be told that there was no room at the inn. The driver said he knew of a hotel where I might get a bed for the night and we drove to the end of another cobbled street, where we got out the car and walked to a large dark door on the side of a flat-roofed building. The door was flung open and as we walked in a smiling, bowing Arab gentleman greeted us. He clearly knew the taxi driver. As they chatted someone showed me to my room. I was so grateful to have somewhere to sleep. It had been a long day.

The next morning I started to explore the city. There was so much to see, the Wailing Wall, the Via Dolorosa (the Way of the Cross), various churches, the Garden of Gethsemane. Also Bethlehem, Jericho, the Dead Sea. So much to see, so little time, and I was fast running out of money.

I was so low on funds I, decided to seek the assistance of the British Consulate. The diplomatic service doesn't generally hand out cash to Brits abroad but the Vice Consul, who was a lovely chap, let me use his phone to ring my dad who kindly wired me some money. Unfortunately, it took some days to arrive and so I lived on houmous and pitta bread for the next few days.

Whilst I was waiting to see the Vice Consul one of the consular staff, an Arab gentleman, invited me into the kitchen and made me a cup of tea. He proudly boasted of his love for the British. He had been in the British army and told me that if I was unable to get any money I was welcome to come and stay with him and his family. Such amazing kindness.

When I returned to the hotel the following evening someone else's luggage was in my room. I went to the reception desk and asked that it be removed.

'No,' the manager said, 'you are now sharing with another man.'

I don't think so. I gathered my bags and left. I don't mind sharing with people I know but I certainly wasn't going to share with a stranger. My recent encounter with the Scotsman in Rhodesia was still fresh in my mind.

Despite the pleading of the hotel owner I left the place and headed out of old Jerusalem through the Jaffa Gate. As I was struggling with my case, still full of heavy soapstone, a group of Israeli soldiers stopped and offered to help me. They then said I should come and stay at their hotel in New Jerusalem. I did. It was a very basic place, the rooms were more like prison cells with little more than a bed and a shower in one corner. It turned out it was a billet for Israeli soldiers so, once again, I certainly felt very safe and it was cheap!

Another thing I discovered in Israel was how easy it was to hitchhike. I only did it a couple of times but I never had to wait long before someone stopped to pick me up. Apparently a young person hitching a ride was assumed to be a member of the Israeli armed forces and therefore you were obliged to give them a ride. I've no idea if that is still the case.

Jericho was the hottest place I had ever visited in my life. It was stifling. On a day trip by bus I noticed goods' vehicles heading for the border with Jordan. I had always assumed borders would be closed because of the animosity between the various Arab states and Israel. I asked someone about this and I will never forget the reply, 'War is war and business is business.'

That same day I went to the Dead Sea. It was pretty quiet and I stripped off to my underpants and waded in. It was true, I floated gently on the water, rich in salt.

Another enduring memory of my brief visit to the Holy Land was to see Bedouin tents nestled in the side of hills and a lone shepherd walking along the road with a little lamb straddled across his shoulders. A biblical sight if ever there was one.

The money my dad wired arrived just a couple of days before I was due to fly out and so for my last 24 hours in the Holy Land I was flush with cash. I decided to go to The King David Hotel for my last night. Jerusalem's most famous hotel had suffered from terror attacks in the past but it was the final place I wanted to be able to say I had visited.

I drank too much that last night and it was a good job that my flight home wasn't until the evening because I woke up with the inevitable and familiar hangover.

All too swiftly my week in Israel had come to an end and it was time to head home. I shared a taxi out to the airport and became quite excited when I saw the British Airways flight to London pop up on the indicator board. Having lived mostly on houmous and pitta bread for the past few days, it was lovely to tuck into the British Airways meal of roast beef with all the trimmings. Who says airline food is bad? I don't agree, sometimes it's just perfect!

I arrived back in London and, to be honest, I felt a bit deflated. My brief time in Africa had taught me many lessons and I hope I became a better person for them. Despite everything I'd seen and everything I experienced, especially the poverty, blatant racism and unfairness of the African continent, I continued to cling to my Catholic faith and, of course, my faith in God. I told myself that surely God worked in mysterious ways.

Chapter 10

Soon after my return from Africa I received many letters from the young people of Mhondoro which were gushing and a far cry from how we would write. Letters would start, "Dearest Beloved Peter," or "Oh precious one, how I miss you." And this was just the boys!

This was how they wrote, boys and girls. It was like a language from a bygone age. I kept in touch with a few of them for a couple of years then sadly lost touch. I was deeply moved by this amazing correspondence and it made me realise what a positive impact I had made on many of the young people at the mission.

Having returned from Rhodesia eighth months early and not required back at my job at the Railways, I took the opportunity to travel and spent time with friends and relatives in Canada. The four months I spent there were amazing and, along with my experiences in Africa, made me realise that there was more to life than working for the Railways. I knew I wouldn't be there for the rest of my life.

I also became aware that everything I did was somehow connected with the Catholic Church. Even my first cycling club was a Catholic cycling club. Dad was a

Catholic trade unionist and there was always the annual visit to Lourdes where I sincerely believe I was at my happiest because I was helping people in a very practical way.

I never missed Mass and, like my father, I was always eager to help the priest.

There was a conclusion to the Helena story, a 'sliding doors' moment. Because I had returned early from my travels, I was able to attend the traditional Boxing Day party thrown by my cyclist friend, Tony. This was the party where I had met Helena exactly a year earlier.

The party was swinging, and I was letting my hair down as I walked into the kitchen for some more booze. I stood frozen in shock as I looked over towards the sink. It was Helena.

'How are you?' she said.

I couldn't move.

'Well, are you going to tell me all about Rhodesia?'

I turned around and walked from the room. A little while later one of her friends came up to me and said she had left the party.

Months later I found out that she hadn't written to me because she didn't want to put temptation in my way and cause me to consider returning home early. She had been distraught that I hadn't written to her but thought it for the better that we had no communication. She went to that party on Boxing Day knowing that I would be there, she was there for me, she wanted to rekindle that spark between us, carry on where we had left off. But, as I so often did, I blew it. I don't know why, I wasn't particularly upset with her. For some reason that night I couldn't bring myself to speak to her and I never saw her again.

Chapter 11

The following year I signed up for the annual pilgrimage to Lourdes. I had been visiting Lourdes every year since 1974 and met some truly wonderful people there who were totally committed to God. It was always an uplifting and yet humbling experience.

I went with a large group known as the Raphael Pilgrimage and I went along as a helper, or *brancardier,* a stretcher-bearer, as we were called in French.

Lourdes is associated with miracle cures but for me the real power of the place was the way it brought people together, and for those who were sick or disabled it was a lovely holiday. On my very first trip I witnessed what I considered at the time a miracle.

One of the sick elderly ladies who I was helping to look after told me she had been coming to Lourdes for years and that she wanted to die there. Spiritually it meant so much to her.

A couple of nights later she got her wish. She passed away peacefully in her sleep. In a strange way I was happy for her but I knew that having one of your party die in a foreign country presents all sorts of problems, and it did.

Another fond memory of my first trip to Lourdes was with one of the older helpers, a chap called Dave.

'Come on Pete,' he said, 'we've been here nearly two hours, we're going to Benediction.'

Well, I knew there was going to be a fair bit of religion as part of this trip but I didn't expect to be dragged to church the moment we arrived. Despite my protests he insisted I walk with him and we left the hospital and walked down the hill into the town centre.

'There you are,' he said as he pointed to the sign above the door: The Joan of Arc Bar.

'I'm parched, I haven't had a pint for nearly 24 hours'

This was what Dave meant by Benediction, a beer or three!

I was greatly relieved, because even at that young age I had discovered the joys to be had from alcohol, particularly in the pleasant atmosphere of a bar. I have to say that this set the pattern for the rest of the week-long trip.

We worked hard, we looked after our sick with great care and compassion then at night we flocked to a bar where we sang, joked and drank until the early hours.

Sometimes we would take some of the willing and mobile sick people with us!

Then first thing next morning we would all be back at the hospital, looking after our people and preparing for some of the lovely excursions that were organised.

The highlight of any trip to Lourdes has to be a visit to the grotto where it is said the Blessed Virgin Mary appeared to a local peasant girl nearly two hundred years ago. Well, I didn't want to visit it for the first time during the day because of the crowds. I wanted to see the grotto when it was quiet, so I went there after the first evening's drinking festivities were over.

It was about one in the morning and practically devoid of people, just a couple of nuns praying in silence. And I'm glad I did go because it had an atmospheric feeling that is hard to describe. It certainly felt very different to any other religious place I had visited. Whether that is anything to do with the Blessed Virgin Mary, or the many good people who were congregated in Lourdes, I have no idea. It is a place I would like to visit again one day.

Lourdes also has a special place in my personal history because I met people there who were to have quite a profound impact on my life's journey. In 1975 there was a priest called Leo Heakin who joined the pilgrimage. We hit it off straight away. He was from Lancashire and a nicer fellow you couldn't meet. He wasn't interested in being called Father, he was just Leo and, like the vast majority of priests, he liked a beer or two.

One evening he dressed up like the pope and entered the hospital wards where our sick people were staying and proceeded to bless them all. It was so funny. Most people took it in the spirit to which it was intended, but one or two of the older, more traditional priests on the pilgrimage didn't think it so funny. But I'm pretty sure God would have approved, it brought joy and happiness to people, some of whom were not going to live for very much longer.

Spending a week with severely disabled and sick people really makes you think. It makes you realise how fortunate most of us are that we do not have to rely on others to do things for us. Basic things, too, like washing and going to the toilet. Things like that. We take so much for granted don't we?

I will never forget one of the pilgrims, a chap called Vic. He was so disabled he could do nothing for himself. He had a 24/7 carer nurse who looked after him and who was devoted to him. There was much more to Vic than met the eye. Turns out he was very well educated. He had even managed to achieve a Ph.D. His disability had not affected his brain and he was a clever chap and he had a great sense of humour.

Vic's body was pretty wrecked and he had to ingest most things through a straw, including booze! One day we were sitting outside one of the pavement cafes in Lourdes town centre. I was drinking a beer and Vic was sipping a vodka and tonic. For his comfort his nurse would tip Vic back in his wheelchair so that he was almost on his side when socialising. A couple of old women, rosaries in hand, passed by us and looked at Vic. You could see the terror in their eyes as they saw this poor chap who was severely disabled apparently hanging from his wheelchair. They both made the sign of the cross as they drew near. Vic motioned to me to come closer.

His speech was also severely impaired but I listened carefully. 'Stupid interfering cows,' he said and laughed. What a guy and what a sense of humour.

This was so typical of Vic. Bless him, he died some years later.

Leo Heakin came from a large Lancashire family and entered the priesthood when he was very young. I think he made up his mind to be a priest when he was barely a teenager.

As well as being an assistant parish priest in Blackburn, Leo was also chaplain in a busy town centre youth club. I visited him on a number of occasions during the next few years and we became good friends. Unlike some priests,

Leo never gave me the creeps, you couldn't meet a nicer bloke.

He would pick me up at Preston railway station and we would head for the nearest pub. There he would remove his priestly dog collar and walk into the pub a civvy. A few hours later we'd walk out and he'd put his dog collar back on. Although not as handsome, he reminded me of Robert De Niro's priest character, Father Bobby, in the film *Sleepers*. He was the type of priest that, if I had ever entered the priesthood, I'd want to be like.

My weekends in Blackburn were great fun. As well as sampling the various local hostelries, which certainly were in abundance in beautiful Lancashire, I would help out at the Catholic youth club and even serve behind the bar in the adjoining social club. And staying in the presbytery of the church where Leo was a priest was very handy for Mass on Sunday mornings!

Over the years I almost lost touch with him but visited him again recently, and it was great to catch up. He was as lovely as ever and very interested in what I had made of Pope Francis when I met him back in 2014. Leo is someone who is a real priest, someone whose love of God is reflected in his love of people. He was aware of what had happened to me and his good question was, 'Who was behind your downfall?'

All I could say is that a few unpleasant people obviously were. They wanted me silenced. They succeeded.

Very recently, at the funeral of a dear friend the officiating priest, a man who normally lives and works in Rome, referred to the Vatican as 'totally corrupt'.

I won't mention his name, suffice to say that there are good priests out there - they are not all abusers. It's just that too many of them are and one is too many. Although I remember this priest's name I will not mention it, because the Church takes a very dim view of anyone who questions it, particularly its own employees.

After my year absence from my job at the Railways I went back to work in my old job at Southern House in Croydon. This was 1978.

During that summer I met someone else I fell in love with. Looking back, I think the only criteria they had to have for me falling in love was that they were good looking and willing to give me the time of day.

I was introduced to a French girl called Marie Christine. She was the niece of very good friends of my parents and her auntie suggested that I might like to show her around London. It was her first visit. She had just turned 18. I was 21. For the next three weeks we became inseparable and I was certain that I was head over heels in love with her.

By that time my brother-in-law George had stopped sexually abusing me but it didn't mean to say that his hold on me was broken. I can't recall the exact time that he stopped his sexual advances, but it was round about the time when I was 14 and I must have put up a particularly good fight one evening when he came into my room.

But that didn't stop him getting to me psychologically, which in many respects is worse than the physical and sexual things that he did.

One day, as Marie Christine and I were walking to a pub on Wimbledon Common, George met us and joined us for some drinks. I remember him making some snide remarks about our relationship but it was the next time I met him that he really turned the knife.

Marie Christine was going to return to France to continue with her studies at the end of the summer. She said we must stay in touch. But when I met George he assured me that someone like her would never marry someone like me.

'She'll marry a pilot or a doctor, you idiot,' he said, 'what makes you think that she's going to end up with someone like you?'

His statement cut me deeply and, despite knowing that I had much love to give to the right woman, I convinced myself he was right. After all, he had predicted I would never win a bike race and he had been proved right. Why would a talented and stunning young girl like her be interested in me? Me, a nobody with two worthless O Levels.

When it came time for Marie Christine to return home and continue her studies, I was convinced that I would never see her again, there was no way would she write to me like she promised.

It broke my heart. I was totally and madly in love with the girl, I thought about her during every waking moment and dreamt about her each evening and the thought of never seeing her again felt like a knife through my heart.

It took me a long time to get over Marie Christine and all the more so because, after I had entered another relationship - with the young woman I went on to marry - she wrote to me, inviting me to come and stay with her and her family in France the following summer. I was devastated. I could not break off the engagement I had entered into because I felt obliged to remain loyal to my fiancée. I was cursing the fact that I had believed George and believed I would never hear from Marie Christine again. He had been wrong.

I was distraught and I was engaged to a young woman I barely knew.

The young woman in question was, and still is, a lovely person. I met her in Blackburn whilst serving behind the bar at that town centre Catholic youth and social club, where Leo Heakin was the chaplain.

Julie and I became inseparable. Her lovely family welcomed me with open arms and in July 1980 we got married. When I look back, I think how unfair it was of me to marry her when I was still harbouring thoughts about Marie Christine and, more importantly, how I had not dealt with the secret trauma and deep psychological scars that I carried from my childhood and youth. We got married in Blackburn and Leo Heakin officiated.

I know that when people split up someone might say, 'It's my fault, you did nothing wrong, it's me.'

Well in our case it really was about me. Julie didn't deserve to go through everything I put her through. If only I had dealt with my issues instead of turning to the bottle and being unfaithful. And I was unfaithful on a few occasions. It was usually around alcohol (you might even say that alcohol became my mistress) and I am ashamed of how I let Julie down. She remains one of the loveliest people I know. She has been an amazing mother to our children, and lately an amazing grandmother to our grandchildren.

But we can't rely on "If only" forever. We have to move on with our lives and if we have not done so because of the curse of abuse, then we really should get help.

I should mention however that some time before I met my future wife, Leo had tried to persuade me to become a priest. He knew it was something I was drawn to but I told him I couldn't envisage life without someone by my side. I had always felt so lonely, not only as a child but also now as I was entering adulthood. He said that God would provide the spiritual company but I was unconvinced. I wanted more of a physical comfort by my side and this lovely Lancashire lass was offering me just that.

Leo recently celebrated 50 years as a priest and I have the greatest admiration for his dedication and faith. Not that he is in any way a slave to the institutional Church, or the "administration", as he calls it. No, Leo is a priest who's only ambition is to serve Christ and his fellow man. As he reminded me, we only need two rules to live by: Love God and love one another. We need no others. Jesus, Leo reminded me, wants spiritual fruit, not religious nuts. A lovely expression.

As is common with many other working priests, I think Leo hasn't much time for the hierarchy of bishops, cardinals and popes. I suspect he would never be interested in having a job that involved wearing a pointy hat.

I returned to Lourdes in 1978, my last ever visit and I have some vivid memories of that trip. For one I nearly fell in love with one of the young female helpers. After returning from France we went on a few dates but she was still seeing another boyfriend and I still harboured ambitions around Marie Christine. So our relationship never really went anywhere but I was so delighted when she contacted me in 2010 to say she had seen me on TV talking about Pope Benedict's visit to Britain. She said I was 'such a lovely chap' and indicated it may have been a mistake to dump me all those years ago. This young lady, I will call her Betty, wasn't the only person to contact me following my many media appearances and I always felt humbled by the reconnection. Perhaps one day I will meet some of these lovely folk again. In my mind's eye they will all be children or young adults but the reality is that they will be like me … approaching old age!

Another memory that sticks from the 1978 Lourdes trip was the night a pretty woman, an older female helper on the pilgrimage, snuck into my room very late after a drinking session and climbed on top of me. I remember who she was but I have never mentioned this before and I will never mention her name. I was sharing a twin room with an elderly priest who was snoring his head off while this woman did her best to have her wicked way with me and I wasn't complaining. Once again it was another test in which I failed miserably and proved to me why I could never have entered a celibate vocation. The reality was that we are all capable of doing stupid things when we have had too much to drink. However, if this had been a man who had entered a woman's bedroom uninvited and climbed on top of a young woman, it would be viewed very differently. The local *gendarmerie* would have been quickly on the scene, I think.

Towards the end of 1990 and at a time when I was between jobs I volunteered to go to Romania with a group of people from the churches I had become associated with. Romania was reeling from its recent past at the time, and its uprising against a communist dictatorship. The Romanians had actually executed their former president in a manner not dissimilar to how the Russians dispatched their royal family more than 70 years before.

The opening up of Romania had also exposed to the world the way in which many of its orphaned children were being treated.

Pictures of these places were beamed around the world and some people thought it would be a good idea to go and help them. So the trip I was a part of was a convoy of three vehicles, packed to the rafters with aid for the orphanages.

Blankets, sheets, toys, washing machines and food were kindly donated by local businesses. The vehicle I travelled in was supplied by a local furniture retailer.

We set off from Stockport and made the late evening crossing from Ramsgate to Dunkirk. We arrived in France late at night and rather than spend money on a hotel we all slept in the cabs of our vehicles none of which, I would add, were designed for overnight accommodation.

It was November and pretty chilly and we all rose very early in order to get some miles under our belts. There was a long way to go. I was driving the furniture van, a beautiful seven and a half tonne Mercedes, on that leg. The seating was luxurious leather and the sound system superb.

My non-driving companion for the trip was a former Catholic monk, who I will call Joe. He was a quiet and gentle chap and, unlike the other people on the trip, he and I were the only two who were Catholic. He had been a monk but had left the order and was looking at other ways of living his faith. We got along.

Our second night was spent near Cologne, where we were guests of a Christian community who put us up in a nice house. They gave us a load of Bibles (in Romanian of course) and the next day we headed to Switzerland and stayed in a nice hotel, paid for by local Christians who gave our leader, Bob, a wad of Swiss francs to help fund the next part of our journey.

After very nearly veering off the road at roadworks we made it to Austria and spent the night in a pleasant traditional hotel not far from the Swiss border. It was now snowing.

We crossed Austria the next day and drove into Hungary. What a cultural difference, we noticed, and how different the roads were. The autobahns of Germany, Switzerland and Austria were swapped for roads that had little room to overtake other vehicles, and a fair number of those other vehicles were horses and carts.

We passed through all the customs checks with relative ease but I remember one customs officer asking me why on earth would I want to help those people. It haunts me to this day that some people have such a dim view of people they see as "inferior" to themselves.

That night in Hungary was a bit of a turning point for me. I had already witnessed some conversations within the group which made me feel a little uncomfortable but the night we spent in a Hungarian hotel was depressingly familiar. It was the first accommodation where Joe and I had to share a double bed. I was not entirely happy with this but we were all sharing rooms and it was too late at night to make a fuss.

I climbed into bed and said good night. Joe suddenly asked if he could hug me. I froze momentarily and found myself, heard myself, saying okay. He leaned over and put his arms around me.

I don't think I felt threatened by him, I don't think he meant me any harm but by the fact that I did not respond to him physically, he knew instantly that I did not want this to be happening. I remember him rolling over to his side of the bed thanking me, and to this day I don't know whether he wanted anything more.

Unlike the man in Rhodesia, unlike the man on the train to Plymouth and unlike the men in my childhood who assaulted me, I will never know if this man was an abuser. I tend to think he was not. I think that there are people who set out to hurt others (God only knows why), and there are those who do it unintentionally. If I were to meet this particular man again I think I would like to have a conversation with him. In my opinion, hugging is something that comes easily to many women but a lot less naturally to men. When we are hugged by someone we don't know it can be off-putting, all the more so for survivors whose early experiences of hugging often turned into something far more sinister.

So this incident really put a damper on the trip for me and I was quite wary of Joe for the rest of our time together. I told the leader, Bob, about the incident because I didn't want to have to share the journey with Joe for the return trip. The rest of the group was going to stay in Romania for a couple of weeks but I needed to get back to the UK and return the furniture lorry. Joe was going to come back with me but after I told Bob he said to Joe that they needed him to stay with the rest of the group, as there was work to do.

There were seven of us on the trip and we stayed in different people's houses when we got to Romania. The town we stayed in was called Hateg, in Transylvania. It was towards the middle of the country and close to the Carpathian Mountains. The day after we arrived we made our first visit to one of the orphanages. To say the place was grim is a gross understatement. Dozens of malnourished children were sitting or lying in row after row of metal cots, which, to be honest, looked more like cages. It was a sight I will never forget and my heart went out to all these little ones who clearly were experiencing a pretty dreadful start to their young lives.

As I drew near a young girl, she stretched out her arms and I instinctively picked her up. She clung to me for what seemed like ages and I practically had to prise her little hands off me before I could move on. I thought she was a baby, so small and light, but she was actually about three years old. One of the nurses said the little girl's name was Maria. I shall never forget her. If she survived she will be in her 30s by now. I hope she did.

Little Maria demonstrated in a most profound way how desperately we need the right kind of hugs and attention when we are little. Some of us still hanker after that as adults. I hope she got plenty more hugs in her young life but my fear as I left the orphanage, and as I left Romania, was that she would not, and that many of these children would once again be forgotten and forsaken.

I was only in Hateg for a few days but I made some friends and I visited a couple of churches. One was the Catholic Church, which I found to be cold and almost empty, and one was the local Baptist Church, which was warm and packed to the rafters.

The shops had hardly anything in them and petrol was hard to come by, unless you were a foreigner bearing a strong currency. Whilst local cars had to queue for ages to get petrol, foreign vehicles were allowed to go straight to the front of the queue. It was the same at the Romanian border crossing. In both directions I was sent to the front of the queue, and the queue leaving Romania stretched for what seemed like many miles.

I was quite excited at the prospect of driving home on my own and I set off early one morning in the December mist. It was very cold but all my travel companions rose early to see me off. Bob gave me enough cash to get me home and I headed for the border which was some hours away. I passed through the city of Timisoara, a place that had seen the start of the Romanian uprising not many months before. I felt quite emotional. It's not often you visit a place where such a recent political, not to mention violent, upheaval took place.

I didn't stop, I drove straight through the city and headed for the Hungarian border. Up until that time I had not realized that many Hungarians lived in Romania. The place has quite a history.

I drove into Hungary and headed straight through Budapest and made for the Austrian border. From Hungary I crossed into Austria and that was the first time I had a problem at customs. The crossing was quiet. I had an empty vehicle and expected to be through in minutes. My passport was in order, I had plenty of money and I was clean-shaven. However, the Austrian customs officer didn't like me at all, he decided I was up to no good.

Perhaps he just didn't like the British, particularly those taking aid to folks in other lands. I will never know. All I know is that he took my passport from me and made me park up while he did … who knows what. I told him a dozen times where I had been, what I was doing and how I was simply heading home but he still didn't like it.

I was there at least a couple of hours, maybe a bit longer, before the officer came over, flung my passport at me and told me to get lost. The delay meant I didn't get very far that day, reaching Vienna shortly after dusk. I couldn't see any cheap-looking hotels or B&Bs, so for the second time I did my best to get some sleep in the cab. It was very cold.

I managed a few hours before heading out of that beautiful city as the sun was coming up. It was a bit eerie but worth experiencing. I was now bound for the German border.

Oh, to be on those autobahns again. The miles flew by. I stayed one more night, in a motel just off the autobahn, then made a dash for the channel ports and Blighty. I arrived in Dunkirk and joined the queue for the ferry. Unfortunately, I didn't have a reservation but because the boat wasn't full they were going to let me on. It was while I was waiting to board, that another lorry driver told me that we had a new prime minister. Margaret Thatcher had been toppled and we now had, in his words, 'Bloody John Major.'

If I thought the Austrian customs people had been difficult, it was nothing compared to what was to come when I reached England.

The ferry arrived in Dover very late in the evening and I headed for the customs queue, which was short. A very polite young customs officer took my passport and told me to drive into one of the big sheds.

Just my luck, I thought, a spot check just as I was nearly home.

The customs officer interrogated me. Had I stopped to pick anything or anyone up, where had I been, what route did I take?

The questions kept coming and the back of the van was opened up. It was empty apart from my small case, which I don't recall them opening. I also remember that they did not search the front cab where, if I had been smuggling something, I might have concealed it. They went round the lorry tapping it in certain places and then decided to start drilling holes in it.

I knew I was carrying nothing illegal but I was starting to worry about what time I might get home. Late night was now turning into the early hours of the next day. They told me to lock the vehicle and wait in their office. I did as I was told, they had my passport and my life in their hands.

I waited and waited. In the end, because I could see very little movement and because all the other vehicles had long left the port, I went up to the office window and with as much calmness as I could muster informed them that if they didn't return my passport soon, I would drive through the gates of the port and on to the road home, because by then I was so tired that the prospect of a night in a police cell held no fear for me.

I sat back down and about a minute later a woman officer beckoned me over, handed me my passport and said goodbye with a smile, or was it a smirk? Either way I didn't really care. I headed out and just accepted that some people in uniform enjoy their little bit of power.

Sad and embarrassing. Embarrassing, because I had to return the lorry to the furniture shop in Macclesfield riddled with holes.

Part Two

Chapter 12

I looked up to my brother Mike, but it was in my teenage years that I realised that he too had many demons. I suspected that he suffered along with me in that cold relationship that we had with our parents, but at the time I only suspected he was also one of the victims of the Jesuits at Wimbledon College.

His school reports at Wimbledon College echoed the hope of his earlier ones, but then it all went downhill. His reports were not good and he ended up passing just one O Level. I'm pretty sure he re-sat some and got more but clearly his time at the college was not a happy one and it was only all these years later that things fell into place.

I remember that Mike was drinking and smoking dope whilst still a schoolboy, and this would tie in with the oppression we suffered at home, compounded by the abuse he was suffering at school. When I actually spoke to Mike, the night before he was sent to prison,
he conceded that the sexual abuse by Father Battersby may have had an effect on his life.

He didn't go into detail and, like many abuse survivors, my brother minimised the effect it had had on him rather than blame the Jesuits for all his failings. This was typical of Mike. He also told me that our brother-in-law, George, had sexually assaulted him on one occasion when he was 19. This made it easier for Mike to believe what our brother-in-law had done to me. It seems George liked to grab young male genitalia.

It was all falling into place.

There is so much I could write about my brother. As a little boy I naturally looked up to him but looking back I can see what a nuisance I would have been at times. I learnt to play chess at a very early age and on a Saturday morning I would set the pieces up and demand a game as soon as he woke. We still shared a bedroom then. I was perhaps 11 or 12 and Mike would have been 17 or 18. He would have been out the night before getting drunk or doing what teenagers did in those days but I would have insisted he play chess.

I loved Mike very much and when he left home I missed him a lot. And he left home young. He went travelling to India when he was about 19. He hitchhiked most of the way.

A few other things about my late brother stick in my head. In 1974 he lived in Portugal for a while. This was at the time of the Portuguese revolution. He had gone over in an old ambulance he had converted into a mobile home. Nothing fancy. A bed. Cooking stove. Candles and curtains. Well, I remember him telling me that as he was returning to his van in Lisbon, after an evening of drinking, there was a pitch battle going on between government troops and the revolutionaries. Mike being Mike, raised a white flag and asked that the fighting cease while he got his van out of the way. And they did! I will never forget seeing the bullet holes in the van when he got home.

Mike never really settled back into what you might call normal life. He had had some terrifying experiences in India. One he told me about was having a knife held to his throat as he was robbed of most of his possessions. Another was when he was thrown into a police cell in Afghanistan for a number of days for, according to him, being in possession of long hair. I suspect there was more to it than that though! But he did return from India with (very) long hair and suffering from malnutrition. I will never forget watching my mum sneak up to him as he lay in bed one morning with scissors to try and cut it. She didn't manage it because Mike instinctively woke up and pushed her away. I think this further illustrates the sort of dysfunctional household we were living in.

Sometime later Mike nearly lost his life living in that converted ambulance. He must have fallen asleep and dropped a cigarette or knocked a candle over because the whole thing went up in flames and he was lucky to survive. He spent some weeks in hospital following this incident.

When he came back from his travels Mike worked in an old folk's home, not far from our home in Wimbledon. It was hardly the right environment but it was away from Mum and her scissors, and he had his own accommodation there. Not very long after working there he got into a relationship with the matron of the home. He ended up marrying her. She was lovely and she was about 30 years older than Mike. He actually gained two stepsons, who were older than him!

Mike's wife was a Catholic woman, which suited our father and although the age gap was certainly a problem for some people (Mum, for example) it didn't stop them from marrying. I remember how they struggled to find a

Catholic priest who would officiate at their wedding with her being a divorcee, but they eventually found one in Portsmouth. I think he was a chaplain at the university down there. And the reason they got married in a Catholic Church was to keep Mum and Dad happy!

It's difficult to speak ill of the dead, but the way Dad treated us leaves me with a lot of questions and makes what happened a few days before he died all the more moving. He said to me that he had hit us all as children and perhaps that was the wrong thing to do. I have no idea what prompted his deathbed confession and I had to fight back the tears as he said it.

'Dad, you did what you thought was right'.

'Yes, it was how I was brought up,' he said.

A day or two later, as he was in his final hours, I said to him I was going to sort our family out. I don't think I knew what I was saying but those words came out and I could see a smile behind Dad's closed eyes.

Conscious that I had spent weeks at his side, Dad said that I must go home that particular night and get some proper sleep.

That was the last time I saw him alive. The next morning I woke and experienced a feeling I'd never experienced before or since. I had a feeling of utter dread. I knew Dad was going to die that day.

I washed, dressed and drove to Wimbledon. On my way through Richmond Park I felt compelled to stop and pray, which I did. Something told me to go see my sister Pauline. I drove to hers instead of Mum and Dad's.

As I entered the house I said to her, 'We need to talk.'

Pauline said, 'Did George abuse you?' Pauline and George had been separated for several years and to this day I still do not know why she asked me that question.

‘Yes, he did.’ Pauline showed no reaction at all and I didn’t know what to say to her.

This conversation took me completely by surprise and as we were having this difficult talk, the phone rang. It was my sister, Mary. Dad had just died. Everything felt a little eerie, a little too coincidental. It was hard to put a finger on what was going on.

I went straight round to Mum and Dad’s and sat with my dad’s body for a while before ringing the undertakers and our church.

I’ll never forget the peace and tranquillity I felt in those moments in that bedroom, a bedroom I rarely dared to enter as a child. I sensed an amazing spiritual presence and I knew what I had to do with such clarity.

After a while I rang the undertakers and explained what had happened. They talked me through the formalities and said they would be there very soon. Then I called the church presbytery.

A priest had visited my dad a week or two before and I remember him saying that Dad didn’t really need a priest as his ‘place in Heaven was assured’. I remember thinking that that was a bit of a cop-out on the priest’s behalf, and he never visited Dad again.

It was the same priest who answered the telephone.

‘Hello Father, it’s Pete Saunders, I’m just calling you to tell you that Dad has just died.’

‘Okay Pete, you need to ring the undertakers.’

‘I’ve already done that, Father, the undertakers just near us in Raynes Park.’

‘Bloody hell no,’ he cursed, ‘we don’t use them, we use so and so.’

I couldn’t believe this man. My dad has just died and instead of saying sorry and offering his condolences, he swore at me for calling the wrong funeral directors. I suspect there was probably a financial arrangement between them and the funeral directors he wanted me to use.

I seem to remember that he then tried to persuade me to change funeral directors but I flatly refused. I was incredibly angry at his total lack of compassion. A great advert for the Jesuits, a great advert for the priesthood.

Chapter 13

Dad died on the 3rd of October 1995. I spent the last weeks of his life by his side. We finally had a close relationship.

All my life I had been scared of my dad. I was never able to talk to him, least of all about what happened to me as a child and as a teenager. But now it was too late to burden him with this as he was dying. As I looked at my own children at this time, roughly the age at which I had first been attacked, I vowed to do something about it. To try and stop it, to speak out, not to remain silent any longer.

I quickly discovered that far from being one in a million I was just one of millions who had suffered abuse in childhood. My silence had been my protection. It was my protection from having to face the unthinkable, to speak the unspeakable. Why did I not speak out as a child? The child understands that perfectly but as you move to adulthood you realise that those who have not suffered cannot understand why you didn't speak out, so we have to explain that to the world, explain why sometimes silence is our protector.

A few days after Dad's death I knew I had to report what had happened to me in childhood. I had kept silent for nearly 40 years and looking back, part of that silence was to protect my family, including my parents, from the truth. But now it needed to come out and, perhaps foolishly, I thought there would be some justice.

The night before Dad's funeral I spoke to my two nephews and my sister about why I was not going to allow their father to attend their grandfather's funeral. I didn't go into detail but I told them he had abused me as a child and that he had recently insulted my dying father and our family in a very profound way. A few days earlier I had bumped into George whilst in a local shop. He snidely asked, 'How's your father?'

'He's dying, George.'

George sniggered and said he hoped we hadn't wasted money on a stair lift. I could hardly believe my ears but then knowing George's capacity for the most insensitive and hurtful of comments perhaps I shouldn't have been surprised. This was one of the moments when it really dawned on me what a dreadful man he was.

My nephews listened in stony silence then one of them said, 'I don't like what you have just told us Uncle Pete, but I believe you.'

The other nephew said something similar and then added that he too had been abused by his father. I was horrified, it was like a knife through the heart but I wasn't surprised either. He said he needed to go to bed but said that he did not want me to do anything about his father at that stage. I think he sensed that I was going to report his father to the police and not only was that the right thing to do - but it was also the only thing to do.

Again Pauline did not react to the revelation and I remained confused.

A few days later I drove to a nearby police station and said I wanted to report a serious crime. After a short wait I was summoned to a room by a very pleasant detective sergeant who said he would take my statement. He was a lovely chap but pre-empted the conversation by saying he was retiring soon because his work with sexual abuse crime had worn him out. Now, many years later, I understand exactly what he was saying. Nevertheless, I made a full statement and he assured me that not only did he believe what I had told him but that there would be a thorough investigation.

Many weeks went by and I hadn't heard anything. I rang the police station and spoke to the same detective sergeant who invited me to attend the police station.

This time I was greeted by both him and a female colleague. As I sat down in the small interview room I was astounded to hear them say that my family, specifically my sisters, were not going to support me.

What? I couldn't believe what the police were telling me and at first it didn't sink in. I didn't know what this meant but with the benefit of hindsight, not to mention years of trying to understand the family dynamics around families and abuse, I understand a little better. But the upshot was that the police were going to do nothing about George and, whilst they believed everything I had told them, they said I should just get on with my life. I remember the detective sergeant saying, 'He's ruined half your life, don't let him ruin the rest.'

I was furious. I told them that he was still working in a school with a thousand pupils.

They acknowledged this and then said that under no circumstances must I go to his school or I might be arrested for harassment. This was an unbelievable turn of events, they put it in plain terms that I could be arrested for telling the truth.

I was shaking and close to tears. They advised me to go home and get on with my life. They even put an arm round me to try and comfort me, they could see how upset I was.

But I had a determination that nobody could shake and I left the police station and drove straight to the school. My old school. They could arrest me if they wanted to but I wasn't going to allow this man to continue to have unfettered access to vulnerable children. He was still a teacher. He was a very real danger to children.

I drove into the school grounds and parked my car. It was the first time I had been on those premises that held such unhappy and haunting memories for over 20 years. I found my way to the administration office and told the receptionist that I wished to speak to the head teacher. I was expecting to be questioned as to why I would be making such a request but, amazingly, this woman looked at me, clearly sensed that it was urgent and told me to wait. Less than five minutes later, the head teacher, a Jesuit priest by the name of Michael Holman, swept into the room and beckoned me to follow him into his office. It turned out he had been teaching at the time of my arrival but something must have told him that this was important.

We sat down.

'How can I help you?' he said.

'I wish to inform you that you have an abuser teaching in your school.'

Ashen faced he looked hard at me, trying to work out who I was. I was clearly an old boy of the school but I could sense he was trying to work out when I had been there. We were of similar age and I guess he may have been thinking, 'Do I know this chap? Were we at school at the same time?' As it turns out we were.

He said he was responsible for the safety and wellbeing of every child in the school and he needed to know who this person was.

I told him I would reveal this information but only in the presence of a witness. He agreed we could meet the following weekend and we set up a meeting for the following Saturday morning. But then he said a worrying thing. He shook my hand and said that whatever had happened to me had happened a long time ago. Not good, not the initial response I had been looking for.

I pointed out that the man I was accusing was still employed at his school and would still pose a threat to children. He sort of retracted his unhelpful comment but I look back and realise now that he is a member of a very exclusive club, a man's club of clergy and they always make excuses or belittle the dreadful experiences suffered by victims of abuse. A 'long time ago.' Does that make it okay?

We met at the school a few days later and I was accompanied by a friend. Father Holman was accompanied by a solicitor. I gave a full account of what had happened to me many years ago and how it still dominated my life today. The solicitor wrote everything down. I was asked if I would be prepared to recount my experience to the school's board of governors and I agreed. The solicitor seemed quite clued up around issues of abuse and I sensed that he had experienced something like this meeting before. I can't remember how much I told them about the two Jesuit priests who had assaulted me, but I knew that one of them was dead and the other one was probably very old by now. In my mind's eye I didn't consider them a danger but that was not the case with my ex-brother-in-law.

Father Holman said they would take swift action but many weeks went by and I heard nothing. Echoes of the police response. I contacted the school and a few days later received a letter from the head teacher to say that they had suspended George the next working day and that he denied all knowledge of abuse. No surprise there. However, as far as I could make out, rather than face his accuser, me, George opted for early retirement. How convenient.

That outcome seems to be the favoured one for so many institutions. Let the accused person walk quietly away or even give them a good reference so they can get a job at another school. I have lost count of how many times I've heard that. I would like to think that things are better today but I am not so sure they are, despite dedicating the best part of twenty years of my life trying to make a difference. Trying to make the world a safer place for children.

The letter I received from Father Holman, whilst indicating some sympathy for me, was clearly written in a legalistic fashion because it said words to the effect of 'Sorry you felt you were abused,' … not the same as acknowledging that abuse took place. Such legalese is quite normal for an institution more interested in protecting itself and its wealth than seeing justice done.

Chapter 14

When I knocked on the door of my principal abuser in 2001, I naïvely thought I could have a conversation with him. Did I have forgiveness in my head? Yes, I suppose I did, but I confronted George that night because I still felt I was somehow under his control. It sounds irrational, I know.

I was now a man in his 40s, not a child anymore, but there was something going on for me that meant I simply had to confront him. I had to ask him why he did what he did to me. Hanging on to hatred is like swallowing poison and hoping the other person drops dead. It's not healthy.

I had recently lost a good friend and I think this had something to do with it. She was a good woman and this idea came into my head about how good people seem to die too young and others, some of the less good people, seem to last forever. I confess I had had a few pints of beer before knocking on his door.

George opened the door. When he saw it was me he stared at the sky.

'Hello George,' I said, 'I want to know why you did what you did to me when I was a child.'

He never gave me an answer. Instead, he said that his headmaster at Wimbledon College had seen the article about me in *The Times* newspaper and the headmaster was supporting him.

I don't know what he meant by that because I know for a fact that the headmaster had suspended George the next working day after I reported him to the school, six years previously. By this time George's girlfriend, the woman he was living with, came down the stairs of the maisonette, carrying a gun. She held it to my face and said that they had been expecting me. Wow, expecting me for six years!

I never thought I would have the guts to go and confront him, but here I was, and for my efforts I was about to get shot!

I was frightened but I was determined to stand my ground. I'm not sure whether George's girlfriend believed that he was an abuser, my experience tells me that abusers are very good liars.

'You'd better pull the trigger,' I said, 'because as soon as I leave here I am calling the police.'

George was shouting at her, telling her to go back upstairs and ring the police. Quite a strange move I thought, but things fell into place a little later.

By this time George was starting to rant about my family, hurling insults at my late father and my mum and my sister - his estranged wife. All the while I noticed that he couldn't look me in the eye. Coward, I was no longer the little boy he could push around.

It wasn't long before the police arrived, four of them. As they came down the garden path I said that there was a woman upstairs with a gun, threatening to kill me, and that she had held it to my head.

Three of them ran straight into the hallway and up the stairs. Another officer told me to wait on the pavement. More police arrived and a senior officer spoke with me.

He said, 'Is he the man who abused you?'

At first I didn't have a clue how he knew that but looking back I guess George's girlfriend may have said something when she called the police.

The policeman was very sympathetic. He said they get a lot of calls about this sort of thing and that he can tell me what they would like to do to these sort of men.

There was a lot of activity for a good few minutes then the officer said that they would drive me home. I told them there was no need because I just lived around the corner but he insisted on driving me home. I was very emotional and angry and he was obviously worried that I might return to the house. Don't ask me why, but by now I had started to cry quite openly.

Very early the next morning the phone rang. It was Wimbledon police station. They asked me if I would like to make a statement about the previous night's incident. 'Absolutely,' I replied. I had a quick bath then got in my car and headed to the police station.

I was greeted by another very pleasant policeman, a plain clothes detective, who was not on duty the night before so he didn't know exactly what had happened. I gave a full account of what had happened and he wrote it all down.

He said that he didn't doubt what I was telling him, but that George and his partner had given a completely different account. They said I had tried to force my way into their flat and they feared for their lives, hence the gun. Of course this was absolute bullshit because I didn't so much as step across their threshold. The policeman reiterated that he believed me, and said it was two words against one.

I told him that I understood, but what about the gun? It was post the Dunblane massacre (another paedophile who murdered lots of children), and handguns were now illegal in the UK. The officer told me that George and his partner claimed the gun was a starting pistol which looked like a real gun.

'Bloody right,' I said, 'when it was held up to my face I was convinced it was a real gun.'

The policeman said he wasn't so sure that it could fire live rounds, but they would be sending it away for a proper ballistics examination. He said that if it turned out it could be fired George and his partner may be charged with illegal possession.

I told him that I had reported George to the police six years earlier but that no action had been taken. The officer suggested I might want to try again to have him arrested. The police had moved on a bit with how they viewed and treated these crimes and he very kindly said that he would see if my file was still in the system. If I wanted, I could start over and pick up where I left off six years earlier. I gave him the name of the police station where I had made my initial complaint, as well as the name of the detective sergeant who handled my case.

True to his word the officer rang me back later that day to say that my file was still there and if I wanted to go after George again I would have his support. I thanked him and said I would think about it.

I never went after him again and there were a number of reasons for this.

Firstly, I didn't want my family and particularly my niece and nephews to suffer for what their father had done and I thought a court case would undoubtedly bring some media attention. It is so tragic that the families of abusers undoubtedly suffer the consequences of their offending relatives' crimes. Put simply, I couldn't put those people, my family, through a court case. I thought the matter ended there. There was a little door that closed in my head because I had finally confronted him, but yes, George in most respects got away with his vile crimes.

There were no further charges brought on possession of an illegal firearm so I can only assume that it was a starting pistol after all. George had his lucrative retirement package and no doubt everyone thought and hoped that would be the end of it.

Little did any of them know that I was to set up an organisation that would give a voice to thousands of other survivors of abuse, or that I would get the sort of media coverage I ended up receiving, as well as a private meeting with the pope.

Chapter 15

One of the other things I did when Dad died was to contact the archbishop of Westminster, Cardinal Basil Hume.

I wrote to him and was amazed to get a reply and an invitation to meet with him.

This happened in December 1995 and the meeting was reported in the *Catholic Herald* newspaper.

I spent about an hour with the cardinal and he seemed genuinely concerned about all I was telling him. I told him about the abuse I suffered at the hands of my brother-in-law and the Jesuits at my school. I also told him I wanted to set up an organisation to support survivors, and he said he would do what he could to support me.

I left the archbishop's house feeling heard and supported, it was another high hopes moment. But it was a premature hope and pretty soon I would encounter the reality of the Church's response. As mentioned above, nothing came of this meeting.

I now know that the Catholic Church is really only interested in protecting itself and minimising the damage. It doesn't give a fig about the people. And, what I appreciate now that I didn't appreciate then, was that the real "Church" is actually the people, the ones who are

Christ's followers. Do we really need an organised body that takes money from us to follow the teachings of Jesus? If God is all powerful why is it that every Christian church on the planet appeals for money? How come God is not so good with the finances?

But they hold all the power and the wealth and woe betide anyone who crosses them.

Many years later, to my dismay, I found out that Basil Hume was also accused of hushing up a sexual abuse scandal at Ampleforth College when he was abbot. He had received a complaint from parents in 1975 about Father Piers Grant-Ferris, who was the son of a Tory peer. Hume had taken the decision not to call the police and the complaints were not acted upon. Years later, in 2005, Grant-Ferris admitted 20 incidents of child abuse. Other monks and lay members were accused of physical and sexual abuse. The local newspaper said that pupils at Ampleforth had suffered decades of abuse, involving at least six paedophiles. They criticised Hume for not calling the police at the beginning of this scandal.

In another little twist in 1984, Basil Hume nominated Jimmy Savile for membership of the Athenaeum Club in London's Pall Mall and his membership was accepted, though they quickly disassociated themselves with him when Savile's abuse allegations were widely reported upon his death. They also criticised Cardinal Basil Hume for nominating him in the first place.

Ultimately, I received no support from the cardinal and instead was fobbed off onto another priest, Monsignor Ralph Brown. He also had an office at the archbishop's house and I was summoned to see him one morning. I was told he only saw people in the morning because by the afternoon he was generally incapacitated because of drink.

Very professional. I found out years later that Ralph Brown was also a canon lawyer.

When I met Monsignor Brown he told me he had never heard of priests abusing children before. I couldn't quite believe the words that had tumbled from his mouth. He went on to say that I should meet up with another fellow who was experiencing similar problems.

I met up with this other chap, a good man called Noel Chardon, an Australian. I think we both realised that we had been fobbed off onto each other. Perhaps Monsignor Ralph Brown thought it was a clever move but one that neither of us really fell for. We could both see how the men in robes just wanted us to go away.

I followed up this rather negative encounter with another letter to Cardinal Hume but his brief response was that he had other things to consider, in other words go away, he was too busy but wished me well.

My feeling at the time was that he had been "got at". I felt he wanted to help me but his officials were telling him not to get involved, that they don't help survivors, they are trouble. I was unaware then that there had been numerous allegations of abuse at Ampleforth during the time that Basil Hume was in charge as chief abbot - enough said.

Around this time I also talked with a female survivor who had been battling the Church for some time. Her name is Margaret Kennedy and she founded a group for survivors of clergy abuse. Margaret, like me, had tried to harness the help of "our" church but to no avail. She battled for many years, and as far as I know Margaret is back in her native Ireland and enjoying a peaceful retirement. At least I hope she is, she certainly deserves that.

I had meetings with both Cardinal Hume's successors, Cardinal Cormac Murphy O'Connor and Cardinal Vincent Nichols. Neither yielded much more than the assurance of prayerful support, which unfortunately does not help pay to run a charity. I was sensible enough to take my wife along to the meeting with Cardinal Murphy O'Connor. You do need a witness at these sorts of meetings. Without one it is likely the event "may never have happened"!

Just like Ralph Brown, Cardinal O'Connor indicated that he was unaware of priestly abuse but would pray for me. Where had I heard that before? He said that he may be able to make a small financial contribution from his personal funds to NAPAC. He sent a thousand pounds.

One thing that sticks in my memory from that meeting, and remembered by my wife too, was that when the question of funding came up, the cardinal shuddered and said quite clearly, 'We don't want to go down the compensation route.'

I hadn't even mentioned compensation during our conversation.

He also said something about not understanding the damage that had been caused to the Church by child abuse allegations in the past.

Later on I discovered that Cardinal Murphy O'Connor had done his fair share of covering up and moving abusing priests from one place to another, the most notorious being the case of Fr. Michael Hill, a prolific abuser who Archbishop Murphy O'Connor protected and moved from place to place within his diocese. Hill was subsequently jailed for his crimes. The man who protected him was promoted to cardinal.

It's hard to explain the freedom I felt when Dad died, but I felt it and having spoken to many other abuse survivors over the years, this is not that uncommon, especially given the relationship I had with my dad. Or should I say the relationship I didn't have with him? I had always been scared of him. He was very strict and although my brothers and sisters said I had an easier time than them I'm not sure that was true. They all had each other but when I came along it was a bit like being an only child. While Dad's death was like a window opening out onto the world, for me it was also a time of great turmoil.

It was just days after Dad's funeral that my brother Mike was sent to HMP Winchester for six months.

When and where had it all started to go wrong for Mike and, more importantly, why? He was an intelligent, bright boy who should have probably gone to university. And this was in the days when only a small percentage of the population did this.

Chapter 16

After Dad's death I dedicated most of my time to setting up NAPAC and had meetings with other interested parties and obtained the patronage of, amongst others, Dame Esther Rantzen, the founder of ChildLine.

Many of the people from those early days remain friends and I intend to keep in touch with them in my life after NAPAC. Many are very dear to me as is my family, though I rarely see some of them. We've always kept in touch by email or phone. In fact, a number of my oldest friends and NAPAC supporters attended the NAPAC anniversary event that I organised in 2017, including Dame Esther and Deirdre Sanders, who sent a lovely video message, as did the prime minister, Theresa May. Valerie Sinason, James Rhodes and many others were there. James is an abuse survivor who turned his life around with his love of music. He is an amazing pianist and played some beautiful music that evening.

Actress Emilia Fox (who starred in the TV series *Silent Witness*), was also there with her daughter, Rose. You honestly couldn't meet nicer people. It was such a shame that only two of the Trustees at the time were able to attend. It was a great night. The venue, The Manor at Bickley, in Bromley, did us proud.

I made sure that our volunteers were invited to this event and was thrilled that a group of them were able to travel down from our office in the Northwest. They had a great time, too.

One of the things from those early days of NAPAC I remember vividly was speaking on BBC Radio 5 Live about childhood abuse. A convicted child abuser was interviewed (in a different studio to where I was), and I will never forget him saying that perpetrators ensure silence in a number of ways and that one of the things they do not want is adult survivors speaking out. They want us to remain silent. And one of the things I've said at many of the conferences and seminars I have spoken at over the years, is that I will not remain silent about this issue. Some people have attempted to silence me but you are reading this book and that is proof that their attempts have failed.

It was also around this time that the chief reporter of *The Telegraph*, Robert Mendick, wrote in an article, 'Mr Saunders is widely respected as the leading campaigner for the rights of abuse survivors.'

Another thing this abuser in the other studio said was how easy it was to spot, and abuse, vulnerable children. And a child who is suffering abuse of some kind at home, is bound to be vulnerable, even looking for affection, and when that child encounters a manipulative abuser, the child stands no chance. I remained silent for over 20 years and the internal pain that caused me remains with me to this day.

I put my energies and passion into setting up an organisation to help others like me and for the next umpteen years I did that 24/7. I gave up my teaching career and devoted all my energies to helping others, and the others flooded forward.

The very first public meeting where the roots of NAPAC were planted, was in December 1995. The same day I appeared on the *Kilroy* TV chat show. The following morning I was interviewed on the *Today* programme on BBC Radio 4.

My ex-wife and my two children leafleted the area where they lived and the meeting took place at Warren Wood Primary School, my children's school. My own children (and subsequently my stepchildren) were very much part of establishing what was to become NAPAC. It was a labour of love and I can never thank them enough.

A few things stick out in my memory of that first meeting, more than a quarter of a century ago. One was the refusal of a child protection officer from the local authority to attend and the other was the intimidating manner of one of the two police officers who did attend. He kept telling me to 'Mind your own business.' I'll never forget him. I have subsequently met and worked with many decent and dedicated police officers but this chap, frankly, scared me.

Chapter 17

I married a co-founder of the charity and without her I may not have survived. I met her under quite interesting circumstances. I was teaching in a large college in West London. I visited the library one day and instead of going to the Business Studies section (my subject), found myself looking at books about social issues and spotted a book about child abuse. I took it home and read it from cover to cover. Some of it was like reading about myself. Some people reading my story will probably, sadly, be able to identify with it too.

The book gave several accounts of adult men and women describing traumatic experiences of sexual abuse in childhood. I was inspired by their bravery which struck a chord with me. I wrote to the author to thank her for such an inspiring book.

Well, I never expected a reply but one afternoon I took a call from the author and she invited me to dinner.

I spent a lovely evening with her at her garden flat in London. She was very supportive of my plans to set up an organisation for survivors and said she would do all she could to help. She later put me in contact with some of the people who were involved in her research and interested in being part of setting up an organisation to support adults who were abused as children, and to my amazement, planned and hosted a dinner party. Tricia, my future wife, was at the dinner party. She shared her experience of childhood trauma with me and I could understand her passion for helping others. You can read about Tricia's experiences in her recently published book, *Because It Didn't Stop When It Ended.*

Already I was beginning to feel less alone. I was now very aware that I was one of many who had suffered childhood abuse. I don't think Tricia and I were a case of love at first sight, but I was certainly struck by her lovely personality and her good looks, and we both shared a Christian faith.

I told the author and Tricia that I was proposing to have a public meeting in the months that followed from which I hoped a committee might be formed, to advance the plans for NAPAC. Both agreed to be speakers at that meeting and barely one year later the meeting took place at the head office of the NSPCC. The meeting was chaired by Deidre Sanders and Tricia was undoubtedly the best speaker. I knew then that she would become a major part of my plans for the organisation. Little did I know at that point that she would become my wife!

The meeting (in January 1997) was attended by over 100 people. It included CEOs and deputy CEOs from some major national charities including the NSPCC, The Children's Society, Mind, Boarding School Survivors, Victim Support, and many more. A few MPs attended too, which was encouraging. It was also attended by survivors who had contacted me following a piece in *The Times* a few months earlier, about the abuse I suffered. The meeting lasted all afternoon and inevitably a fair few of us ended up in the pub afterwards. Indeed, a feature of many of the subsequent NAPAC committee meetings would conclude with a pint or three in a local hostelry.

At the end of the meeting I asked for volunteers to form a committee. Well, there was no shortage of people who wanted to be involved and so, for the next year or two, too many of us attempted to take the whole thing forward. At that first committee meeting, attended by about 20 people, there was a proposal that I be made chair. I reluctantly accepted the nomination and was voted in, but there was one slight hitch. One person on the committee said she could not be part of an organisation that had a man as its chair. I look back on this with sadness because she, like some other less-informed people, seem to think that men are only ever the abusers. As I mention elsewhere this is patently not true. To this day I am saddened when I hear talk of violence just against women and girls. That is appalling and must be challenged, but there is also a lot of violence and abuse perpetrated against boys and men.

Although the committee was too big in the early days we did get a lot done. One of the first tasks was to think of a name for the new organisation. That, I can tell you, was an interesting and sometimes humorous discussion. Given that one of the main priorities was to establish a telephone help line for survivors (a sort of ChildLine for adults) we had some interesting suggestions. I won't bore you with them all, but I always remember one which was that we call ourselves the Adult Abuse Line. Can you imagine the response to this? We thought about those Monty Python sketches like the Ministry of Silly Walks and we thought about people calling our helpline and hearing a load of abuse! As I often say, you have to maintain a sense of humour in the murky world of abuse otherwise you might go mad. We all had a good laugh about this suggestion, not necessarily received too well by the person who suggested it, but they did get it in the end. When we settled on NAPAC everyone signed up and agreed. We were to become the National Association for People Abused in Childhood. It may not have been the most dynamic or exciting title but it said exactly who we were.

I drew up a business plan and others worked on different projects and papers. Tricia spent many hours filling out the paperwork for the Charity Commission (these were the pre-online days) and Companies House. This was 1997 and in May 1998 NAPAC became a registered charity.

As well as being chair I had also committed to organising a march and rally in support of survivors. Part of me wishes I had never taken that on because it was a lot of work. On the same morning that we had the march and rally in Trafalgar Square, I had made a live appearance on the BBC News Channel, but I think it was too early to reach many people on a Saturday morning. One of our committee had put out a press release to all the main British media but our event was mostly ignored. As had the previous incarnations of the same event in past years. Child abuse and survivors were still not a popular or cosy cause.

I do remember seeing a very small group of people in Hyde Park (not far from where we were gathering), who were demonstrating in support of the legalisation of cannabis. I spotted at least two TV cameras and a handful of journalists covering that event, but they totally ignored ours. Sad, and an indication of the past and present attitude towards child abuse.

NAPAC started life as a charity in a bedroom in my mum's house. As well as writing to all and sundry, government ministers, Members of Parliament, agony aunts *etc.*, I also drew up a short business plan and sent it to as many organisations and individuals who I thought might be interested. It drew quite a lot of interest and a fair few donations, and with those donations we were able to buy a computer, printer, filing cabinet and nice headed paper. Being pre-email days I thought it important to present a positive image and that included quality headed stationery. We may have been living on a brown ale budget but I was determined to present a champagne style company and it certainly appeared to have worked.

Donations came in and I received a large number of very supportive letters from people, like the late Claire Rayner. Claire was a leading light in the rights of patients and one of the UK's best known and loved "agony aunts". She sent me a beautiful reply urging me to get on with it, it was a "much needed" organisation. I only had the pleasure of meeting her once, but her loving support remains a vivid memory for me. I received many letters of encouragement and I really thought I would get the charity up and running quite quickly. I was wrong. These things don't just happen overnight. They take weeks, months and years of hard work.

The first three years of NAPAC saw me doing other paid work alongside my role as a volunteer at NAPAC. Firstly, it was as a lecturer at the college in West London, then at AVMA (the charity for survivors of medical accidents) and then for a while as a labourer on a building site. The latter was not especially what I would have chosen to do but as the charity didn't have money to pay a full-time worker, I continued to make the whole thing progress whilst humping bricks and cement up and down ladders.

There was one day that typified how difficult it was to keep the plates spinning. I was up on the scaffolding in Wandsworth when I got a call from the World at One, BBC Radio 4's lunchtime news. Was I available for a live interview that day? 'Well,' I said, 'I would be if I wasn't stuck on a building site in Southwest London.' They said they would send a Radio van to me, which they did. I can't remember what aspect of abuse I was being asked about but I got some funny stares from the neighbours in the street who were used to me climbing up and down ladders and mixing cement. Suddenly they saw me climbing into a big BBC truck to broadcast to the nation.

That reminds me of all the other times I have done live or pre-recorded interviews from some weird places, including my living room at home. It's always a curtain twitching moment when one of these Radio/TV trucks parks in your street and up goes a massive satellite dish!

Chapter 18

I can honestly say I was working pretty much round the clock those days, paid work during the day, NAPAC work for half the night and often into the early hours of the morning.

But some serious donations did come in and the Trustees of the charity offered me a full-time position. My dream was coming true. I was working for an organisation that was my heart, my soul and my passion.

A Labour Government had swept to power in 1997 and I got an early meeting with Jacqui Smith, the Health Minister who approved some serious funding for our helpline.

But that funding didn't last as long as we had hoped. We subcontracted our service (and the funding) to another provider, an organisation that was also a charity and specialised in providing helplines. It was an expensive arrangement, based in Manchester and some distance for me to get to easily. The brief time there was nevertheless a success and our team of call takers (which NAPAC actually recruited) became long-standing friends of the charity, even after that operation had to close down. And although it closed down we managed to resurrect it quite quickly by recruiting volunteers in London, cutting out the 'middlemen', and cutting out the large monthly management fee we had been paying to the previous provider.

They say a good volunteer is worth two and a half times what a good paid worker is. I'm not so sure. Yes, we had many brilliant volunteers but because we were still a relatively small set up, it was quite difficult to control what was going on. And if a volunteer decided they could not do their shift, there is not a lot you can do about it. So we moved towards a system where we had a mix of some paid staff and volunteers. But these weren't just any volunteers, ours were very special. They needed to be able to handle the most difficult, distressing and delicate calls. They needed to be strong enough to do that and they needed good external support so that they didn't absorb all that pain they were hearing. And this was the tricky part … making sure they got that support.

I remember in the very early days, despite the excellent training we provided, losing one or two volunteers because they just weren't able to handle what they heard. And if the volunteers were survivors themselves, triggering became a major concern. So, we needed people tough enough to handle it and to leave it behind when they finished their shift, but at the same time understanding and sensitive enough to provide what we were offering, a safe and caring place to offload the pain.

What we didn't anticipate in those early days was just how many unpleasant calls might come in. By 'unpleasant' I mean nasty callers. I cannot for the life of me understand why people go to such lengths to make life difficult for others. In those days I used to take calls myself and on a couple of occasions I experienced these nasty calls. One chap in particular used to ring up and I can only describe him as a ghastly individual who was clearly getting off by talking his filth on the phone. I called the police on a few occasions about such callers, my assumption being that they were probably abusers. One policeman told me that we must expect such pervert calls to a support line, especially one that is free of any charges. I think most free telephone helplines have to put up with similar unpleasant stuff.

There was a couple of times when we thought we were getting genuine calls and that these were so serious we had to call the police. I remember one chap saying he was a wheelchair-bound survivor and living with an abusive partner. I called the police and they followed it up. He was not wheelchair-bound and he lived on his own. The police had a word with him. We never heard from him again, but you wonder if he was making the rounds of the various free helplines we have in this country. Tempting as it is to describe these people as sick, in most cases they really are not, they are just plain nasty and sometimes I fear, potentially dangerous.

Throughout the years of setting up NAPAC, I neglected to look after myself. NAPAC was my life 24/7, my family and close friends will confirm this. They suffered because of it. NAPAC always came first. I had a few brief encounters with counselling but they didn't last very long. One chap I used to see would fall asleep halfway through our session. Now, I know I am capable of boring the socks off people, but I was paying this guy to help me. Looking back I should have picked up his glass of water and tipped it over his head.

Another thing I remember about him was that he sometimes smelled of alcohol, beer, in fact. My session was in the afternoon on a Friday and I figured he must have had a liquid lunch. Not good and not professional. In all my years of teaching I never went drinking during my lunch or early evening breaks. I knew a few lecturers who could have a couple of pints at lunchtime and then teach in the afternoon, but not me. The only time I drank when I was on duty, was when I took students away on trips such as those I organised to the major institutions of the European Parliament and NATO headquarters in Belgium. These were really fun trips but because all the students were over the age of 18, social drinking in moderation was permitted.

However, my wife Tricia's constant pleadings of, 'You need help too, Pete,' fell on deaf ears. I was helping countless people. I was in the media breaking the silence almost constantly. NAPAC was gaining support and funds were emerging, I believed that the world was changing for the better and that survivors were being heard for the first time. I dared to dream that I had made a difference and that our children may be a little safer.

If I had got the right kind of support when I was urged to do so, the things that happened in 2008 may never have happened. But unfortunately, we can't turn back the clock and I was to learn a very harsh lesson in just how nasty, unkind and dishonest some people can be.

Chapter 19

We all mess up occasionally, none of us is infallible despite the claims of a certain church. While I try my hardest not to be judgmental in life I do have to remind myself of my own failings, of which there are many. I also look at the people who I have judged and wonder what their backstories are. When we look at the old man sleeping rough in a shop doorway in Fulham, how can we possibly judge when we don't know what he has been through in life? How can we make judgements if we are acting on limited knowledge?

They say the love of money is the root of all evil. I'm not so sure about that. I think alcohol comes close to taking the title but, as with money, I suppose it is what you do with it that determines whether it becomes a problem or not. Me and my two brothers all struggled with alcohol. I have been asked a number of times whether my parents were drinkers. The answer to that is a resounding no. So, one might conclude that drinking is not in our genes. I have no idea if such things, as a propensity to addiction, are in one's genes, but I suspect it is not. Having said that, we know that babies born to drug users can be born with life threatening addictions. It is, I suppose, the earliest form of child abuse to poison your child in the womb. And "drugs" obviously include alcohol. We know that whatever Mum ingests and inhales, so does the baby.

I cannot speak as to why my brothers were both alcoholics but I can certainly guess as to why they started drinking and whilst my older brother, Anthony, moved out when I was very young, my other brother, Mike, was living at home. I remember him drinking as quite a young teenager, and indeed he was smoking dope then as well. He went on to harder drugs (you name it, he took it), but it was alcohol that eventually killed him at age 56. My other brother also died at the very young age of 52.

Anthony was physically abused by our dad when he was young, as was Mike. Mike was also physically and sexually abused at Wimbledon College by Father Battersby SJ and, I suspect other priests too. There were certainly other priests at the college who were abusers.

I was introduced to alcohol by my brother-in-law, George, when I was about 8 or 9 years old. He sometimes gave me a bottle of cider when I babysat for him and my sister. Part of my remuneration for babysitting. That's the way I saw it back then. I didn't really know anything different, so alcohol became a part of my life from an early age and from my experience of meeting other survivors this is not that unusual. Abusers know that if they drug their victims they tend to be easier to abuse. I have read two books recently, Shannon Clifton's powerful account of how she was repeatedly raped by her father from six years of age, and Jessica Harrington's bestselling memoir of how, she too, was abused and raped by her mother's boyfriend. Both young girls suffered terrible ordeals over numerous years. Shannon's father regularly plied her with alcohol during the abuse. Jessica's tormentor injected her with a drug.

Alcohol is a very powerful drug and in British culture we are introduced to it at an early age. I remember being in pubs from age 16, breaking the law. But it was exciting and I loved the experience. My brother-in-law was also in those pubs on a regular basis. He was a heavy drinker and many of the times when he assaulted me was when he had consumed alcohol. To this day I can still remember his smelly drink breath and his body odour when he sneaked into the bedroom and assaulted me when I was a child.

A couple of years ago I was on a tube train in London. It was crowded and a man was standing way too close to me and was rubbing up against me. His body odour and drink breath took me back to those dreaded moments in childhood and if the train hadn't stopped at the next station, allowing me to get off, I think I may have hit him.

I have drank too much over the years, I've often asked myself whether I'm an alcoholic. There are always others who are willing to answer such questions on your behalf but most people who know me declare that I am not. Their blissful ignorance usually comes from a place of … well, blissful ignorance. But I am not so sure.

One description of the disease (and I have no doubt it is a disease) is that someone who has no control over alcohol is an alcoholic. To be one does not necessarily mean you wake up every morning desiring drink. I certainly don't fit that category, unlike my brother Mike who drank from the moment he woke. But once I start drinking, now that's another question. For too many years drink has been my crutch, even, dare I say, my friend, but alcohol is not the sort of friend I would ever encourage.

Mike's marriage to his first wife didn't last very long and he soon met another, much younger, woman who was to become his next wife and the mother of his four beautiful children. Mike met her whilst he was training to become a psychiatric nurse. This was at one of the last big psychiatric hospitals we used to have in the UK at Banstead in Surrey. One evening there was a party at the hospital and Mike asked if I wanted to come over, I could meet his new girlfriend.

I went to the party, got very drunk and remembered wondering how the devil I was going to get home. I had taken the train there but they all stopped well before midnight. As the party petered out in the early hours of the morning, people were disappearing and I found myself in the bedroom of the nurses' home where Mike and his girlfriend were sleeping. I think I was invited to sleep on the floor but I really didn't fancy that, and took my brother's car keys from his pocket

Bearing in mind that I still had not officially learned to drive, I got into his little Fiat and set off into the night. I was drunk and I dread to think what would have happened had I caused an accident. But this was the early hours of the morning and luckily there was no other traffic on the roads.

I drove to Box Hill, one of my favourite bike training routes and steamed up there like I was Sterling Moss. There are a couple of hairpin bends on Box Hill and I'd always wondered what it was like to go round them fast. Luckily I managed to work out how to change the gears by the time I got there and so I didn't have any mishaps. Then, as I headed for home, I put my foot down to see how fast I could go. This was on a road that is locally known as the Mad Mile, from Banstead crossroads to just outside

Sutton. Again, I can't believe what I did and I also remember how the accelerator kept sticking. I remember watching Mike have to pump it a couple of times to make it come loose and so I did the same. I was experiencing twin emotions of excitement and sheer terror but then I realised I needed to get home. I couldn't go back to the nurses' home and certainly couldn't go to Mum and Dad's. I went to my sister Pauline's where I slept on her settee.

When I woke a few hours later I asked my sister if I could use her phone to ring Mike. I rang him and one of the nurses answered and a few minutes later a very sleepy sounding Mike came on the phone. I told him I had taken his car the night before. He muttered something along the lines of , 'Okay, bring it back later will you, I need to go back to sleep.' Well, I couldn't take the car back because I hadn't passed my driving test and now I was as sober as a judge.

A few hours later a very different sounding Mike rang me at Mum and Dad's. The penny had dropped. I'd driven his beloved car home pissed as a newt and he was furious. He had obviously sobered up, realised his car was missing and then remembered me telling him I had borrowed it from him. His language was a little blue, he told me I could have killed myself.

Booze has got me into much trouble over the years and whilst it can do a marvellous job of blocking out the pain of childhood memories, it is a painfully short term and a quite ineffective way of dealing with it.

I certainly lost two of my jobs because of drink and if, I am really honest, I can say that the only time I have taken days off work sick has been because of a hangover, though this hasn't happened for some time I am pleased to report.

But yes, drink has certainly caused me many problems over the years and having brothers and a brother-in-law who were heavy drinkers probably didn't help. Neither did the Catholic upbringing if I am honest. I refer to my visits to Lourdes and visiting my dear priest friend in Blackburn and to how many Catholic parishes there are that have a social club attached to them. Ours in Wimbledon certainly had one and I remember that when visiting my cousins in the Northeast, a pint or two after Sunday Mass at the adjoining social club was very much seen as an essential church activity.

One thing about alcohol and its misuse is that it can open you up to all sorts of vulnerabilities. It can play havoc with your boundaries and when alcoholics (or people who are intoxicated) get together it can lead to all sorts of problems. It certainly lead to a massive change in my life.

Some of my closest relationships have been deeply and adversely affected by my behaviour around drink. I am one of those sad men who has constantly wondered about whether the grass is really greener on the other side. Every time I was in a relationship I would inevitably expect it to go wrong. 'What do they see in me?' I would ask myself because I was a product of the psychological abuse that my brother-in-law instilled in me, a failure.

Deep down I was thinking, 'When will these people see through me and leave me?' My response was to cling to someone else before it happened and hope that I could make that relationship work. More often than not it was when I was in the pub or at an alcohol-fuelled party. It was insecurity in its basic form and that insecurity came to the fore when I was around alcohol.

But you cannot run away from yourself. Alcohol may be a temporary fix for that, but it doesn't last and it can certainly be a very dangerous temporary fix.

One thing children need above anything else is love. To grow up feeling unloved is to be open to abuse, and abusers can spot this very quickly. I will always be convinced that when George married Pauline he knew he was getting me into the bargain. He would have seen my love and devotion to my sister and my loneliness as a child of parents who were past caring, or so it seemed.

I mentioned above that I lost a couple of jobs because of alcohol. The reason was that these two jobs in commercial industry involved meeting clients. During both jobs I failed to make proper connections with clients because I was hungover. On another occasion I almost got into a fight with a co-worker, who I would plead was more drunk than I was, but no excuses. I was drunk and out of control. No one apart from me really knew how I let myself down in these work situations but I most certainly did.

In a strange way (or perhaps it's not so strange) I am writing this book to set the record straight. It's not easy admitting you are probably an alcoholic. It's not easy admitting how many people you have let down over the years, and I put my children at the top of that list. It's not easy admitting my lack of determination to stick with Alcoholics Anonymous when I was privileged enough to be able to attend some of their meetings. I admit that alcohol is still a crutch I hang on to this day but I do my very best to drink in moderation. But in my heart of hearts I know it is a false crutch. A deceitful crutch.

I mentioned that my brother Mike served time in prison. I remember him telling me that he never met any inmates who were really bad people. Many were alcoholics and many more were survivors of childhood abuse. There are exceptions, of course. Rose West was up the corridor in another wing in the same prison at the time.

Like my brother, I would like to think that I am not a bad person. I have never set out to harm anyone, quite the reverse. It has been in reaching out to help others that I have fallen foul of those intent on hurting me. I will never know the motivation behind people who set out to hurt and destroy others, but there are plenty of them out there and I suffered as a result of one brief encounter.

Chapter 20

In 2008, I met up with two women in Manchester who I thought were interested in NAPAC. They said they were survivors and wanted to be involved. One of them had been on a TV programme talking about her experience of abuse in childhood. We arranged to meet for morning coffee in Manchester and later moved on to a nearby pizza restaurant for lunch, which turned out to be extremely poor judgement. After an awful lot of drinking, one of them attempted to seduce me. We'd had lunch and had been joined by my teenage son, who was studying at a nearby university. He did not drink any alcohol.

Towards the end of the lunch, I needed to go to the toilet and when I came out of the loo, one of the women was waiting for me. She made her intentions clear and dragged me into the women's toilets. Within a second or two she was on her knees and began to perform a sex act on me. I was too drunk to resist and equally too drunk to be in the least aroused by this woman's attentions. I quickly came to my senses saying, 'This is madness,' and put a stop to it. It was a stupid thing to do and an encounter I had not wanted. We returned to our table, my son left, and we continued to drink and socialise, eventually leaving the restaurant and going our separate ways. I never saw or heard from either of the women again.

As much as I beat myself up about this stupidity, nobody had been hurt and the only person who I harmed that day was my wife, and she did not deserve that. Alcohol had once again led to a moment of madness. As an old friend, Dame Esther Rantzen said to me, 'This is the sort of thing that hurting survivors of abuse do, they inflict further harm on themselves.' She is right. However; I concede that being the head of a charity I should have conducted myself in a far better way

I thought no more of the incident. Six months later I had a note through my door from the police saying they needed to speak to me urgently but didn't say why. It wasn't unusual for me to receive communication from the police. I worked closely with various police forces across the country, supporting adult victims and survivors of child abuse. It was unusual for them to meet with me at home which I thought odd but agreed a time for them to come to my house.

My wife was at home and she, like me, had no idea why the police were there. One of the officers asked if they could speak to me privately and the official tone in his voice told me this was personal. I told them whatever they had to say they could say it in front of my wife. I had nothing to hide.

You can only imagine when one of the officers said, 'There has been a rape allegation against you, Mr Saunders,' what was going through my wife's head. And mine. I am sure you will understand my utter astonishment when I learned that both the women I had met for lunch many months before, had accused me of orally and anally raping them in Manchester, in the middle of the day. I hadn't disclosed anything to Tricia about what I had felt was a "stupid encounter" because I felt so ashamed of myself for drinking far too much alcohol and for being momentarily unfaithful to her.

I was taken to the police station and placed in a cell where I had to wait two or three hours before being interviewed. I was feeling bewildered and confused, wondering who would accuse me of such a terrible crime and why? And I was very distressed at what might be going through Tricia's mind. I couldn't speak to her, I wasn't even allowed a phone call until after my interview had been concluded.

As ridiculous as this might sound, as soon as the police interview started I began to feel a little better. Needless to say, I told them everything, from the beginning of the story when I first met these two women, the drinks we had and even the pizzas we ate, leading up to the encounter in the toilet and when we parted. As the interview progressed, I sensed the police knew that I was telling the truth.

After I had given them my account of events on that day the police disclosed the full details of the allegation against me. They then told me those two women had accused me of anally and orally raping them, while drunk, at lunchtime in the toilets of the busy pizza restaurant.

At the end of the interview, they told me I could go home and said, 'We do not expect to be seeing you again.' I took that as meaning they were satisfied that no crime had been committed.

And yet I wasn't satisfied, I felt violated if that's the right word. It was so preposterous that it was almost laughable, but it was far from funny. From the beginning of my police interview it was clear that it was all a huge waste of valuable police time.

When I arrived back home Tricia was waiting for me. I knew the situation must have caused her similar feelings of bewilderment, confusion and pain and it was the last thing I wanted. I also knew I had some explaining to do. Telling my wife the details of the lunchtime encounter with those women was one of the most challenging things I have ever had to do. Her distress and hurt were clear to see. I had let Tricia down by my heavy drinking, poor boundaries and then by not telling her about that stupidity straight away. The situation was made worse for us both by the many weeks that passed before I heard anything further from the police.

That said, the police were extremely polite and professional in their dealings with me, and I later learned this professionalism continued in their thorough investigation into the allegations against me. I learned from my son that they interviewed him as part of their investigation. He informed them that when I was upstairs, 'Allegedly orally and anally raping both these women,' that one of the women had in fact remained downstairs with him and said to him, 'Do you want to fuck my brains out?' The woman was a mother in her 30s, my son barely 18, and a lovelier more innocent young lad you couldn't wish to meet. He had been horrified by her suggestion and came upstairs to the toilets to find me. He left the restaurant without telling me what had happened and went back to university.

I don't know who else the police interviewed but six long weeks after being interviewed I was informed by the investigating officer that they were satisfied no crime had been committed and there would be no further action. I asked the police officer whether any action would be taken against these women who had made a blatantly false accusation for reasons only known to them. The officer told me that as far as they were concerned, they had closed their files and told me to get on with my life. If only!

One thing became crystal clear to me; these people were out to destroy me and I couldn't understand why. I actually put that very point to the police and the response from one of the officers was, 'There are some evil bastards out there.' The same officer added, 'We know about the great work you do Mr Saunders, please get on with it and forget about these nasty people.' Easier said than done, of course.

On learning the outcome of the investigation Tricia's instant reaction was one of anger. She wanted to hear directly from the police what they were going to do about the two women whose allegations had put us both through a living hell for the last six weeks. I couldn't face dealing with any more of this horrible situation and asked the investigating officer if they would talk to Tricia and gave consent for them to answer any of her questions.

Tricia later told me that the police officer shared all I had told them with her and informed her they were satisfied no crime had been committed. She told the officer she found it impossible to imagine me raping anyone but knew for a fact that I could not have committed that crime because she had phoned me that afternoon and I was so drunk, I couldn't string two coherent words together. She knew in that state it would be physically impossible. Tricia said she was dealing with the pain and hurt of my actions that day but said it was a private matter between me and her.

Tricia told me she had also asked the officer what action they would be taking against the two women and was told, 'As far as we are concerned a sexual act between two consenting adults took place and there is no case to answer to'. Tricia repeated her question and the officer said, 'The person concerned maintains she was raped, we will not be taking action against her.'

It was clear the police did not believe these women but it was a most unhelpful and confusing conversation from Tricia's perspective. We were both left feeling extremely distressed about the whole situation.

As part of the process of trying to put this behind us we spoke to the Chair of Trustees of NAPAC. Tricia was a co-founder and Trustee and, although she felt strongly that it was a personal matter for us to deal with, the allegation was made against me during a work-related meeting.

It wasn't an easy meeting to have but the chair was supportive towards me. We were an organisation of survivors working to support survivors and needed to be more aware of how vulnerable that made us. From an organisational perspective it highlighted the fact that we needed tighter processes in place regarding the consumption of alcohol during work meetings, the use of the charity debit card and more thought about when and where meetings should take place and who should attend them.

Trust is important for all relationships but for survivors it sits on a completely different level. Tricia had tried to help me with my drinking, and we were both struggling with how I used it to blot out my pain. She was hurting too but used therapy to deal with her pain and couldn't understand why I chose such a destructive route. I really didn't know if my marriage would survive and nor did

Tricia. We got on with our lives the best we could. Our family and our careers kept us very busy.

Then in September 2014 just as I was due to speak at a conference, one of my colleagues called me into a room and presented me with an e-mail. It was from the partner of one of these women.

The e-mail said:

Dear ---

My wife found out about this event and was very enthusiastic about attending until she saw that one of the speakers was Peter Saunders. In 2009 my wife met with Peter Saunders in Manchester to discuss the possibility of launching NAPAC in the Northwest. Subsequently during that day he sexually assaulted and orally raped her. This matter was reported to the police who interviewed him and he admitted the offence. It did not go to court, however my wife was compensated from the Government's Criminal Injuries Compensation Authority due to him admitting the offence. We are both survivors of sexual abuse and are astonished that at such an important event the keynote speaker can be a man of such little integrity. Also that he can still head a charity which does so much good to help survivors of abuse. We would be grateful of a response and should you require any further information do not hesitate to contact me on the above an e-mail address.

I was absolutely stunned as I read the email again, line for line. I pointed out to my colleague that it was all lies and explained exactly what had happened and how this woman and her friend had falsely accused me of rape back in 2008.

'It's nonsense,' I said, 'if I had admitted raping two women orally and anally, it would have certainly gone to court and I would have been banged up for twenty years.'

The mention of this woman receiving Criminal Injuries Compensation, was another blatant lie. The police had confirmed that no criminal offence had taken place.

This email was another attempt to discredit and lie about me.

I would have been sitting in a cell in Strangeways or Wormwood Scrubs! The sentencing guidelines as laid down by the Sentencing Council UK suggest a category range of between 10 and 15 years for each rape!

Needless to say my colleague gave me the green light and I spoke as a keynote speaker at the conference, despite the e-mail which once again had turned my life upside down. I couldn't quite get my head around the motives of this woman (and her husband), who claims that she, too, was a victim of child abuse, a survivor. I haven't named her, but not for legal reasons (because I have copies of the emails that she and her husband have sent). From a legal point of view, I have every right to name and shame her, the lies and accusations against me in statements to the police and written in emails are beyond doubt. I haven't named her because if she is truly a survivor then I assume that she is suffering great mental anguish.

Sadly that's not the end of the story, because a few days later, the woman herself wrote an email to the same colleague and this time brought my wife into the mix when she stated:

' ... It was enough for me at the time to get an apology from him and his wife and to be believed by the police and supported by them'.

Once again I was stunned into momentarily silence as I tried to process it. An apology from me and my wife? Where had that come from? This woman was making stuff up as she went along and digging a deeper hole for herself with every lie.

To say Tricia wasn't best pleased would be an understatement. She was absolutely livid, but now at least she knew first-hand the lies that this woman was capable of because she had never met her, so how could she have given her an apology?

We went straight back to the police station to make a complaint about this woman. This had gone on long enough, she had to be stopped. We both wanted to make statements about the malicious gossip and damage she was peddling.

I don't think I slept for the next two or three nights. I mulled over the situation and realised how damaging it could have been for my marriage, my career and my reputation had the police not carried out a thorough investigation. I was frightened and later that week, after discussing it with Tricia, decided to go back into the police station and ask for the officer who had originally interviewed me.

I explained my concerns to them, that I was really worried and also angry at the lies these women had told about me. I said I wanted to take it further and I wanted them charged with wasting police time at the very least. The officer said that one of the women was known to the police and it wasn't the first time she had made malicious accusations. I nearly fell off my seat. Surely, she should be charged with something and at least it might put a stop to her behaving in this way. The police officer accepted my point and said, 'We can go round to see her and give her a stern warning.'

To be honest, I wanted this woman to get more than a "stern warning" because she had put me through hell again and if I hadn't had such an understanding wife, her lies may have put an end to my marriage. A few days later I was advised that the woman had moved to a different part of the country and the local police in that area had paid her a visit. They had warned her that if she continued to harass me she risked prosecution.

The police told me the woman had apologised for her behaviour. And for the second time, I was told to forget about it and get on with my life. This was serious and while I understood where the police officer was coming from, I still wasn't happy.

I shared this information with Tricia and she sent the following email to the police officer dated 27/1/2015:

> *'... I am very unhappy with the situation as a whole and also about what has been said about me. For the record; I do not know this person, I have never spoken to her or met her and have never and would never apologise to her or anyone else for the behaviour of another person.*
>
> *Pete has told me this woman has apologised for what she said.'*
>
> The next day Tricia sent a follow up email to the police officer:
>
> *'It is important for you to know that I am not willing to be left in the position of having an accusation against me left unchallenged - no matter how trivial it may seem in the context of your job and the things you deal with - because I am a registered professional and the email xxxx sent to xxxx says that Pete's wife (I am*

Pete's wife) apologised to her for what she says he did to her. That is a complete and utter lie, and it greatly offends me at my core. My integrity, my values and my character are being slandered.'

I considered taking legal advice. Tricia, on the other hand, asked the police officer for a meeting with the woman and possibly her husband at the police station to talk to her about what she had said. She also wanted her to write a letter to my colleague, who had organised the conference, and to us, with a retraction and an apology.

Because of the experiences this woman said she had suffered as a child, namely that her father had raped her, we were well aware that she was highly vulnerable and clearly hurting, but we wanted her to understand the devastating impact of her lies.

The next day, Tricia received an email from the police officer. It was short and to the point.

'Hi Tricia

Basically xxxx could not be compelled by any party into a meeting, nor could she be required to make any written statement.'

And that was that. From the beginning of October 2014 to the end of January 2015 we had tried everything within the law to get this issue resolved and we didn't get so much as a written apology from this woman who had tried to destroy not just me, but Tricia as well. We had countless sleepless nights, discussions into the early hours of the morning and I had numerous conversations with my colleagues from NAPAC. We had tried to reach out to this woman, to be sympathetic to what she said she had been through as a child. However, the police made it clear that this wasn't the first malicious accusation this woman had been involved in. But, without bringing about a private prosecution which would have cost me thousands of pounds, the police said that there was nothing they could do. They said the woman had apologised, and it was best that we left it at that. Once again, I was told to close that chapter of my life and devote my time to what I do best, speaking up for survivors.

I am more than aware the damage that false allegations do to the genuine victims of sexual abuse who are thinking about coming forward. I felt a duty to bring these two women to book. But my sense of belief in the British justice system was short lived. I spoke to a lawyer specialising in slander and defamation. I was determined not to let these women get away with what they had done, not just from my point of view or my wife's, but to stop them doing it again to someone else. The lawyer was an honest man, and while he could have taken my money and pursued a case against these women on my behalf, which he said I would win, I would face hefty legal costs which we could ill afford. For the second time in a week, a professional person told me to forget about what had happened and get on with my life.

I mention elsewhere that on more than one occasion I was warned to, 'Watch your back, Pete.' I should have been more aware than I was, that there would be people out there who wanted me silenced. I always thought that because I was a good person and because I was doing lots of good work that I would be safe. I also believed at the time that God would protect me.

Part Three

Chapter 21

I've already said, the Jimmy Savile scandal certainly put NAPAC on the map, big time and for the few months after the story broke, barely a day went by without contact from one media source or another.

I think it's fairly safe to say that the country, and indeed the world, as the news filtered out internationally, was stunned at the revelations that poured out from the media.

The average person probably couldn't believe the scale of abuse, the turning of a blind eye and the cover-up of Savile's systematic abuse of young people over the decades. And while the numbers of people who had been abused by this celebrity predator did at first shock me, the cover-up did not.

A total of 214 criminal offences were formally recorded across 28 police force areas in which Savile was a suspect, dating from 1955 to 2009. Within the recorded crimes there were 126 indecent acts and 34 rape/penetration offences alleged against someone who was awarded an OBE in 1971 and knighted in 1990 (at the insistence of Margaret Thatcher, and against strong advice). He also received a Papal Knighthood. Savile was made a Knight Commander of St Gregory the Great, by Pope John Paul II. It is the highest civil award a pope can bestow. Savile was a devout Catholic.

And as incredible as it may sound, even in the light of the disgusting allegations against him, there were some in the Catholic Church who were still trying to focus on the good side of Saville and his charity work. There is no doubt that the man raised millions over his lifetime, no one can dispute that. However, the Catholic newspaper, *The Catholic Herald*, had the audacity to suggest that there was a conspiracy of silence surrounding the TV presenter's religion at the time of his death. *The Catholic Herald* noted that few newspaper obituaries mentioned that he was a practising Catholic, who attended Mass on a regular basis.

The Catholic Herald asked its readers – and I quote verbatim, 'Why not mention that an important part of his life was attending daily Mass? There's a deep dedication in the life of a man who gives away 90 percent of everything he earns and so tirelessly does all the other things he did.' And there's a little twist relating to Jimmy Savile and the knight commander of St Gregory the Great. After his death there were many calls for him to be stripped of the papal knighthood. I personally asked a cardinal of the Church if this could be the case and was told, no! The Vatican's response was that this was not normal protocol. They said that a permanent official list of persons who have received papal honours in the past does not exist, that the papal knighthood dies alongside the knight. It is therefore not possible to strike anyone off a list that does not exist.

The Vatican's official spokesman, Father Federico Lombardi SJ, said 'The Holy See firmly condemns the horrible crimes of sexual abuse of minors, it is deeply saddened that a person who has been soiled in this way could in his lifetime have been proposed for an honour by The Holy See, which in the light of recent information should certainly not have been bestowed.'

A point well-made Father Federico, but I find it hard to believe that a list of former knights does not exist, especially in the Vatican. A simple Google search of Knight Commander of St Gregory the Great throws up around 150,000 results. Jimmy Savile's name appeared on the first list I looked at. Of course, such lists exist. The Vatican writes everything down.

As mind-blowing as the figures relating to Savile are to some people, they were not particularly mind-blowing to me. As I have alluded to many times in this book the vast majority of people abused in childhood never come forward and never disclose the crimes that have been committed against them. It's difficult to put a number on the silent ones but I fear the people who have the courage to come forward and disclose what has happened to them is a very small percentage.

When the Savile scandal broke, I remember a woman sobbing on the phone as I took a phone call at NAPAC. She thanked me for speaking out about childhood abuse and said she could never do it. And she told me her husband had no idea that she had been raped as a child by the great and saintly Sir Jimmy Savile. And even though the story was now all over the national newspapers and on every television channel in the land, she said she still had no intention of telling him. I completely understood her reasoning. Like many victim/survivors she blamed herself for the crimes committed against her.

There will always be a backlash where so many allegations are made against one individual or an institution. Because we live in a victim-blaming society there will always be those who question the credibility of victims' accounts of abuse. Some will challenge the point of pursuing allegations against someone who is dead. I understand that. If the victims cannot obtain justice then what is the point? Well, the point is that some abusers have collaborators and if they are still alive they should be pursued. This was certainly the case with Savile and victims may feel some sense of being able to move on with their lives if what they suffered has been acknowledged. I am not a great fan of the term "closure" but I hope you know what I mean when I say that an investigation may help people move on.

The offences reported against Savile were broken down as follows; 82% were female, most in the 13 to 16 age group, 57 allegations implicated hospital premises (including hospices), 33 related to television or radio studios and 14 identified schools.

I remember speaking with another former government minister who carried the title of Lady who, upon hearing that my work involved working with survivors of abuse declared, 'Oh! I suppose they are all after compensation, are they?' I cannot begin to express how angry that comment made me feel, but I had to accept that she may well have been genuinely ignorant of what this is all about and simply needed some re-education. But I was not so sure. She was married to a judge. Another time I was talking to a retired judge who was referring to the 'apparent stiffness' of a sentence passed on an abuser. I talked to her for about an hour about my work and about the consequences of these crimes on the victim. At the end of the conversation this person, this former judge, conceded that the sentence imposed was actually, in the light of what she had just heard, quite lenient.

I'm afraid that we have too many judges who, for one reason or another, don't seem to want to take the abuse and rape of children seriously. There was the infamous comment by one who said that it was understandable that a man raped his child because his wife was denying him sex. I am not making this up.

And there were some journalists and columnists and media men and women from around the world who gently reminded us that Jimmy Savile wasn't all that bad and asked us not to forget about the millions of pounds he raised for charity.

There are others who have heaped praise on perpetrators for their many 'good works' and then passed ridiculously lenient sentences. Robin Peverett OBE was a man who walked free from court having pleaded guilty to multiple offences but who had glowing testimonials from the adult children he did not abuse. I am not making this up! Peverett was headmaster at the countess of Wessex's prep school, Dulwich College, and an adviser to the Thatcher government. He was also chairman of the Independent Association of Preparatory Schools.

He was convicted of nine counts of indecent assault in 2000, and received a two-year prison sentence, suspended. He was a man of prominence with the best lawyers money could buy. When you read the court papers and see what was said about him, it's unbelievable. He is practically painted as the victim of the times and because his reputation was in tatters, 'Hadn't he suffered enough?' to quote one prominent lawyer involved in the case. Not a word about his countless victims.

Little wonder so many victim/survivors end up taking their own lives when such miscarriages of justice are hoisted upon them.

Watching the news reports or reading the newspaper articles at the time when Savile's many indiscretions and rapes had come to light was very distressing for me personally but it also threw me into a sort of mild depression. Certain sections of the press were never particularly interested in the abuse of children but the sensationalism of the story. When it involves a celebrity it is a different story and when it is sexual abuse, it adds to the media's obsession and it becomes headline news. The Savile scandal was second only to the London Olympics in terms of media coverage during 2012. And because of Savile's BBC connections it attracted worldwide attention.

Because abuse was out in the open, so to speak, it also gave many more survivors the strength and courage to come forward. Many who had been assaulted by Savile came forward. Other so-called celebrities were also accused. The BBC's Stuart Hall was one. Rolf Harris was another.

Here's a scary thing. Some years ago I was attending a function at the Houses of Parliament and I found myself in conversation with Rolf Harris. He was charming and most interested in my work. So interested that the next day his personal assistant rang me to say that Rolf had enjoyed meeting me but he was too busy to become involved. He wished me good luck. How kind, I thought. Well, it is just as well that he was 'too busy' because I dread to think of the consequences for NAPAC had he become a patron or some such thing.

Some years later Rolf Harris was convicted of child abuse and went to prison. After that brief meeting, but long before he was convicted, I received a letter from a young woman who claimed that Rolf Harris had raped her whilst she and her family were on holiday in France. I didn't doubt what I was reading but as there were no contact details for this person, all I could do was hope that she had gone to the police with this allegation. But I will never know whether or not she did. I just hope she is okay today.

Whilst it is true that some sections of the press are not that interested in the abuse of children, many more see it as something more than just a news story. As one journalist at the BBC said to me, 'Pete, this is more than just a news story, this is about the protection of all our children'. And they would be right. At the end of a live interview on the BBC News Channel, when we went off-air, the presenter said to me, 'Keep up your good work, Pete. I was abused too as a teenager.' And that sort of comment from colleagues in the media was by no means unusual.

Sometimes investigators might need to exploit the power of the media spotlight. Jimmy Savile is dead, but a string of celebrities have been questioned in the same inquiry, grabbing headlines. If a victim who feels isolated, reads in the newspapers that their abuser is being questioned over similar charges, the hesitant may then come forward and so publicity becomes a forensic tool for collecting evidence. I remember seeing Stuart Hall (a former BBC personality) standing in front of a courtroom protesting his innocence and attacking the motive of those who came forward to accuse him. The result of his protestations was that more victims came forward and he was duly imprisoned for his crimes.

Standard police methods are somewhat limited in tackling crimes against children. They need to have as many means as possible which they can use to pursue abusers. Savile and his ilk quite often achieve a lifetime of abuse and get away with it. But he was by no means an aberration. Many offenders offend on a similar scale as him.

What made him different was his celebrity status, which he used to great effect to not only abuse but also to intimidate everyone around him who dared to question him, including the police.

One man who did question him was Johnny Rotten of the Sex Pistols. In an interview as far back as 1978, Johnny had compiled a death list of people who he wanted to do away with. He stated during the interview that, 'I would like to do away with Jimmy Savile.' The interviewer was puzzled and asked why. Johnny replied that we all know that Jimmy Savile is up to all sorts of seediness and there are many rumours. Now known as John Lydon, the musician claimed that he had made noises in the correct places about Savile, told the 'big boys' at the BBC all about Savile's behaviour and that as a result, the BBC banned his records for so-called contentious behaviour.

Lydon said he was in no doubt that the BBC banned his records because of what he had said about Jimmy Savile. It appears Savile was protected by people in very high places who knew all about what was going on and did nothing about it.

That 1978 interview was repeated during a Piers Morgan interview with John Lydon in 2015. It is still on YouTube and worth a look.

Chapter 22

Most abusers get away with their crimes. Not only are these crimes difficult to investigate but they are unique in that they often leave the victim feeling guilty, shameful and alone. And victims, again uniquely, find it slightly easier to talk about the crime the greater the time lapse. In other words, it is not uncommon for victims to remain silent for weeks, months and most often years, before they can speak of these things. I stress again, it is the only crime where the victim often feels the guilt that should be borne by the perpetrator.

People like Savile who hurt children, are rarely obviously disturbed or dysfunctional. They are rarely the stereotypical dirty old man in a filthy raincoat lurking in children's playgrounds or by the school gates. That isn't to say these characters don't exist but they tend to be rare. Many abusers are pillars of the community, Savile being a prime example. They are often highly intelligent, confident, respected, family people and successful. This disjunction in the public imagination over what they should look like and behave, makes policing and detection very difficult. Abusers do not have horns and tails.

In Jean Renvoizes' book *Innocence Destroyed*, her research indicated a number of common denominators amongst those who abuse. They are generally (but not exclusively) male. In fact, recent research would seem to indicate that abuse by females is a far bigger problem than has been acknowledged. And little wonder. Women are generally seen as the nurturers, the caregivers, the 'gentler sex'. Both male and female abusers tend to be married with families, are often hard-working professionals and many go to church. In other words, it is hard to characterise them by some obvious trait. The one common denominator shared by them all, of course, is that they all hurt children.

June Kelly, the respected BBC journalist once visited the NAPAC office to interview me. I remember her telling me she had just visited a UK prison that was populated almost entirely by 'sex offenders' (to use that slightly misleading term), and she mentioned speaking with inmates who were doctors, pilots and other professionals. By no means is the abuse of children a "working class" problem.

In the very early days of setting up the charity I had a chat with a senior official of the charity ChildLine (then independent, now part of the NSPCC). This chap had been a child protection social worker but he left because he said he just couldn't 'do his job properly'. He described how it was relatively easy to identify some abusers and thus protect children but at other times it was very hard. He cited the example of how relatively easy it was to apprehend and prosecute a father who lived in social housing, had minimal intellectual capacity and was beating the hell out of his children. He compared that to visiting the detached house of an eminent and successful individual who social services were certain was sexually abusing his young daughters but had no chance of proving it, such was the burden of proof needed to pursue such an individual, and the stranglehold this individual held over his family, including his wife. I remember him saying, 'I drove away from this big house knowing that the children were being abused and I could do nothing about it.' And so he went to work for ChildLine where he thought he could do more good.

I don't think it's usual to include a full newspaper editorial in a book, so I hope my readers will forgive me for this next inclusion. It was in *The Guardian*, the headline was "Curbing Sex Abuse at Home" and I remember thinking that it was very uncanny timing as it came just at the time when I was heading up my plans to set up the organisation for survivors.

A true story doesn't need to be sensationalised on TV.

Unlike homelessness in the 1960's, child sex abuse is not a hidden problem. A succession of scandals in the last decade have received wide publicity. A Cathy Come Home *documentary is not needed to arouse public concern but the producers of last night's* No Child of Mine *were right to recognise the need for a "true life" drama to correct continuing misconceptions about abuse. Three of the most prevalent delusions about abuse were scotched by last night's powerful film. The biggest threat to children is not "stranger danger" but abuse within the family - by parents, step-parents, relatives or their friends. Secondly, the typical paedophile is not the monster portrayed by the tabloid press. That is what makes them so dangerous. They don't grow horns, they look quite normal and can appear, like the father in last night's drama, likeable in many respects. Finally, the victims themselves, the children, are often good at covering up their abuse and don't wear "victim" stamped on their foreheads.*

No wonder children's organisations were embracing the production team even before release. They were not only serious about relaying the real situation but they had the commendable idea of pushing for policy goals too: a proper network of refuges for children who run away from abusing parents and carers plus a new national organisation for adult survivors. But two fatal mistakes were made by the producers. The first was to choose such an extreme case of abuse - a girl who was sexually abused by her mother, her stepfather, her care worker as well as being coaxed in to prostitution by her father and a pimp promising a better life. The phenomenon of "repeat victimisation" is familiar to professionals but by choosing such a sensational case the team eroded the programme's credibility with the public it was trying to persuade. Worse still, they failed to corroborate their facts, as we documented on our front page yesterday, thus giving apologists a chance to deny the seriousness of the social problem. If, for effect, drama producers want "real life" cases then they must apply the strict journalistic rule of standing up their story. A statement from the Health Department has added to the doubts about the claims in the drama.

Yet the underlying message of No Child of Mine *is absolutely true. Children are being robbed of their innocence every day. Sexual abuse is one of the largest categories in the 10,000 calls which ChildLine receives every day. Almost 8,000 children were given extensive telephone counselling last year. If they had wanted more intensive therapy they would have had to wait 18 months in most areas. That is a scandal. We do need an organisation for adult survivors. They have many needs. There are still only four refuges for children who run away. There should be a national network funded by the government. Not even the rise in child prostitution has prompted ministerial action. If only a TV drama could'.*

While I take issue with some of its content, it couldn't have come at a better time. The language used is not always appropriate. For example we should not refer to child prostitution. There is no such thing. There is child trafficking and child abuse and rape. NAPAC was right at the start of its journey and one of the first people to make contact with me was the director of the drama mentioned. His name is Peter Kosminksy. He rang me to ask whether we could link the creation of NAPAC to the film drama in a way similar to how *Cathy Come Home* in the 1960's was closely linked to the creation of two charities for the homeless.

Shelter, the launch of which took place within days of the broadcast was not in any way linked to the drama but *Crisis*, launched the following year (1967), most certainly had its roots in the tragedy of the Ken Loach-directed drama. *Cathy Come Home* remains one of the most powerful and highly rated pieces of British TV drama of all time.

I told Peter that it would be disingenuous to link his drama to the creation of NAPAC, which was already on its way well before *No Child of Mine* was screened. But I said I would welcome his support for our fledgling charity.

While on the subject of homelessness, a survey by the University of Southampton found that 100% of the street homeless they interviewed reported coming from abusive households. Certainly, when I used to give money to homeless folk on the street and spoke with them, they almost always disclosed abuse in their past. A scary but not altogether surprising fact.

Predators abuse their positions of authority and respect to get close to victims and avoid detection. They deploy a number of intimidatory methods to silence those they target. I have heard many disturbing accounts from survivors. 'No one will believe you'. 'If you tell on me you will be taken into care,' or, 'Your mother will go to prison'. There is no end to the number of things that a sly perpetrator can say to a young victim to ensure their silence. They target the vulnerable, some of whom will have been abused before and this, plus the mind games abusers play, mean victims frequently end up believing they "caused" the crime, "colluded" with the abuser or in some way "deserved" it. So when a victim/survivor encounters a medical professional who, as happened to me, challenges the person with, 'Why did you let it happen?' it is little wonder they tend to keep quiet.

Another tactic is to point out to their victim that if they, the abuser, is apprehended, the family will lose its breadwinner. It is known that Jimmy Savile used his long history of fundraising for good causes to intimidate people into silence. Individuals like him can point to a cause and say, 'Look what I have done for this or that,' or ,'Who will fundraise if I'm not around?'

These are powerful and to a vulnerable child (or even vulnerable adult) compelling messages to remain silent. Abusers are masters of distracting witnesses and a community from their true machinations. We know that Jimmy Savile appeared to the outside world as a lovable eccentric. Thus, idiosyncrasies such as apparently driving everywhere in a "campervan" were viewed through this lens. In fact the campervan now emerges as a key tool in his sexual abuse strategy. He took his place of safety, where he could abuse with impunity, on the road with him.

Savile was friends with some of the royal family, he spent a lot of time with Prince Charles. They had a 30-year friendship and even during Prince Charles and Princess Diana's troubled marriage, he was brought in as an unofficial marriage guidance counsellor. Incredible. Whether it was Jimmy Savile who manipulated Prince Charles or just a genuine friendship we will never know, and, of course, Charles is now our King. The former prince was an avid letter writer and sought Savile's advice on many occasions. In 1990 it is documented that Charles wrote to Savile asking him to, 'cast an eye over' a speech that he was working on and after Charles had delivered that speech wrote back saying, 'Dear Jimmy, I can't tell you how grateful I am for the most useful assistance you have provided for my speech in the Guildhall the other day. It was really good of you to take the trouble to put together those splendid notes and provide me with considerable food for thought.'

Savile spent Christmas at Chequers as a guest of prime minister Margaret Thatcher on more than one occasion. Did he woo and dupe Margaret Thatcher as well? By all accounts they were certainly very close and met on numerous occasions, both on official business and privately. Recently released letters (although heavily redacted), are available online and make interesting reading, although quite chilling too, as he talks about his 'madly jealous girl patients' and his 'paralysed boys.'

He courted newspaper headlines over his good causes, so who in their right mind would go after such an eccentric and saintly man, a man who my generation listened to on the radio, watched on *Top of the Pops*, and later on in his massively popular TV show *Jim'll Fix It*. He was also a cunning man who chose carefully when he entered advertising deals. He is remembered (by those of us of a certain age) as the face of the *Clunk Click Every Trip* TV advertising campaign to encourage the wearing of seatbelts. He was also the face of British Rail for a while, where he kept on referring to 'this is the age of the train'.

Nothing very controversial about all that. He could rightly boast that he was a well-protected individual and woe betide anyone who crossed him. And as a former cyclist, wrestler and coal miner, Savile was an imposing, if somewhat weird-looking, figure who you might not pick a fight with.

Some years ago the writer and broadcaster Jonathan Maitland wrote a brilliant play about Savile. It was called *An audience with Jimmy Savile*, in which Savile was played eerily and brilliantly by Alistair McGowan. Maitland kindly donated the proceeds from the play to NAPAC and I was invited to attend the post play discussion with the audience at Park Theatre in London. The play was a massive hit but I am unsure it ever went on the road to other venues. Maitland, who remains a friend, also had success with another of his astonishing plays about the downfall of the prime minister, Margaret Thatcher. That was called *Dead Sheep*, referring to the famous and barbed speech made by Thatcher's sacked Minister, Geoffrey Howe. The speech was the beginning of the end of Mrs Thatcher's term as prime minister. That play did indeed go on tour following its record-breaking stint at Park Theatre.

Victims are generally selected because they are isolated and vulnerable and they may sometimes believe that the abuse is the price they have to pay for the privilege of getting attention from a famous and respected person or be in the audience of a TV show. I remember speaking with some of the women who attended the boarding schools that Savile would visit in his Rolls Royce. At first it was exciting that the great Jimmy Savile was coming to their school to visit them. But it quickly turned sour when they realised that there was a heavy price to pay and that his visits were in no way whatsoever for the benefit of the pupils. The purpose of these meetings was entirely so that Savile could abuse young girls who he knew had been dubbed "troublesome", which was why they were at that particular school in the first place. The girls didn't really stand a chance and those who dared say anything were quickly rebuked and told not to 'tell filthy lies'.

This reminds me of another young woman I used to work with, who told me that when she was a small child at school she drew a disturbing picture of a "monster" abusing a child. When the teacher asked what it was about, the little girl said, 'This is what my daddy does to me.'

The teacher's response? 'How dare you tell such filthy lies about your father?' That little girl did not speak of the abuse until decades later and her father eventually went to prison. But how many other children did he abuse in the intervening years? And all because the teacher took no action and, in fact, did a lot worse by condemning the little child who was simply telling the truth. And we all know that children rarely lie about such things. This reminds me of a meeting I attended at the Houses of Parliament some years ago when one of the female peers stated, 'We all know children lie about these things.'

I would love to name this peer, but for legal reasons I can't.

One of the attendees at that meeting, a female clinician, responded with, 'Madam, I have worked with children for over 40 years and I have never known them to lie about such matters.' That shut her up. It's just a shame that at the time of writing this book, she is still one of our legislators.

Chapter 23

The Metropolitan Police investigation of the crimes of Sir Jimmy Savile was called Operation Yewtree. It represented an opportunity to transform the legal landscape so that never again a marauder such as Savile could manage to escape detection. Well, it wasn't that he escaped detection, he escaped justice, he escaped being stopped in his tracks as he should have been. What needs to be acknowledged, and to a great extent this is what the Yewtree report did, was that abuse was happening and continues to happen right under our very noses and mostly we don't recognize it. Or at least we don't want to recognise it - that's the scary part.

It is also worth mentioning that much of Savile's offending took place in a time before the establishment of Esther Rantzen's ChildLine, which was set up in 1986. Prior to this there was no free telephone line that children could call when in need, and ChildLine was undoubtedly a major step forward for child protection.

There are many things we as a society could do to keep children safer. Giving them the means to speak out is one of those. Abusers' primary fears are detection, arrest and conviction. If every child knows that they can speak out if something bad is happening to them then that is a big step in the right direction. And what must follow is swift action to protect that child, and swift action to challenge the abuser.

We, society, must not be distracted from what is happening by making excuses. Some people defend the filmmaker rapist Roman Polanski because he had a tough childhood. So what? Many of us had rough childhoods but we would never inflict on others what was done to us. But some do and we have to find out why. We have to actually try and get into the minds of the people who commit these appalling crimes. Many times over the years I have been asked about the leniency or otherwise of sentences passed down to convicted child abusers. This is not an easy question to answer. Yes, some sentences are ridiculously lenient. Other times they can seem appropriate, rarely are they excessive.

Be in no doubt, people who are a danger to others belong behind bars. But I have also on many occasions said that I would prefer a "lenient" sentence, where an offender is given the right kind of support such that they are less likely to reoffend (hence my support for initiatives like Circles UK), to a stiff sentence where the offender is released and re-offends.

The former CEO of Circles UK is someone I have kept in touch with. Stephen Hanvey has remained a great friend to me and since leaving the employment of both Circles UK and latterly Victim Support he has embarked on a PhD, looking at the lack of support for and understanding of victims of sexual abuse crimes in court. This is an area that has been much neglected and Stephen, with his vast experience and knowledge, will be able to throw some much needed light on this area of criminal justice. Many times I have heard how the experience of giving evidence and the lack of specialist support can leave some victims wishing they had never reported the crimes committed against them.

There are countless tragic stories to back this up, one of which I heard first hand in the very early days of setting up the charity. A woman came to the first meeting in Stockport to encourage me. She was the mother of a young boy who had recently taken his own life after being stalked by his abuser. The mother had begged the local authorities and the police to allow her son to have some counselling or psychological support because he was not coping. He was waiting to give evidence against his abuser. But because these authorities denied this young man any support he ended up hanging himself. He was just 13 years old and the man who he was to give evidence against ended up serving two years in jail for abusing three other children. Declan Curran lost his life and his family is left with a lifetime of grief, regrets and what ifs. The other boys the pervert abused have to live with the consequences for the rest of their lives. Justice? I don't think so.

A similar tragedy surrounded the untimely death of the musician Frances Andrade in 2013. She had given evidence against her former music teacher, Michael Brewer OBE, who was a senior staff member at the renowned Cheetham's School of Music in Manchester and the founding director of the National Youth Choirs of Great Britain. The cross-examination she had to endure in court drove her already fragile self to the edge and she died from a prescription drug overdose a week later. She left a husband and four children. Another victim not only of an abuser but of a criminal and mental health system that let her down. Her abuser, Brewer, was sentenced to six years in prison.

I suppose it's about balance. There are some people who will always pose a threat to children. Mercifully they are in a minority but a minority that may need monitoring for the rest of their lives. Then there are offenders who can genuinely change their behaviour to such an extent that they no longer pose a threat. The trick is knowing the difference. That is the big challenge. Can we ever really trust an adult who has violated a child? As I've said many times, abusers can be charming, plausible and highly manipulative.

I could write an entire book, a very long book, about all the abusers and alleged abusers I have been asked to comment on over the years. It wouldn't make for particularly uplifting reading but if you really want to see how many are out there, and I just mean those accused or convicted, you only have to scour the internet.

A common question I was often asked is, if someone contributed something positive to society but was then found to be an abuser, do we condemn their work? Do we tear their works down if they were a great artist? Stop playing their music? I don't think these are easy questions to answer but I would say that if victims or survivors of these people's crimes are still alive then that must make a difference. I know Jimmy Savile was not an artist of any kind but is it right to delete him from the BBC archives? You bet it is. Unless, of course, other perpetrators could be identified using the footage.

If Leonardo da Vinci was now exposed as a child abuser would we demand the Mona Lisa be taken down? Probably not. If a pop singer admitted to abusing kids should we stop buying his records? Gary Glitter springs to mind. If you have watched the American TV documentary *Leaving Neverland* about Michael Jackson's alleged abuse of young boys you might think twice about playing his records. Or maybe you won't.

Some years ago I was approached by Nathaniel Hepburn, who is the director of the Ditchling Museum of Arts and Crafts. He told me the museum was planning a special exhibition of the work of Eric Gill. Gill was one of the most influential British artists of the 20th century and his works include the famous statue of Ariel from *The Tempest*, mounted on the BBC's Broadcasting House in London and the Stations of the Cross in Westminster Cathedral. Gill, who died in 1940, also made no secret of the fact that he had abused his own daughters and admitted bestiality with the family dog. I can't help thinking that his Stations of the Cross do not belong in a place of worship but who is to say whether they should be removed or not? The owners, the Catholic Diocese of Westminster, is unlikely to do so and, as my friend Margaret Kennedy said back in 1998, 'They were created by the same hands that abused, they should be removed.' I agree. But then where do you stop?

It was good that Nathaniel contacted me. It is far better to discuss these matters than to just fall out about them. We had a good discussion and the outcome was that I went to speak to the staff at the museum in Ditchling to give them some thoughts about handling difficult questions, and also to make sure there was a supply of NAPAC leaflets in the museum for people to take away.

My understanding is that charities are not allowed to reject donations without very good cause. I guess this is why people like Jimmy Savile and Gary Glitter were able to donate to children's charities like the NSPCC , even though suspicions ran high about some of these characters.

I will now describe what I thought was going to be one of our biggest funding opportunities. In the aftermath of the Jimmy Savile scandal I contacted the BBC, specifically the director-general. I believe in going straight to the top! The negative media exposure around the now deceased Savile and his long association with the BBC meant that the latter had become a target of a great deal of criticism. How did Savile get away with so much for so long? Who knew about his crimes? Who covered up his crimes? Why was he not stopped and, crucially, why did the BBC not show a documentary, subsequently finished off by ITV, that exposed Savile for what he was?

And what was he? A predatory abuser who's sociopathic offending went unchecked for decades. He ruined the lives of many with his sexual assaults and over the years I have been contacted by several women whose childhoods were stolen by that man.

I was invited to meet the then director-general, George Entwistle. I liked George. He was deeply upset by the revelations about Savile and wanted to help NAPAC in a meaningful way. He said the BBC would make a "substantial" donation to our organisation so that we could handle the massive increase in calls coming to NAPAC. As stated earlier, the Savile scandal was a huge media story in 2012. When the documentary, cataloguing Savile's history of depravity, was shown on ITV the producers put the NAPAC logo and phone number on the screen at the end. From that evening and for many months to come the NAPAC Support Line phone did not stop ringing. I was doing media interviews for weeks on end. Early mornings, late evenings, the middle of the night sometimes when it was Australia, New Zealand or China! Yes the whole world was interested in the story and that was primarily because it concerned the BBC, which is hugely respected all over the world.

Sadly, the Savile scandal cost George Entwistle his job. The pressure on him was immense and he resigned, but not before something quite peculiar happened. I was invited to another meeting with him which was also attended by the Chair of Trustees of the NSPCC. Following this meeting the offer of "substantial" support was withdrawn. Apparently some conversations had taken place and the NSPCC had said that NAPAC didn't need the support because the NSPCC intended extending their helpline offering to survivors of abuse. At least that is what appeared to have happened. It was clearly a case of Big Brother pushing us out of the way and it made me very angry. And part of that anger was because of one or two things that happened whilst I was working at their London head office a couple of years before. The other thing was that many of the people who rang our support line over the years were very unhappy because in the past some of them had been taken by NSPCC staff back to the abusive households from where they had "escaped".

Chapter 24

When I first founded NAPAC, I had a simple goal; to create an organisation for survivors of child abuse. I wasn't green, I knew that child abuse throughout the previous generations had been largely concealed but as I read and researched during the next two decades, never would I have believed the sheer scale of child abuse that had been swept under the carpet across the continents and how many organisations were complicit in deliberately protecting individuals within their midst.

I was genuinely shocked at the scale of the cover-ups involving my own church and as I dug deeper and met with more of the men at the top - bishops, cardinals, archbishops and even the pope - I felt a deep-seated shame as I realised that my childhood, my youth and early adulthood had been a religious sham. I gave my religion every chance to right the wrongs of the past, to turn over a new leaf, to condemn and bring to justice the paedophiles who had brought what I thought was a noble organisation into disrepute.

But it wasn't just the Church and as the Jimmy Savile story unravelled and the media sensationalised every aspect of the crimes he had committed, I sat back and wondered just how many organisations like the BBC and the Church were out there. How many "untouchables" like Sir Jimmy Savile were there?

While NAPAC clearly benefited from the publicity surrounding the Savile revelations, it was also a very depressing time but I dug deep, seized the moment and was determined to be heard. Newspapers, magazines and television stations clamoured to interview me. I became, I suppose to many people, the unofficial spokesman for people abused in childhood.

I was working more hours than I had ever worked in my life and the research was taking up several hours each day. I heard more rumours, names were being whispered to me on a daily basis, names that I couldn't quite believe. Top policemen, judges, even MPs and yes, more celebrities like Max Clifford, Gary Glitter and Michael Jackson.

And across the pond more revelations from Hollywood. There is a substantial list of actors, producers and directors allegedly abusing their positions or using their positions of power to coerce, blackmail and force young men and women to engage in sex to further their careers or in some cases abuse and rape them knowing that the chances of any police complaints and charges, let alone convictions, would at very best be slim. Bill Cosby, Harvey Weinstein, Jeffrey Epstein and Ghislaine Maxwell shocked Tinseltown to its very core.

Weinstein was sentenced to 23 years in prison and has recently been given a further 16 years for rape, criminal sex acts, sexual abuse and sexual misconduct, following allegations dating back to the late 1970s. The allegations against him sparked the Me Too movement.

It's not altogether surprising that Weinstein publicly spoke against efforts to extradite Roman Polanski from Switzerland to the US on the proven charge that he had raped a 13-year-old girl.

Weinstein too, believed he was untouchable such was the sphere of influence he wielded in Hollywood. But when the allegations broke he hired a British Israeli intelligence firm to try and stop the publication of the allegations against him. He is now incarcerated in Wende Correctional Facility in New York and although he has appealed against his verdict and sentence it is expected that even more charges may follow.

Back in 2015 *The London Evening Standard* ran a headline that said, 'Child charity, NAPAC tells New Scotland Yard to Investigate Prince Andrew sex claims.'

I was the chief executive of NAPAC at the time and my comments were clearly noted and *The Evening Standard's* headline was far more dramatic than the conversation I had had with one of their journalists. I never told New Scotland Yard that they had to 'investigate Prince Andrew,' I simply passed on papers that had been sent to me from America. These included a deposition by a young woman who claimed to have been sex trafficked to London and coerced into having "sex" with a member of the British royal family.

A US attorney, acting for one of Epstein's victims, had contacted me and sent NAPAC details of the allegations made against Prince Andrew, specifically how this young woman, a minor, had been trafficked to London some years earlier. I did what I considered the only thing I could do and that was to forward those papers to the police at New Scotland Yard. Two police officers flew to the USA to interview the woman and whilst they had no problem believing her account, these alleged sexual encounters were with someone above the age of consent (16) and they took place before sex trafficking legislation had come into force. It was a case of No Further Action, but I won't repeat what one senior police officer said about the conduct of Prince Andrew.

It wasn't until some months later, after Jeffrey Epstein's death, that Prince Andrew gave the car crash of an interview to the BBC. I'm sure I am not the only person to have squirmed so much as I watched that interview with Emily Maitlis. It had been five years since I'd originally received the paperwork from the American attorney.

The word "untouchable" doesn't even come close now we know that a settlement of $12 million was negotiated by the best lawyers money can buy. The settlement means that the case was dismissed which avoided a lengthy, public trial. Virginia Giuffre claimed she was sexually abused by Prince Andrew in three different locations; Ghislaine Maxwell's London home, Epstein's Manhattan townhouse and at an "orgy" in the Virgin Islands. Not only can Prince Andrew not remember the orgy, but he also can't recall meeting Virginia at any time. Nevertheless, he agreed to the $12 million settlement.

Andrew has taken a back seat now. He is rarely seen in any official capacity and has been stripped of his titles. However, far from ruining him, his financial net worth is still estimated at around £30 million.

Prince Andrew's association with Ghislaine Maxwell and Jeffrey Epstein dates back many years, and allegations of Jeffrey Epstein's sexual assaults began to surface when he served a prison sentence for child abuse in 2008. Several years later I received documents from an American attorney containing allegations against a member of the royal family. Even after Epstein served a 13 month sentence for child abuse in 2008, it appeared that the two men still remained good friends as they were photographed together in Central Park, New York in 2010.

Another photograph released in 2010 shows Prince Andrew inside Epstein's Manhattan mansion. Prince Andrew, during the Maitlis interview, said he attended a small dinner party while he was there but denied it was to celebrate Epstein's release. The prince said that he regretted staying at Epstein's house during the visit, saying he 'let the side down,' and when pressed on reports that many young girls were coming and going from the house at the time, he said 'I didn't see any.'

Epstein apparently took his own life on August 10, 2019, but suicide, in my opinion, was far from conclusive. A four-hour autopsy performed by forensic scientist Doctor Michael Baden on behalf of Epstein's brother, claimed that in his opinion, evidence pointed more to murder than suicide because of the unusual fractures he saw in Epstein's neck. Baden said, 'I have never seen three fractures like this in a suicidal hanging.'

Epstein was on suicide watch and the two guards assigned to him should have been checking him every 30 minutes. They had checked on him at 19.49 the previous evening but then allegedly both slept through their shift and didn't see him again until 06:30 the following morning. The camera footage that was supposed to show the guard's movements outside Epstein's cell door that night was apparently corrupted.

Of course, the conspiracy theorists have been out in force since Epstein's death. He was connected to a long list of rich and powerful people and a prolonged court case was the last thing that any of them would have wanted.

Whilst I am not a conspiracy theorist, there are undoubtedly many questions to be answered. Don't hold your breath though, and it should be noted that Epstein's victims did not get justice in court.

We will never know the extent of Epstein's abuse and sex trafficking nor will we ever find out about the other paedophiles and perverts connected to the case.

Once again, it appears money talks.

Chapter 25

The former Liberal politician Cyril Smith was another case in question that made my blood run cold. Smith was the member of parliament for Rochdale from 1972 to 1992 but after his death it was revealed that he had been a prolific child abuser.

I can recall Smiths parliamentary years. He was a larger than life character who always seemed to walk around with a smile on his face. He was very popular in his constituency, again in 2012, yet another *déjà vu* moment as the Greater Manchester police force said that there was overwhelming evidence that he had sexually and physically abused young boys and there was no doubt that Smith should have been charged in his lifetime.

A total of 144 accusations had been levelled against Smith but all attempts to prosecute him had been blocked. As I researched the case against him I couldn't believe what I was reading. The cover-up was on an unprecedented scale, evidence had been destroyed and many of those collecting evidence against him were threatened with invocation of the Official Secrets Act. What the hell was going on? Had the Establishment moved in quickly and acted?

Once again, in a Savilesque repeat performance, the rich and famous, the all-powerful, rallied to support him. The Liberal Party leader at the time, David Steel, played down the allegations in 1979, claiming, and I quote, 'All he seems to have done is spanked a few bare bottoms.'

Nine years later Lord Steel, as he then was, even proposed Cyril Smith for a knighthood.

And then, as I read my own research notes, it took a sinister turn. An allegation of MI5 and Special Branch cover up. Those two words again!

Channel 4's *Dispatches* programme had taken up the case and discovered the file which accused Smith of a sordid series of indecent episodes with young boys. It was handed to prosecutors as early as 1970. The *Dispatches* team interviewed the policeman in charge of the operation. He was visibly upset and said that, 'People had accused the police of not caring and not bothering.' He continued with a tear in his eye, 'But we did care and we did bother and we compiled compelling evidence and plenty of it and then one day I received a phone call from MI5 who ordered me to pack up all the original case files and send them in a box by special courier to their headquarters.'

The evidence in that box accused the politician of eight counts of sexual abuse, including six offences at a care home he set up in his Rochdale constituency. He had a key to the care home, strong parallels with Jimmy Savile who also had his own keys and access to patients at Broadmoor, Stoke Mandeville and Leeds General Infirmary.

Just what else was in that box? What information had the police gathered and who was implicated along with Smith? We will probably never find out but I would suggest that, because of the intervention of MI5 who only operate in matters of national security, there were people implicated who were at the very top of government. MPs and cabinet ministers and it wouldn't surprise me if Edward Heath, the prime minister at the time, had one or two mentions in that file.

There had been allegations against him, none of which related to his time as prime minister. He was accused in 1961 of allegedly raping an 11-year-old boy. In 1962 he allegedly indecently assaulted a 10-year-old boy in a public place. In 1964 he allegedly indecently assaulted a 15-year-old boy during three paid-for encounters. Two years after becoming leader of the opposition he allegedly indecently assaulted another 15-year-old boy during a chance encounter in a public building. It must be pointed out that all of these accusations were never followed up and never proved but a distinct pattern was definitely emerging.

In 1976 he allegedly indecently assaulted another male while he was MP for Sidcup and much later, in 1992, he allegedly assaulted a boy aged between 12 and 14. Later that year he allegedly assaulted an adult man in what had been a paid, consensual sexual encounter.'

Something that became abundantly clear to me over many years is that certain people who abuse children are undoubtedly protected and they are often protected by very powerful forces. I remember having a chat with another Member of Parliament who I had just been on Sky News with a few years ago, and he said that when he was growing up in the area of north Manchester, 'Everyone knew that Cyril Smith was dodgy.' Again it begs the question; if everyone knew why didn't anyone do anything about it? Well, now we know a few brave souls did speak out but they were silenced and side lined and Smith was protected by very powerful political forces. Just like the late Sir Jimmy Savile, Cyril Smith received his knighthood during Margaret Thatcher's premiership.

It was claimed that Cyril Smith was part of a VIP paedophile ring but it's unlikely that we will ever find out the truth.

I was asked many times to comment about such cover-ups, and many times I was warned to 'Watch your back.' When you are dealing with powerful, and I would say sinister, forces, you must be careful. I have to confess that I didn't ever feel threatened. I, perhaps foolishly, thought that most people, most right-thinking people anyway, would abhor the abuse of children as much as me. I forgot that there are a lot of abusers out there too and they certainly don't want attention that will shine a spotlight on their sordid offending.

On many occasions I was asked about certain so-called celebrities who had been accused of abuse. My response was always to stress that obviously people are deemed innocent until proven otherwise. However, there seemed to be too many occasions when I got the sense that the police would be told to back off if it was someone on, what we might call, the "untouchables" list. People so high up in the Establishment that they could pretty much get away with murder, or something close to it, like child abuse.

The case of the late Lord Janner was one I was asked about on a number of occasions. NAPAC had received numerous allegations against this man and there is little doubt that a full and proper investigation should have taken place. It did not. I was quoted on the BBC website in January 2016 responding to the decision not to hold a trial of the facts after Janner's death. I said, 'It was a disastrous day for child protection'. Peter Garsden, a lawyer representing many of the alleged victims said that they were immensely frustrated that they haven't had the chance to have justice done and for them to give their version of events to a court of law.

Sir Richard Henriques KC, a man I was privileged to meet, later agreed, saying that there were strong grounds to have brought a prosecution against Lord Janner many years before, when he was still alive.

Another former Member of Parliament who was accused of abuse was Harvey Proctor. He was never charged or prosecuted. He had, however, been convicted of acts of gross indecency which ended his Parliamentary career.

I attended a press conference in August 2015 that Proctor held after one of his accusers, Carl Beech, had been charged with perverting the course of justice (lying to you and I), and I remember a conversation I had with one of Proctor's friends after the event. The friend told me that he never thought that Proctor was an abuser but that 'everyone knew' that another prominent former Tory MP (a man who had held very high office) was an abuser. That individual was also never charged or prosecuted.

It seemed that deals were struck behind closed doors and because abusers come from all walks of life (and from political parties of every persuasion) some of those deals were politically motivated. Frankly, the whole thing stinks.

When I was questioned by the Home Affairs Select Committee under the chairmanship of Roman Catholic former Member of Parliament Keith Vaz, I stated that I was aware of the serious allegations that were being made against some very senior former or current politicians and I stated that I had no reason to suspect that those allegations were untrue and therefore needed thorough investigation. I sat next to lawyer Alison Miller at that Committee hearing and she said much the same thing.

Little did I know then that the machinations of some sinister forces were already at work and those forces were determined to silence me. It's one thing to make comments about the likes of Rolf Harris, Stuart Hall, Max Clifford or Sir Jimmy Savile but when you start talking about very senior Establishment figures, watch out.

I had already criticised Prince (now King) Charles for his friendship with a Church of England bishop (this was on *Channel 5 News*) who had already been convicted of child abuse. I also had the audacity to send papers which I received from America implicating another member of the royal family in an abuse scandal to New Scotland Yard. I mentioned that earlier.

So, when journalist David Rose (friend of Daniel Janner KC, son of the late Lord Janner) of the *Mail on Sunday* rang me in 2019 whilst I was on holiday in Switzerland with my wife and expressed his anger at how I had supported serial liar Carl Beech, I told him I had done no such thing. I had simply taken Beech at his word as had the police, who did their job and investigated his claims.

NAPAC always took people at their word. It was not for us to judge.

David Rose persisted, asking me when I had last spoken to Beech. I had never spoken to him but I had had some limited email contact. He asked me again when I had met Carl Beech. I told him that he wasn't listening to me and repeated that I had never met him. I also told him that when it came to light that Beech was being investigated by the Northumbria Police I forwarded that correspondence to them.

Beech was another man who decided to take on the Establishment via his online claims. Initially he only ever mentioned two names, one of which was Jimmy Savile and the other that of his stepfather Major Raymond Beech. Beech was on safe ground, but he also talked about other Establishment figures (though he didn't name them) and made claims of cover-ups, missing dossiers of evidence and at one point called for a national inquiry into child abuse. There were also teasers about which famous figure would next be revealed as a paedophile.

It appeared that Beech's online posts were being noticed and in some quarters taken seriously. A retired child protection manager, Peter McKelvie, got involved and brought the posts to the attention of the BBC. Articles about Beech's claims began to appear on the *Exaro News* website.

Mark Conrad, a reporter for *Exaro News*, met Beech and went through his claims. Conrad claimed to have shown him many images of the people he had accused as a form of a picture test and Beech picked out people he had already named. The journalist must have thought he was uncovering a hugely explosive story as the names that Beech dropped into the mixing pot were revealed to him. However, it needs to be pointed out at this stage that neither the journalist nor *Exaro News* published any of these names. We now know that Beech accused Lord Bramall, Sir Roland Gibbs, and another senior general, Sir Hugh Beach. He named the former chiefs of MI5 and MI6, Sir Michael Hanley and Sir Maurice Oldfield, as well as the former prime minister, Sir Edward Heath, former home secretary, Lord Brittan as well as ex-MPs Harvey Proctor and Lord Janner. And now it appears that the police also were taking his claims seriously.

In what was described as a massive *faux pas* at the time, Detective Superintendent Kenny McDonald informed the media at the outset of the investigation in 2014 that officers assigned to the case believed the claims made by Carl Beech were, 'Credible and true.'

Needless to say the media was all over it, and what is not under any dispute is that the Establishment figures mentioned in the previous paragraphs were pitched into a living nightmare, many of them quite rightly describing their lives as 'ruined.'

Beech's claims were sensational, alleging that he was the victim of a VIP paedophile ring who had also murdered three boys. Beech had claimed that his stepfather had handed him over to the VIP group who used chauffeurs to collect him from school. Police described his recall of incidents as strong, and yet they began to doubt his story about the various drivers and witnesses and non-famous abusers as he was unable to offer anything tangible.

Beech's story began to unravel. Harvey Proctor called him a liar and a fantasist and said the inquiry (Operation Midland) was a homosexual witch-hunt and, while confirming his homosexuality, he said he was not a paedophile and had paid the price of his misdemeanour back in 1987 when he pleaded guilty to four acts of gross indecency with young men.

Other men accused by Beech labelled him a fraudster and began picking holes in his claims. Carl Beech claimed his stepfather had handed him over to Lord Bramall in Wiltshire, where they lived. Lord Bramall countered that he had never ever met Major Raymond Beech.

And then the bombshell. Beech's house was raided and images of child abuse were found on his computer and it was also discovered that he was covertly filming a teenage boy.

The game was up for Carl Beech, his credibility was in tatters and the tide turned against him.

Almost overnight the media and Establishment turned the screw and all of a sudden it was Carl Beech in the dock, accused of 12 counts of perjury and one of fraud which related to a criminal injuries payment he had received after the Jimmy Savile abuse scandal.

Having studied the case in detail I am very much of the opinion that Carl Beech was abused at some time in his childhood and early youth. Whether he is a fantasist as was claimed or whether he exaggerated his claims, we will probably never know. Some survivors of child abuse have been documented to be exaggerators. Beech was sentenced to an astonishing 18 years in prison for perverting the course of justice, fraud (the Jimmy Savile pay out) and the offences relating to images on his computer. Rapists, murderers, violent paedophiles and armed bank robbers receive sentences far less harsh than what Beech received.

While I don't downplay the damage he has caused to countless lives because of his false accusations, I am at a loss to work out why accusing somebody of abusing and raping carries a stiffer sentence than carrying out actual abuse and rape.

I refer to Judge James Goss, who sentenced Beech to 18 years. Checking out some of Justice Goss's cases from recent years, I note that when he presided over the case of Maxwell Laycock, an 18-year-old man who had raped an 86-year-old woman in a care home, Judge Goss sentenced him to three years in a young offenders unit. In 2010 the paedophile David Bryant was convicted of kidnapping four young girls aged between three and five years of age during the 1980s and 1990s and subjecting them to horrific sexual ordeals. Bryant was sentenced to 16 years in prison. And in Newcastle, in 2013, Abdul Miah raped a teenage girl at knifepoint in the West End of the city. Judge Goss sentenced him to 12 years in prison.

The compensation factor is also weighted heavily in favour of those who are falsely accused of crimes as opposed to those who have actually been victims of crimes. Here I speak directly from experience of hearing from many survivors. The level of monetary compensation some of them received for years of abuse at the hands of adults working in institutions such as Church-run schools, boarding schools, children's homes to name a few remains pitifully low.

Lawyers maintain that we must hit the organisations where it hurts the most, in their pocket, and only then will they take the necessary steps to do anything about it. That makes logical sense to me and is the reason why have I have advocated during my time with NAPAC that the United Kingdom's compensation awards should be brought in line with that of the United States.

As a case in point contrast it with the award that Harvey Proctor received. Mr Proctor's house had been raided by the Metropolitan Police at dawn. Mr Proctor said his life and reputation had been damaged beyond repair. After Beech was jailed, Harvey Proctor received £900,000 from the Metropolitan Police and an apology from Chief Constable Cressida Dick, even though The Independent Office for Police Conduct watchdog found no evidence of misconduct or criminality by the officers during Operation Midland. Go figure.

Chapter 26

Writing a book which has, at its heart, the dreadful scourge (I've sometimes called it a cancer) of childhood abuse is always challenging and painful. Memories are brought up and the constant question I keep asking myself is, why haven't we done more to tackle this man-made, deeply troubling phenomenon?

More precisely, why did no one spot that I was in trouble when I was a little boy. Why did no one spot the signs and symptoms of abuse that I must have been displaying? I suppose the truth was that no one knew what to look for and when I did display any kind of unchildlike behaviour they would just have put it down to me being "naughty". The quote below does, I believe, go some way to explaining this. Society simply does not want to see something so disturbing and so tragically common in our midst.

> *'Imagine a childhood disease that strikes one in four girls and one in six boys before they reach 18, a disease that can cause dramatic mood swings, erratic behaviour, and even severe conduct disorders among those exposed; a disease that breeds distrust of adults*

and undermines the possibility of experiencing normal sexual relationships; a disease that can have profound implications for an individual's future health by increasing the risk of problems such as substance abuse, sexually transmitted diseases, and suicidal behaviour; a disease that replicates itself by causing some of its victims to expose future generations to its debilitating effects.

Imagine what we, as a society, would do if such a disease existed. We would spare no expense, we would invest heavily in basic and applied research. We would devise systems to identify those affected and provide services to treat them. We would develop and broadly implement prevention campaigns to protect our children. Wouldn't we?

Such a disease does exist. It's called child sexual abuse.

Our response, however, has been far from the full-court press reserved for traditional diseases or health concerns of equal or even lesser magnitude. Perhaps the perception of sexual abuse as a law enforcement problem or our discomfort in confronting sexual issues contributes to our complacency. Whatever the reason, we have severely underestimated the effects of this problem on our children's health and quality of life.' Dr James Mercy, researcher with the Centre for Disease Control and Prevention, Atlanta, USA: Mercy, J. A. (1999). Having New Eyes: Viewing Child Sexual Abuse as a Public Health Problem. Sexual Abuse: A Journal of Research and Treatment, 11(4), 317-321.

My personal view about Dr Mercy's figures* are that they are way off the mark in terms of abuse incidences. I am personally convinced, based on decades of listening and research, that far more children suffer abuse than any official figures indicate. I have spoken to literally thousands of people who told me they had never spoken of their suffering and so would never show up in official figures.

* Updated from Dr Mercy's original speech in 1999. Some studies estimate sexual abuse is as high as 1-3 girls and 1-5 boys.

The truth of the matter is that we will never know the extent of this curse of abuse. It very much remains a taboo in most societies. Where I might differ slightly with Dr Mercy's assessment of sexual abuse being a 'public health problem' is if you say this to some survivors they may understandably state that being raped, assaulted and abused is also a criminal justice problem. As one survivor said to me, 'Is being beaten and raped as a child a public health problem?'

I think the point being made is that abuse is much more than one thing and for the victim it is a life-shattering crime. And it is a crime that creates an enormous economic burden on society in terms of those who, quite literally, do not survive. They are never able to contribute to society. Many victim/survivors have severe physical or psychological problems that prevent them from working. Millions of pounds are spent on drugs and hospital in-patient care. The list goes on. The reality is that the real "cost" to the economy of child abuse and its consequences are incalculable.

In the early days of setting up NAPAC my work covered a multiplicity of activities. These included campaigning for the rights of survivors, attending and speaking at seminars and conferences, meeting politicians and government ministers, fundraising and at the same time responding to the hundreds of survivors who were getting in touch.

In 1998, as mentioned earlier, I organised the NAPAC Hope After Abuse-rally in Trafalgar Square. The march and rally had previously been referred to as the CROSS march. CROSS stood for the Campaign for the Rights of Survivors of Sexual Abuse. There was a good turn-out but for the amount of effort that went into organising it, it was a relatively low key affair. The abuse of children was, and still is, a taboo subject and people tend to steer well clear. Though having said that, as we walked down Park Lane towards Trafalgar Square many people stopped to applaud us and shout encouragement. Deidre Sanders ("The World's Favourite Agony Aunt" and NAPAC patron) had organised banners for her fellow agony aunts and quite a few of them attended, at least half a dozen.

Our speakers in Trafalgar Square included Father Shay Cullen, an Irish Catholic missionary priest revered for his work with street children and the underprivileged in the Philippines. He spoke very passionately on the subject and pointed out that in many respects the United Kingdom was 'way behind' some other countries when it came to child protection. Other speakers included Ken Livingstone MP (later to become mayor of London) and Christopher Cloke from the NSPCC. Unlike previous CROSS marches I made sure there was some entertainment as well. This was provided by two bands. One was called Slinkyhead and they brought a wonderful and vibrant sound to Trafalgar Square, and the other music was provided by Paul and Jayne, two NAPAC stalwarts who also had their own band.

The music certainly set the place alight and was a great distraction from the sombre subject of the occasion. Child abuse is no laughing matter but we all need a distraction from the seriousness of it, if only to keep us sane. Slinkyhead was actually the band of the brother of one of NAPAC's founding members, Katie John. To this day Katie does an amazing job of monitoring what is being said in the media about child protection issues and if she feels something needs saying she will go into action. Many years ago I spotted a letter she had written to *The Guardian* newspaper and this was one of my first encounters with her brilliantly proactive presence.

Another of our Trustees, a communications specialist, produced and distributed an excellent press release ahead of the event but as is often the case, particularly then, it was mostly ignored.

But it was a great day and many survivors spoke from the platform at the foot of Nelson's Column and many more danced and sang their way around Trafalgar Square, much to the delight of the thousands of tourists who flock to that place.

But back to fundraising. Some funders shy away from supporting the big, well-funded charities and one example of those was the Body Shop Foundation, sadly no longer in existence. I had done an interview on TV about our work and out of the blue I got a call from their grants manager, asking if we could meet. You don't say no to such an offer.

A few days later I met three of their team in a coffee shop in Victoria station in London. They said they were impressed with the interview and were keen to help. Whilst wanting to jump in and grab their kind offer, I played it cool and said something about how much we would appreciate their help with our unique work.

The help was forthcoming. NAPAC and the foundation enjoyed a long and fruitful relationship and it was such a shame when the Body Shop company was taken over by a multi-national and ended the foundation's work. But before that happened we had some fun. I visited the foundation in Littlehampton on a few occasions and had the pleasure of meeting their founder, the late Anita Roddick and her husband, Gordon. Another time I met Will Travers, son of film star and animal rights activist, Virginia McKenna. He was there representing the Born Free Foundation and as I recall, he turned up by helicopter. I remember having lunch with him and saying how much I had loved his mother in the film *Born Free*.

That particular visit to the foundation was memorable for another reason. During the visit I was called by the BBC. They wanted me to be a guest on *Moral Maze* that evening. *Moral Maze* goes out live on BBC Radio 4 at 8 p.m. on Wednesday evenings. This particular edition was one about hitting children.

I had long been an advocate for outlawing physical punishment of children, everyone in the know knows it doesn't work and I've yet to meet a parent who is glad they beat their kids. Discipline is not about punishment, it is about leadership. "Do as I do not just as I say", and I have yet to meet a child (or a grown-up for that matter) who really appreciated being hit.

Let's look at positive parenting rather than punitive action and for me it is not just about changing the law, about criminalising parents, it is about changing a culture that currently says it is okay to hit children. We all know that violence tends to breed violence and whilst many parents will have hit their children in the past with no obvious detrimental effects, for many the beatings can be deeply damaging and lead to life-long problems. I liken it to the law on wearing seat belts. A few people were very put out when compulsory seat belt laws came in. An infringement of their civil liberties, some said. It was opposed, but the fact was it saved lives.

Some people think they have a right to hit their children. Well, we protect adults from such assaults, so why don't we afford the same rights to children? They are people with an equal right to protection, yes? I know this is something that draws venom from certain quarters and some commentators, including some former breakfast TV and radio presenters. They think that we should have the right to hit our children while they dress it up and downplay it as smacking or a gentle tap on the bottom, and it suddenly doesn't sound so fearful. But I instinctively know it is wrong. Let's teach each other to be good parents or better still, let's ask our kids what they think.

Let's do our best to take violence out of society, for adults and for children.

I suffered at the hands of bullies at my school. As much as I hated what they did to me I can't help but think those kids probably didn't return home to loving, caring parents and if a clout around the ear, or perhaps even worse was par for the course in the confines of their own family environment, then it follows that they are going to bring that violence to school. To them it's a normal part of life and they have suffered at home, so why not make someone else suffer too?

I was ready and willing to get all these points across on *Moral Maze* and took copious notes on the fast train to London once I had left the foundation. Time was pressing and this was live radio. When I got to Victoria there was a security alert, the Underground was closed off and the queue for the taxi rank was ridiculous. I rang the studio, which was at New Broadcasting House and they began to panic. 'Jump in a cab, do anything but get here.'

Well I was really fortunate. As I turned a corner outside the station I spotted an empty black cab which I waved frantically at. The driver swung round and picked me up.

I got to the studio just minutes before the programme was due to air. Poor Michael Burke was pacing up and down, worried that I wasn't going to make it. But I did, just. Fortunately I wasn't the first witness to go before the panel of inquisitors. That fell to a young woman from the NSPCC. I was up second, but while I was waiting for my turn I had an enlightening chat with another guest, none other than Rachel Johnson, sister of Boris, who at that time was some way off becoming prime minister. And the member of the panel who I remember most vividly as an arch opponent of legislation to ban hitting children was a journalist called Michael Gove. Yes, that's right, a Conservative Member of Parliament, a minister (I think) these days and a future education secretary who opposed legislation to stop beating children. It's amazing who you meet at the BBC sometimes.

That was a late, late night and having set off for the Body Shop in Littlehampton early that morning it became a very long day. I was exhausted by the time I got home, but that is what you have to do when you are setting up and keeping a fledgling charity afloat. It's hard work but incredibly rewarding - most of the time.

Chapter 27

There are hundreds of thousands of people who turn out for causes they feel strongly about, fox-hunting supporters spring to mind, but when it comes to child protection, particularly in the UK, people are worryingly absent.

I visited and spoke at the European Parliament in Belgium a few weeks after a million people had taken to the streets of Brussels to protest about the child abuse scandal that was engulfing that small country. A million people. The turnout amazed me, we had managed a few hundred at best.

The scandal unfolding in Belgium included allegations against some very senior politicians and reminded me once again that child abuse and paedophilia has no social, economic or political boundaries. The scandal erupted after four young girls were found dead in a warren of underground concrete caves and cages beneath the house of the known paedophile and convicted sex offender, Marc Dutroux.

He had previously been jailed for the abduction and rape of five young girls in 1989.

The poor girls had been kidnapped and used as Dutroux's sex slaves, but there were also allegations that other men had visited the children while they had been kept prisoner although this was never verified.

Two of the girls who died, were buried alive, the other two starved to death after Dutroux had been jailed for a different offence.

Two other girls were miraculously rescued, one of them had spent nearly three months in chains while Dutroux raped her on an almost daily basis. She was 12 years old, and her rescuers were left in no doubt that the two girls found alive would have been murdered had they not been rescued.

During the investigation, which discovered a warren of underground concrete cages, it was suggested that there was an existence of paedophile networks in Belgium. The investigators said that there was evidence that orgies involving drugs and underage children had taken place. Clients included VIP's, judges, politicians, police and members of the clergy.

The investigation, which lasted 15 months, and ended in 1998 pulled no punches. It claimed massive incompetence and corruption by the authorities. The Belgian public were horrified and one newspaper wrote that the inquiry had left the country scarred. It was only after the results of the inquiry were published that the police started to take the very real issue of organised paedophilia in Belgium seriously and conducted a series of raids on prominent figures and their institutions.

Many of the places raided were churches and other places of worship. The Vatican responded by calling the raids a witch-hunt. Pope Benedict XVI called the raids deplorable. Cardinal Tarcisio Bertone, the Vatican's secretary of state, said the raids were unprecedented.

They were indeed, and the public were demanding even more of them as the scale of the abuse filtered through the media and sympathy for the Vatican waned.

The Vatican's top deputy for foreign relations, Archbishop Dominque Mamberti, stoked the fire. He had the bare-faced cheek to call in the Belgian ambassador to the Holy See and give him a dressing down. He said someone had leaked that the Belgian police had nicknamed the raids Operation Church, and he insinuated that the police were not really interested in the real perpetrators of the abuse, only determined to go after the Catholic Church.

This did not go down well with the Belgian public and the newspaper, the Flemish daily *De Morgen*, applauded the clear signal sent out by the police, that the Church was not above the law.

The daily newspaper *Le Soir*, went even further, suggesting that the Vatican 'prefers the tombs to the victims.' It said that the police were well within their rights to target clergy who they believed to be involved. And we now know that a lot of clergy in Belgium were very involved.

The tide had turned for the Church, their relationship with the Belgian public cooling day by day. A 2008 study found that only seven percent of Belgian Catholics attend Mass on a weekly basis and only half of new-born children in the country were baptised.

I can relate to the winds of change exactly. I speak from experience. Only a couple of decades earlier I was a devout Catholic, who wouldn't have a word said against my guiding organisation. However, the older you become, the more you look at the organisation and the more you realise what it is it stands for. Over the years I have given them the benefit of the doubt again and again and begged them to prove their sincerity in dealing with a very real problem. I came to the conclusion that it was mostly a waste of time.

After the Belgium sex abuse scandal it appears that Belgians are beginning to wake up too. Around the same time of the Belgian sexual abuse scandal Pope Benedict made some remarks on his way to Africa which didn't help his cause. He said words to the effect that condoms make the problem of AIDS worse. The national Belgium parliament formally voted to censure the pontiff in an overwhelming majority of 95 to 18.

In a sickening twist to the story, it appears that child killer Dutroux is making a bid to be freed from jail, composing sick letters to the parents of his victims. Dutroux is claiming that it is a human right to be set free and he is not the cold monster that he was once referred to.

I'm all for human rights but when a person violates and murders a child or children they forgo those rights in my opinion.

Chapter 28

The Belgium scandal proves yet again that abusers exist in all strata of society and right across the world, but as we were to discover here in the UK some years later, pinning anything on well-connected politicians or even members of the royal family is extremely difficult, and ultimately cost some of us our livelihoods.

When the Labour Party swept to power in 1997, as mentioned earlier, I had very high hopes that things would change, that child protection would move swiftly up the political agenda. In some respects they did and I was able to secure an early meeting with new health minister, Jacqui Smith MP. Jacqui became an ally and was instrumental in helping NAPAC secure its first big government grant. That enabled us to get our first telephone helpline off the ground. It was a huge success and we received hundreds of calls as soon as it opened – largely thanks to some amazing TV coverage courtesy of Sky News and the BBC. Oh, and I nearly forgot; the very first corporate donation we received was actually from Channel 4 TV.

Years later I managed to secure another meeting with a government minister, this time it was the Conservative secretary of state for health, Jeremy Hunt MP. Meeting Secretary of State Hunt was interesting. I went with a couple of colleagues to the department of health in Westminster and when we walked into his office he greeted us, then sat on his chair behind a big desk, put his arms behind his head and asked me, 'What can I do for you Pete'? A fair question. I replied that it wasn't what he could do for me but what could we all do together to support survivors and to make the world a safer place for our children. As often happens in such meetings the minister (in this case the secretary of state) says some encouraging things then states that we need to meet with his officials. And sometimes that happens and sometimes it doesn't and in this case very little happened afterwards. Large organisations that have a large staff to follow up such meetings and dedicate time to these matters are one thing but when you are a tiny organisation like NAPAC and, as chief executive you are trying to do everything, you tend to run out of steam and patience. Then you think, 'What's the point?' The "big boys", the NSPCC's, the Save the Children, the Barnardos of the world have all the power and influence, not to mention the funding and you know you are fighting a losing battle. At least it feels like that at times.

Organising marches and rallies and meeting government ministers may sound glamourous but I can assure you it is not. It is a lot of hard work and all too often the outcome is not what you hoped for. I've often been asked if one kind of abuse is "worse" than another and my response always was that all abuse is insidious and nasty and they all tend to merge into one, at the worst of times. Hence sexual abuse is also a physical assault but the lasting effects tend to be profound and psychological.

People who are physically abused can suffer consequences similar to those who suffered sexual assault and people who are "only" abused psychologically can also be no better off than anyone else. I don't think it is always helpful to categorise abuse. They all have dire consequences but the effects of those consequences will inevitably affect individuals in different ways. I have met people who suffered an entire childhood filled with degradation and abuse and they have survived relatively well. I have met some people who were assaulted just once in their childhood but can never seem to break free of the pain they were left in.

I also remember one individual saying that he suffered more than all the other boys who had been abused at his Catholic boarding school. My response to that was, and is, 'How can you say that?' How can any of us know what others have gone through? I have spoken to people, some of whom are or were serving prison sentences, who went through almost unbelievable childhood trauma. I used to belittle, or maybe a better way of saying it is 'used to understate', the abuse I suffered. I wasn't ever beaten to within an inch of my life, but I was held down by my brother-in law and went through moments of sheer terror. I was held down and sexually assaulted. I was a very small child. I didn't know what was happening. But it was horrible and I prayed for it to stop. For him to stop. And what I suffered has affected me profoundly and it has taken me over sixty years to begin to come to terms with it all.

Will I ever have real self-esteem? I doubt it. Will I ever have total confidence in myself? Probably not. Will I ever know what life might have been like but for the abuse I suffered? Of course not. I am not unusual in that respect.

None of us can say how life would have turned out for us had we not suffered as we did. And I never forget that many children who suffered abuse did not survive. I think back to the victims of Myra Hindley and Ian Brady in the 1960s, the abuse and murder of children over half a century ago. How many investigations, inquiries, conferences and laws have we seen about this and other atrocities over the decades since then? Very many indeed. But have things really changed? Are our children really much safer today than we were as children? The experts seem to think not. Again, it comes back to this often cited point that we, society, do not want to address this disturbing aspect of human behaviour. It is best kept swept under the carpet.

Over many years I have spent a lot of time at various broadcast outlets, including the BBC, ITV, Sky News, CNN, most of the European media outlets and even Vatican Radio, and whilst the majority of people who work in these places are lovely there are a few who have given me the creeps. These tend to be individuals who, for one reason or another, clearly wish they were interviewing you about something else.

For legal reasons I will only mention the celebrities who I have found to be decent people, I was once threatened with legal action by a high-ranking cardinal of the Catholic Church, purely for offering my opinion about his conduct and I don't want that experience again. As I am sure you appreciate, legal redress tends to only be available to people with money - not the rest of us. A couple of celebrities I did cross swords with I will mention. I say we crossed swords, but I doubt they would know me from Adam. One was Stephen Fry, one of Britain's most popular, not to mention brainy, people and the other was former *Top Gear* presenter Jeremy Clarkson. Fry attacked Operation Yew Tree when speaking at a Labour Party fundraising event in July 2014. He was quoted as complaining angrily as he urged guests to 'remember that people are innocent until proven guilty' and was thought to be referring to the treatment of his friend DJ Paul Gambaccini, who was on bail following his arrest amid allegations of child abuse. Clarkson was reported for cracking a joke in relation to the Stuart Hall abuse scandal, saying, 'No one in the BBC had ever put his finger in my bottom'. These are things that outraged survivors of abuse and on each occasion I was asked to comment.

My comment about Mr Fry made a headline in the *Daily Mail* as did my comment about Mr Clarkson. These two people share some similarities. As far as I am aware both went to private schools and I'm told that many people who attend these institutions tend to have a sense of entitlement that the rest of us don't, and the other thing they share is a tendency to say or do outrageous things. But I suppose that is why they are popular. Outrageous can be fun but I do think that sometimes people should think before they engage their mouth. And I raise my hand to sometimes being guilty of the latter!

Of course celebrities are not the only ones who sometimes say quite worrying things. I have encountered individuals who have said things about abuse that made me seriously question their motives. A priest who claimed he had been abused as a child said, 'Oh, you just get over it.' Seriously? Did he believe that or was he simply defending the actions of his church? Indeed, was he really a survivor?

Defending the fact that Church officials, principally priests and nuns, have got away with murder for years and been protected by the institution is a disgrace I struggle to come to terms with. And I agree with my friend, Father Tom Doyle, that the abuse of a child is tantamount to 'murder of the soul'. I have met very few survivors of abuse who claim that they have really "got over it". It is something that stays with you forever. It doesn't have to define you forever but I fear few of us ever truly forget. One of the most outrageous things a panellist on *Moral Maze* (you can try and work out who) said during the programme some years ago, was that he did not recognise the scale of abuse I had been describing and that sometimes child victims 'act provocatively'. He was referring to a 6 or 7-year-old as I recall. Beyond scary, particularly as this man had been a former member of the British government.

One of the things that the internet and social media has done has been to connect people like never before. Victims have contacted other victims. Abusers who thought they had got away with it were no longer doing so because people were coming forward with similar accounts. Most abusers still, I believe, get away with their crimes but more of them are now being identified because of our ability to connect with one another, not just locally or countrywide, but globally.

Chapter 29

As you have read I was born and raised Roman Catholic and as far back as I remember I was told and believed that the pope was God's man on Earth. I believed that the pope had some sort of direct communication with the Almighty. How wrong could I be? But this is what Catholics are told and when something is drummed into you from a very early age, you grow up believing it. It's a bit like young lads who are taken to football matches even before they can walk or talk and are brought up to believe that Dad's team is the greatest thing since sliced bread. Even if that team happens to be in the lowest league of the football world! My devotion to God and my church was absolute throughout my childhood and youth and through many decades to come. Yes, I am a slow learner and it took me a long time to see through all the lies and deceits perpetrated by organised religion and how it, far from being the loving unifying body that it purports to be, is in fact the complete opposite. A very simple example I cite is how my parents wouldn't let my brother marry the woman he loved because she was not a Catholic. It's almost worse than racism. It is also the worst kind of misuse of power and control and that, again, is what religious institutions revel in. I was brought up to believe that my faith was superior to everyone else's.

Fast forward many years to when I was setting up NAPAC and battling with various institutions over their handling of child abuse issues. The institution I did battle with most was, as it turned out, the very institution to which I had been so devoted over many, many years: the Roman Catholic Church. When Pope Benedict resigned the papacy (and we'll never be told the truth behind that move) in 2013 and Pope Francis was elected to replace him, I thought that things might change, that we may finally have a radical pope who would take action on the issue close to my heart, the protection of our children.

This hope was strengthened when I heard that the new pope had set up a papal commission to look into the whole sordid affair. It was called, to give it its full title, The Pontifical Commission for the Protection of Minors. Little did I know at the time that I would end up being a member of that commission or that I would be sitting chatting to the new pope barely a year later. But that's what happened. I took a call from a senior British Catholic to ask if I would like to meet the pope and a few months after that meeting I was invited onto his new commission. I still have the official letter of my appointment, duly signed by the Vatican secretary of state, another high-ranking cardinal. Trouble is, it's all in Latin so I have no idea what it says.

From the start of my involvement I sensed that this papal commission was not what I had thought. It became obvious early on that little would change as a result of this initiative and the fact that it was only to meet once or twice a year was a strong indication that the Vatican was not taking it seriously. Furthermore, there was virtually no budget for the commission and during the entire time I was there, not once did the pope come and visit. He was willing to go to other things but child protection was clearly not on his list of priorities. My time on the commission was brief.

I was appointed at the beginning of 2015. Just over a year later the commission said it could not work with me. I regularly spoke to the media about what was going on and the commission members hated that. My suggestion that we had more openness and transparency about our meetings was met with derision. One member, a Polish woman who had apparently been Polish prime minister said, 'We need secrecy.' I couldn't believe my ears. I stated that it was this secrecy that went a long way to why the Church had got away with so much. It thrives on secrecy. Fear and secrecy.

Abuse thrives on the same things. There were a few things that I said or did that clearly infuriated the Vatican. I gave an interview to Australian TV about the scandal surrounding the former archbishop of Melbourne, Cardinal George Pell. I met with people who had experienced what they described as his callous and cold attitude. I also went on British TV, a BBC Sunday morning chat show hosted by Nicky Campbell, where I recounted what Cardinal Pell was alleged to have said and that was if a lorry driver raped someone his company was not responsible for his actions. This was his clear and sinister justification for getting the Church off the hook when its priests and nuns abused children. The cardinal was wrong. A company is in fact responsible for the acts or omissions of its employees, and the courts have established that these people are indeed employees of the Church. But the crunch part of this is that whereas a company will undoubtedly remove such a dangerous employee, the Church will just move the abuser/rapist to another parish, diocese or country. The attitude of the Church at times is quite unbelievable. I think this was around the time I heard an interview on Radio 4 during which a cardinal of the Roman Catholic Church was defending a convicted priest, saying that perhaps the priest was confusing love with abuse, or was being overly affectionate! There is nothing wrong with being appropriately affectionate. There is nothing wrong with loving someone but there is a world of difference between affection and the rape and assault of a child. When the two priests at my school were rubbing my tummy and genitals there was nothing affectionate or loving about it. They were doing it for their own sexual gratification and these events, suffered by many others, will play on our minds for the rest of our days. Of course, when you are a child you don't really understand what is happening to you and because these characters are often authority figures you dare not question them.

A day or two before my removal I challenged my fellow commission members over a case that had come to light whilst we were there in Rome. Two Italian priests had come forward to report one of their colleagues who was abusing children. They went to their bishop, their boss. He told them to do nothing, to remain silent. These brave men then went to the police. The police referred them back to their bishop. So much for child protection in Italy. What happened next? I do not know. One of the priests on the commission just shrugged his shoulders as if to say, 'So what?'

From day one I had been told the commission doesn't engage in individual cases. Most convenient. Especially as people were contacting me from all over the world reporting abuse and saying that their local church was doing nothing to stop it. And also reporting that when they tried to make contact with the hierarchy, or even the Vatican itself, they were ignored. I think it's also worth mentioning the Oscar-winning film *Spotlight* (if you haven't seen it you really should), the dramatisation of the Pulitzer Prize-winning team of journalists at *The Boston Globe* who exposed the full extent of abuse in that predominantly Catholic city, a cover-up presided over by the late Cardinal Law, the former archbishop of Boston. Cardinal Law who was going to potentially face criminal proceedings over the cover-ups and who, by chance, was whisked away to the Vatican where he lived the life of luxury afforded those with "Red Hats" – to the uninitiated – cardinals of the Roman Catholic Church.

Although I had been "ejected" from The Pontifical Commission for the Protection of Minors for speaking out, I was refusing to resign. Cardinal Sean O'Malley, commission president, knowing that I was in that part of the USA (Tricia and I were attending a wedding in Maine, this was Spring 2016), invited me to meet him at a hotel in Boston. In fact, his officials booked Tricia and I into a very smart harbourside hotel where we had a fabulous suite furnished with cheese, wine and fresh fruit on our arrival! How the other half live, eh?

Cardinal Sean, who is the archbishop of Boston and his assistant (I've discovered that cardinals, like senior politicians, never seem to be allowed to go anywhere alone) came to the hotel and we had a light lunch and a chat together. He told me that the commission needed me to resign. I said I had no intention of doing so, the pope had appointed me. The pope could disappoint me! The cardinal didn't seem too perturbed by this, even saying he was glad I wasn't going to resign. All a bit odd really. But what I know about church officials, and they don't get much higher in stature than a cardinal, is that they all tend to toe the party line, even when they know that that is crazy. I think Cardinal Sean could see the sense of having me, a survivor of abuse, on the pope's commission but he was sent to do a job and that was to get rid of me.

So we had an interesting conversation in the specially opened dining room of this fabulous hotel (which it turns out belonged to a friend of the cardinal) and my wife was also able to make a few points of her own to the archbishop. And that was quite interesting too!

Tricia was for many years deeply involved in her local Evangelical Church and she has always had a healthy disregard for most things Catholic. Her and the cardinal had a good exchange of views. The cardinal acknowledged the failings of his diocese 'in the past' but said that Boston was now a beacon of good (child protection) practice. Tricia asked why his good practice was not rolled out throughout all Catholic dioceses. The cardinal said that he, as a cardinal, had no jurisdiction over other dioceses and therefore could do nothing. Tricia pointed out that her understanding was that the pope did have jurisdiction over all his bishops (and hence their dioceses) and so he could do something. She quite hilariously asked the cardinal, 'Have you heard of a tablet?' adding, 'Not the Tablet of Stone with its Ten Commandments that would take years to distribute and be costly, I'm referring to the electronic type where it takes moments to write a message and seconds to send it to the entire world!' In other words she was having none of his excuses and we all know if the Vatican was serious about protecting children, the so-called "beacon of good practice" the cardinal boasted about in Boston could easily be implemented across the so-called universal church! Quite simple really? You would think so. But if all the priests and religious within the Catholic Church who did not stick to their vows of celibacy were to resign, or be dismissed, about half their number would disappear overnight.

I was sitting with Tricia back in 2016 watching the BAFTAs on TV. We were absolutely delighted when it was announced that *Spotlight* was one of the winners and despite being in our lounge and nobody able to hear us, we couldn't help but breakout into a spontaneous round of applause! We watched as the director and screenwriter, Tom McCarthy, delivered his acceptance speech. To my absolute amazement towards the end he said, 'I'll give a shout-out to Pete Saunders, a UK citizen and survivor, for all the great work you are doing in this country here and at the Vatican. You are an inspiration to us all, truly.'

Wow. I sat in stunned silence, hardly able to comprehend what I just heard and a little part of me thought, perhaps I am getting through to people, perhaps I am making a difference.

A couple of months later, *Spotlight* won the coveted Academy Award for Best Picture at the Oscars.

During my last visit to the Vatican as a member of the papal commission, the producers of *Spotlight* contacted me and offered to hire a private cinema in Rome where I could show the film to my colleagues. It was a huge surprise.

Most of my colleagues did not want to watch the film and instead of taking up Hollywood's kind offer, the Vatican got hold of a pirate copy of the film and insisted on showing it in one of their less comfortable rooms! When I look back, I realise some of them would have found it very uncomfortable to watch a movie that clearly demonstrates the deliberate failings of their church to protect children. The sceptic would say that was the reason why the Vatican orchestrated a viewing in such uncomfortable surroundings. I suppose the fact that fewer than half the members bothered to watch *Spotlight* was indicative of how much interest they really had in actual child protection..

A comment I heard from one commission member about *Spotlight* was that the only reason *The Boston Globe* pursued the matter was because the 'editor was Jewish'. A stunning statement, and there was I thinking that these antisemitic views had long been banished from the Catholic psyche.

At the end of the film another commission member said, 'We really must look after our priests.' One of the nuns from the African continent who was on the commission turned to me a few days later and said, 'I do not think that we have sexual abuse in my country', and this from a papal commission member for child protection.

Another member said, and I quote, 'There are children running around in priests' houses all over the world where celibacy has not been followed. And it's not seen as an evil thing in many of those places.'

As the comments tumbled out of the mouths of the people who had watched the film, it was clear, once again, that the majority of the members were not really interested in child protection.

So, to hell with the victims of these evil creatures, it's the priests we need to look after. As I say time and time again, you couldn't make this up.

A number of the characters and names mentioned in the movie were, and still are, friends and colleagues. I met with *The Boston Globe* reporters when I visited the city and have their permission to mention them in this book. The American organisation Survivors Network of those Abused by Priests (SNAP) that I talk about earlier, is mentioned in the film. Over the years I was privileged to attend a number of their conferences in America and they were always amazing and powerful events.

Regular speakers at the SNAP conferences included people like Tom Doyle, Jason Berry, Phil Saviano, Mitchell Garabedian and Walter Robinson. These are all amazing people whose characters are depicted in *Spotlight*. Tom Doyle is a Catholic priest who has been speaking out on behalf of clergy abuse survivors for over four decades. He first alerted the Church hierarchy to the impending financial disaster that would befall it if it didn't take action against its abusing employees. It took no action and many Catholic dioceses in the USA were subsequently bankrupted following civil lawsuits. Tom is a truly inspirational individual who sacrificed his chosen vocation to speak truth to power. He is now in his mid-seventies but he is a sprightly man who still travels extensively in order to provide his compelling testimony and expertise. As well as being a priest Tom is also a Cannon Lawyer. He is an amazing friend to me and it is a great privilege to know him. He also happens to own his own light aircraft and I have great hopes of having him fly me one day!

Jason Berry is a journalist who has also worked tirelessly to bring out the truth behind the abuse scandals in the Church. He has written numerous books and articles about the subject and I had the pleasure of meeting him on a number of occasions.

Phil Saviano, whose character is central to *Spotlight* was a survivor of clergy abuse and has spent most of his life fighting for justice. There is a heart-breaking scene in the film where Phil describes being 'preyed upon by a priest.' He emphasises he means 'preyed' upon not prayed upon. Very powerful.

Sadly, Phil died quite recently. A tragic loss of a true humanitarian.

I can't say I really know Walter Robinson or Mitchell Garabedian but they were both very powerful conference speakers. Robinson was the head of the Spotlight investigative team at *The Boston Globe* and Mitchell Garabedian is a lawyer who has represented hundreds of victims and survivors of clergy abuse. The thing they have in common is their humility, their determination to do the right thing and their refusal to stay silent on these issues. Between them they have done an enormous service for the cause of survivors and, by implication, the cause of child protection.

At the SNAP conference in 2016, I had the privilege of having lunch with Marty Baron, the former editor of the Boston Globe (who went on to be Editor-in-Chief at the Washington Post) and was keen to assure him that I found the anti-Semitic comment made by my former papal commission colleague completely unacceptable.

Another man who must be mentioned is the late Dr Richard Sipe. Richard was a former monk who, like Tom Doyle, dared to speak out about the scandal of abusive clergy. Not only did he speak out but he also worked with offenders and carried out extensive research into clergy abuse. Richard is not seen in the film but his voice is heard. He is asked by one of the Spotlight team about the prevalence of clergy abuse. He points out that it is far higher than anyone dares to imagine. He also points out that his research indicates that more than 50% of Catholic clergy do not lead celibate lives. Of course this does not mean 50% of priests abuse children but it confers on the whole organisation a cloud of secrecy which itself helps to perpetuate the incidences of abuse. Sipe also points out that the imposition of a truly unnatural rule of celibacy is bound to lead to rule-breaking. Most human beings do not respond well to the imposition of such a law and while some people may well be able to live a celibate life, Richard's research would seem to indicate that for Catholic clergy at least, half of them don't manage it.

So, my time on the papal commission was short but a great deal happened around that time and a great deal more work followed.

In 2018 I travelled to Chile to stand with survivors of abuse as the pope visited their country. I then flew to Lima in Peru where I met with more survivors of clergy abuse. Funnily, the pope decided not to visit his home country of Argentina although we know that survivors of clergy abuse would have made a warm welcome for him there. I was very conscious of how the pope had hurled insults at the people of Osorno in southern Chile, when he was questioned about the appointment of the Bishop of Osorno. This was in St Peter's Square and the pope was heard to call the people of Osorno dumb.

I met many of these good folk in Santiago, they made the ten hour bus ride to come and protest at the pope's visit and they were far from dumb. They were angry and they knew they had been betrayed. These were people who had been so dedicated to "their" Church but who were now being let down so badly by the institution many had given their lives to supporting.

In an article in *The Guardian* in 2016, the respected journalist and author Paul Vallely wrote, ‘Peter Saunders, one of the world’s most forthright anti-abuse campaigners, whose sacking last weekend (from the papal commission) is a signal that, behind the scenes, the Catholic Church is reverting to its old bad habits.’

Paul was and is correct, but in my opinion it never really began to deal with its old bad habits. The papal commission was and is nothing more than window-dressing, a public relations exercise.

I suppose I should have known that the institutions, of which I had been highly critical, would one day seek revenge. The Catholic Church did that when it sacked me from its papal commission in 2016.

Technically I wasn’t sacked, I was placed on leave of absence and eventually resigned of my own accord. But in reality I was sacked.

Chapter 30

In 2018 I was a founding member of ECA – Ending Clergy Abuse. I spent a number of weeks with my fellow survivor Miguel Hurtado, another founding member in early 2019. We travelled around Spain and received a great deal of publicity as I supported Miguel in his fight for justice and, just as importantly, his fight for better measures to protect children. We then flew to Rome where we met other members of ECA and staged protests outside the Vatican. The pope refused to meet with any of us even though he was convening a so-called child protection conference that weekend. It really was nothing more than a joke. What wasn't a joke was just how many armed policemen and security services turned up to make sure we didn't protest too loudly. Once again the power of the Church was visible in a profound and most intimidating way.

My friends at ECA told me that a member of the papal commission had tweeted my story with a comment along the lines that the Pontifical Commission knew nothing of the rape allegation. Why would they? And how would this person know that anyway? This is called fuelling an already tragic situation. Likewise with the independent inquiry, IICSA. I underwent a thorough security vetting by the Home Office. There is nothing on me - because I have committed no crime. Why would I bring this up years later knowing that we had all moved on? Well, I thought we had.

This particular papal commission member and I clashed over the workings of the commission. When I joined, she claimed she had 'never heard of me'. I think she was wondering how I qualified to sit on the commission. She lives in another country and although I have done a lot of international media particularly around the pope's visit to the UK in 2010, why would she have heard of me and why would she make that point?

But I will not sit back and let people smear my name without responding. Tell a person whose life has been blighted in the worst possible way, by abuse, to stay silent and not fight back? I did that for nearly 40 years. I stayed silent for nearly 40 years. I am paying a heavy price for that error of judgement in Manchester many years ago, but as I say it's not really about that. It's about survivors speaking out.

The Establishment is hitting back. How dare we speak out.

I continue to get messages of support. I grew up thinking and believing I was bad. I was older than 60 when I finally began to believe that I was not a bad person. Like most people I have made a few mistakes in my life. It goes with the territory, survivors are often self-destructive. Speak to the ChildLine founder, Dame Esther Rantzen, about that.

But I am not a bad person and whilst it breaks my heart to see what has happened, I wanted NAPAC to treat me the way our wonderful people in Stockport, and colleagues in London, treat survivors; with respect and dignity and perhaps, like my amazing wife, with forgiveness.

I have been honoured to give 24 years of my life to supporting survivors and speaking out about child protection but now I move on.

IICSA

Independent Inquiry into Child Sexual Abuse

Before I speak about IICSA there was an earlier major "coming together" as I was planning NAPAC. This was the National Commission of Inquiry into the Prevention of Child Abuse (NCIPCA, HMSO 1996) This, the largest ever inquiry of its kind, was under way in 1996 and one of the key members of the Inquiry, Deidre Sanders, got in touch with me and proposed a meeting. Deirdre was one of dozens of agony aunts and uncles I had written to during 1996 about my proposal to set up a survivor's organisation. She thought it was an extremely good idea and told me that the bulk of her weekly postbag was letters from survivors of abuse. She wanted to have somewhere to send them, she wanted an organisation that was specifically for survivors of abuse because at that time there was no such national body and she didn't have any place she could direct survivors to. Just about every other cause you could think of had a national charity or a Helpline, but adult survivors had nothing.

I met Deidre in a restaurant in Soho in the summer of 1996. She also invited Christopher Cloke, the secretary to the National Inquiry. At that meeting they both pledged to do their best to support me. Deidre eventually became a patron of the charity and to this day she frequently mentions NAPAC in her Problem Page in *The Sun* newspaper. Chris Cloke went on to become instrumental in helping NAPAC develop by securing a regular meeting place (at the head office of the NSPCC) and some early media and legal contacts. I was sitting in a studio alongside Chris during one of my first ever radio interviews, on BBC 5 Live!

For a brief time, the NSPCC provided NAPAC with a desk and resources at their head office in London. They also allowed NAPAC to use that address for its registered office. This was a great help and something that was supported by Jim Harding, the director and chief executive at the NSPCC. Not everyone in that organisation was as supportive and it wasn't long after Jim retired that I was told they needed the desk space and NAPAC could no longer be accommodated. Friends who worked for the NSPCC informed me the desk was still empty more than a year later.

There are many people who said that I was directly responsible for the next inquiry, the Independent Inquiry into Child Sexual Abuse. Home Secretary Theresa May set up the inquiry on 4 July 2014 after many years of MPs and politicians being pressurised. I was delighted that after years of cutting through yards of red tape and generally banging my head against a brick wall it had eventually happened. I had initially requested a royal commission, which make the recommendations from such an inquiry mandatory and legally required to be implemented. However this was not to be and eventually Home Secretary May implemented a statutory inquiry which meant that witnesses had to appear by law if called upon by the inquiry panel. For reference purposes, a non-statutory inquiry means that anybody requested to appear in front of the panel has the right to refuse, therefore a non-statutory inquiry isn't really worth the paper it's written on. At least not for a subject as serious as this.

The one thing that I wanted the inquiry to recommend was mandatory reporting of sexual abuse. In this day and age, I can't get my head around the fact that there is no law against burying and sweeping under the carpet sexual abuse that has been witnessed by a person in a position of power or responsibility.

It's madness. But what is even more infuriating is that during my many battles to try and influence certain organisations that mandatory reporting should be implemented, it was the NSPCC who more than once stood in the way. They claimed it would be a hindrance to victims coming forward. I never understood that argument because I have yet to meet a victim/survivor who doesn't think that reporting a known or suspected abuser is a good idea. If all the known abusers I encountered in my childhood had been stopped in their tracks I wonder how much misery would have been avoided. How many lives may have been saved?

The first two chairs of the original inquiry were Baroness Elizabeth Butler-Sloss and Fiona Woolf. However both had to step down because of their perceived closeness to establishment figures who would likely fall within the investigation of the inquiry. In February 2015, Theresa May announced that Dame Lowell Goddard, a New Zealander, would chair the inquiry. I liked Dame Lowell Goddard from the outset and she announced that 12 separate investigations would be undertaken as part of the inquiry. She set up a survivors panel within the inquiry and I was invited to be part of that. Having called for the inquiry in the first place I was only too happy to assist.

Dame Lowell always kept us informed about how the inquiry was going and once a week she made a point of meeting with the survivors panel for a cup of tea.

To my dismay, Amber Rudd, the new home secretary announced on the 4th of August 2016 that Dame Lowell had resigned. I never really found out exactly why she decided to call it a day, but she pulled no punches and quoted the inquiry's legacy of failure. A few days later Amber Rudd appointed Professor Alexis Jay as the new chair.

My initial impression about Professor Jay, the 4th chairman of the inquiry, was that she lacked charisma. That's no crime. I don't claim any for myself but I think the head of such an important inquiry should have a bit more about them. She was distant from the survivors, the weekly cup of tea with the chair pretty much ceased when she was appointed.

In June 2017 it wasn't any surprise when one of the other survivor groups, Survivors of Organised and Institutional Abuse (SOIA) withdrew from the inquiry. They said it was not fit for purpose and that they had been totally marginalised. They went on to say the inquiry was just a 'costly academic report-writing and literature review exercise.'

During 2016 and 2017 the inquiry had published a series of interim reports, indeed by September 2021 they had published 16 of them. Every single report that I read came up short and told us nothing that we didn't already know. I was beginning to side with SOIA about it being an academic writing exercise. As for the cost? £186m! Think what NAPAC and survivors groups everywhere could have done with that money.

I was interviewed on Sky News, speaking on behalf of the victim and survivors consultative panel. I said that the inquiry had serious shortcomings and I was also very disturbed by the way in which Lady Justice Goddard had been dispatched from the inquiry. In our opinion she was the right person for the job, she certainly placed great store on our involvement and would regularly meet with us to discuss issues, as mentioned above. Her successor rarely consulted the victims and survivors panel and I will be very interested to see if one of Alexis Jay's sternest critics on the victims panel keeps her word and tells Professor Jay 'what she thinks of her,' when the inquiry ends. I somehow doubt that happened.

The inquiry panel was furious with me for making such a bold statement but I have always done that. I tell it how it is, in plain language, in black and white. One of the few things the inquiry did say that resonated with me was that the Catholic Church of England and Wales swept allegations of sexual abuse under the carpet and that the people in positions of responsibility such as priests, monks and volunteers did not acknowledge any personal responsibility.

They were particularly scathing of cardinal, archbishop of Westminster, Vincent Nichols, the most senior cleric of the Catholic Church in England and Wales. They said he was more interested in protecting the reputation of the Church than the victims. Tell me something I don't know, I thought to myself.

Another interesting piece of the report stated that they had examined 38 religious groups and sects from Christianity to Orthodox Judaism and Islam and found shocking failings and blatant hypocrisy in the way major UK religious groups handle child sexual abuse allegations. Needless to say, I agreed with everything they said, but even back then I had no confidence in anybody implementing any recommendations the inquiry eventually came up with. Only days before writing this I heard a bishop of the Catholic Church in England saying that they (the Church) would ignore the mandatory reporting of child abuse if it was disclosed within the confessional.

Someone who I remember being visibly irritated by my presence in the survivor world was a woman at a Catholic safeguarding seminar at which I was speaking. She didn't like what I was saying, rolling her eyes at any comment I made. This same woman was criticised by the Independent Inquiry into Child Sexual Abuse for her handling of certain abuse allegations against priests.

Another disturbing aspect about the inquiry was the way in which I was treated when the *Mail on Sunday* did its worst. I go back to the conversation I had with the secretary to the inquiry whilst I was on holiday in Switzerland. As soon as he called to say the *Mail on Sunday* had been in touch I panicked as that awful nightmare permeated my entire soul once again.

I reacted in a similar way to most survivors. It was one of the worst periods of my life, the despicable actions of those women had pushed me to the brink and I didn't want to be transported back in time. I had explained myself to the police and my wife. Both had believed me and I didn't want to go through it all again. I found myself momentarily back in that police cell behind a locked steel door. It was the worst day of my life and I didn't want to go back there.

I took the line of least resistance.

The reporter had told the NAPAC Chair of Trustees that they were still considering whether or not to run the story (it's pretty obvious they were always going to do it) and he believed them. The reporter also promised to ring him back and it transpired he never did. The next call I got was from secretary to the Independent Inquiry into Child Sexual Abuse. The secretary rang me to say that they needed to distance themselves from the slurs.

I said I didn't want this to harm the inquiry and offered my resignation over the telephone. I know now that it was a knee-jerk reaction but I was in a state of shock reliving an incident from nearly a decade before. But instead of saying to me, 'Pete, let's discuss this when you get back from holiday,' or 'Take some time to think about what is happening and let's talk later,' they decided to act on a few stuttering, jumbled words over the phone while I was under duress and almost hyperventilating.

I have not had a single communication from the inquiry since the day I resigned.

To say their duty of care to me was absent is an understatement and given that I was partly (some would say almost wholly) responsible for getting the inquiry off the ground in the first place I am saddened at how swiftly I became a non-person in their eyes, how quickly they turned their backs on me. They should know that survivors sometimes endure chaotic episodes in their lives and, crucially, how certain sections of the media set out to destroy people, particularly people rocking the boat.

It confirmed everything that I had suspected from the day that the police came knocking on my door. I had been set up, it was something that some people in high places could hold over me and when the time was right they could act. And the time was right. Once again I was making my views known, daring to speak out against a government inquiry. I had spoken out against everyone, against celebrities, churches, government officials, policemen, social workers, schools, politicians and establishment figures, priests, cardinals and bishops and, yes, even criticised two popes. How dare I?

But had I committed any crime or serious wrongdoing? Absolutely not. Did the inquiry give me the opportunity to state the truth of what had actually happened? No. Did they contact the police to confirm that no crime had been committed or that I received any form of caution? They did not.

Even the Victim's Panel of which I had been a member from the start of the inquiry issued a statement that said something about how disappointed they were and that I had indulged in victim blaming. *Et tu, Brute?*

Victim blaming is something I most definitely have never done. Again, it was so sad to see people behaving in such a way, people who really should know better. It appeared that I had pissed off all and sundry and they couldn't believe their luck when I had blurted out my resignation over the telephone.

Ah well, I thought, at least I will be able to concentrate full time on NAPAC and give the organisation the attention it deserves.

Little did I know that I would get another phone call the following day.

A weird coincidence. The person who "replaced" me on the Victims and Survivors Consultative Panel at the Independent Inquiry into Child Sexual Abuse was Christopher Shellam. Chris attended that first meeting at what was to become NAPAC at the NSPCC head office in January 1997. He had seen the piece in *The Times* about me the previous year and got in touch. He attended the meeting with his wife and afterwards handed me a book, *Sleepers*, by Lorenzo Carcaterra. He wrote a lovely message in the book, referring to me as a brave brother to be taking up this cause. I still have the book and it was good to know that a founding member of NAPAC was still going to have some influence on the inquiry.

I doubt very much if the inquiry knew that Chris had been an early supporter of setting up NAPAC.

Another weird coincidence is that the man who replaced me on the pope's child abuse commission, the Chilean survivor and activist Juan Carlos Cruz had also given me a book a few years earlier, also with a loving inscription. I still have that one too.

While on the subject of books, I recently came across the one written by Dame Esther Rantzen about the history of ChildLine, the charity she founded. It is called *Running out of Tears*. The penultimate chapter is about me, a very potted history of my life and how I was inspired to set up an organisation for survivors. But the thing that caught my eye was the two inscriptions inside the front cover. One was by Dame Esther and the other one was by the actor Robert Powell and his beautiful wife Babs, who was one of the original members of Pan's People, a dance group who appeared on *Top of the Pops* throughout the 1970s and 1980s.

Babs wrote, 'To Pete, our inspiration.'

So sweet. My wife and I met Robert and Babs at the launch of Esther's book which took place in the Speakers House at the Houses of Parliament. Other guests we spoke to were the opera singer Lesley Garrett and the late, and ever so charming, Nicholas Parsons. Esther had kindly mentioned and pointed me out in her speech and as we were leaving the venue I bumped into Nicholas, who said he wished he had come and talked to me earlier. So do I. He passed away not long after that.

I met many so-called celebrities over the years in some of the work situations I found myself in. As my wife will testify, I am easily starstruck. When I meet people who are famous I tend to be a bit in awe of them, but over time I have discovered that some "celebs" have an entirely different persona in real life to the one when they are on stage, screen or behind a microphone. I remember being quite shocked when, on an early appearance on *Breakfast TV News*, the language turned quite blue when the cameras were on another story (i.e. not on the studio). I look back now and think how dumb I must have been to think that these folk we see or hear on our devices everyday don't cuss and swear like the rest of us.

Chapter 31

I am conscious that for some time I was the unofficial media voice of the inquiry, and that a senior advisor to former Prime Minister May said I was the person responsible for getting the inquiry set up in the first place. It is perfectly true that following Australia's royal commission into child abuse I had publicly called for something similar to be set up here. That was at the beginning, and I believed in the inquiry then. I believed it could achieve great things in terms of child protection. But as time went by I learnt that many of those involved with the whole thing were pretty clueless about the issue. When I was interviewed by Sky News following the inquiry's interim report one of the IICSA staff told me that the inquiry panel was "furious" with me because I dared to say how disappointed I was that there had been no mention of support for adult survivors.

My silencing, followed by the COVID-19 pandemic have been the abuser's answer to prayer.

When one is unceremoniously dumped it is perhaps natural to display sour grapes, but I want to say a couple of things about IICSA and the Victims and Survivors

Consultative Panel (VSCP), of which I had been a member.

A good friend and former senior police officer always said that the inquiry would be a waste of money because we all know what needs to be done about child protection. It's having the political will and doing some innovative work to make it happen. Inquiries tend to change very little and are often a very expensive way of putting things away on a shelf to gather dust. What we really need is a total change of culture around how we view and treat children. And there must be absolute zero tolerance of abuse.

When I sat on the victims panel and attended on official business, I was awarded a payment of £300 per day. I had no idea we would be paid when I volunteered to be a panel member. I remember thinking at the time that was a ridiculous amount of money. I'd never earnt that sort of money in my life, and when I voiced my opinion to one of my fellow panellists he told me that some of the lawyers advising the inquiry were probably on about £5000 per day. I didn't believe that at the time, I didn't think it was possible to earn that sort of money. However, as I write these few lines in October 2022, the results of the inquiry have just been published. The cost of the inquiry? A staggering £186m.

And sadly, there is nothing "independent" about the inquiry. It is entirely dependent on government funding and we already know Boris Johnson's view of it. In his words, 'It is spaffing money up the walls.' Johnson also once referred to child abuse and rape as 'malarkey', so his comments are not entirely surprising.

We have to remember that people like Mr Johnson were packed off to prestigious boarding schools when they were pretty young and we all now know that most of these schools were hotbeds of abuse. But, as many of the public schoolboys I have met over the years say to me, 'You don't rat on your old school.' I believe Mr Johnson went to Eton, a favourite with royal families from around the world.

The old boys network remains strong. The old school tie is very much held in place with a good old-fashioned Windsor knot and let's not forget that these people mostly come from families that already own most of the country so why would they rock the boat?

Thankfully it appears that some people at these elite private schools do take child sexual abuse seriously. One has only to look on the internet, punch in a search engine "public school sexual abuse", perhaps filtered down to Eton College and you will see many examples of ex-pupils who had the courage to come forward and talk about the sexual abuse they suffered. Some, but not all, ended up in court.

Matthew Mowbray was recently jailed for five years for downloading 4,500 indecent images of children onto his computer, and eight counts of sexual activity with a child. I refer back to my point about the disproportionate sentences being handed out on this occasion by Judge Heather Norton.

Mowbray, an Eton College teacher, regularly visited boys' rooms late at night on the pretext of discussing their homework. While in their bedrooms and dormitories he abused children for his own sexual gratification. At Reading Crown Court he pleaded guilty to 26 counts of making indecent images and one count of voyeurism where he covertly filmed a boy getting undressed at the school. He denied nine other sexual activity charges against four boys and a girl over a period of several years.

Robert Montague, the son of the 10th Earl of Sandwich, also came forward and was brave enough to talk about the abuse he witnessed at Eton College. He even described how he had stopped a boy from committing suicide after he was raped by two prefects. He spoke some years back at the Oxford Literary Festival while discussing his book in which he revealed years of systematic abuse. He made an astonishing claim that some aristocrats even feel entitled to abuse young boys and girls, that it's part of the culture. Mr Montague said that sexual abuse at public schools such as Eton was nothing new and incidents known as fagging sprung up in the early 1960s, a practise in which young boys act as sex slaves to the older ones. They are stripped naked and fondled in degrading acts. It is normally the smaller boys who were targeted, or those who were considered effeminate. Mr Montague said that he and a few of the other boys had banded together to try and protect the younger boys from the gangs of bullies but the fagging culture was rife and it was not uncommon for prefects of 17 or 18 years of age to sexually abuse boys as young as 13 and 14. Nor was it just a problem at Eton College.

As recently as March 2022, an online campaign invited users to post anonymous testimonies of sexual assault and harassment. To date more than 8000 accounts from boys and girls as young as nine have been posted anonymously in the online campaign. Many youngsters tell of a rape culture within many public schools and universities. Eton, St Paul's, Highgate and Dulwich College are some of those referenced.

I'm not suggesting for one minute that Boris Johnson ever suffered any type of this abuse but I find it difficult to believe that he didn't witness any of it either. However, that's just my opinion, it could well be that Mr Johnson breezed through his Etonian years, that it was all sweetness and light. I certainly hope so. I wouldn't wish my worst enemy to suffer the way I did. I also feel for those who witnessed that sort of abuse and were powerless to do anything about it. I grew up in a generation where priests and teachers were respected members of society and the word of a child counted for nothing.

Nor do I blame Mr Johnson if he simply doesn't want to rock the boat. No, it's up to the mere mortals like me to rock the boat and I will continue to rock the boat until my dying day.

I rocked the boat when I visited Seattle a few years ago. This was in the early days of setting up Ending Clergy Abuse (ECA).

I was furious that a Jesuit church where I had attended Mass insisted on doing a big celebratory Mass for a dead paedophile priest.

Reverend Father David Jaeger admitted to 'inappropriately' (I hate that sanitised word) touching 8 to 10 minors at Catholic youth organisation camps in the 1970s. The Seattle Archdiocese settled two of those cases and after investigations took place, the Vatican accepted Jaeger's request to leave the priesthood, known as voluntary laicization.

In Jaeger's case, the archdiocese's case-review board and the bishop had recommended he be permanently barred from ministry, one step short of defrocking. Jaeger decided instead to petition the Vatican for voluntary laicization. He was quoted as saying, 'At this point, it just seemed like a good thing to move on in a spirit of peace for the good of my own soul and the good of others.'

What a noble chap!

Dave Hamilton, a 40-year-old furniture maker in Seattle said Jaeger molested him one evening at a CYO camp in 1978. Hamilton said he was 'disappointed in the entire system and how it's treating people'. I couldn't agree more. Arranging a celebratory Mass for a priest who has openly admitted to abusing youngsters under his care is rubbing salt into the wounds. The vigil and Mass with 20 celebrant priests and a full choir was held in July 2014 at St Joseph Parish after family and planners received permission from its pastor, Jesuit Fr. John Whitney. Whitney said they had told him that Seattle's other Jesuit-staffed parish where Jaeger attended, St Ignatius, would be too small to accommodate the number of people expected.

And it seems there was no end to people willing to come forward and say what a wonderful man and priest Reverend Jaeger was.

At the time of the archdiocese inquiry Kathy Kirschner, a member of the St Anne Parish council, said she had known Jaeger for nearly 25 years. 'He was the most wonderful guy, understanding and tolerant. He listens to you and did what he could to help you and was known throughout the community for his ministry with the gay community and for being involved in the recruitment of priests.'

As Kirschner continued to support him during the inquiry she said he would be a great loss to the archdiocese if he were expelled. And then she came out with one of the most amazing statements I have ever heard in my time fighting the Catholic Church in their attitude to paedophile priests and child abuse. She said, 'It just makes me wonder, are we going to kick out everyone who touched someone inappropriately?'

A few years later I attended Mass officiated by Father Glen Butterworth at St Joseph's RC Church, Seattle. My dear friends George Mead and his wife Cheryl used to attend Mass at this church. Glen Butterworth acknowledged my presence in his congregation. He went on to liken me to Francis of Assisi because I was a big thorn in the side of the Church. Francis respected and obeyed the Catholic Church's authority but had no desire to take the title of Priest. Without the Church's blessing, he was labelled by some members of the Church as a heretic for his unorthodox teaching. What's more, Francis had turned to poverty which was a radical notion at the time. The Church was tremendously rich as were the people heading it, and Francis rejected the now decadent Church, setting out on a mission to restore Jesus's original values.

I was truly humbled at Father Glen's comparison and welcomed his support from the pulpit.

I wish those parishioners who questioned the big celebration of a dead paedophile could have been afforded the same support from their fellow parishioners, but St Josephs was divided, and they were ostracised by much of the religious community in Seattle.

Chapter 32

One thing became abundantly clear to me when I started out on the road to setting up NAPAC and that is the sheer scale of the problem. It was far bigger than I had ever dared to imagine. Once my name and contact details were out in the public domain I started to receive a lot of correspondence and quite a bit of that came from people who were in prison.

I'm not sure prison is necessarily the best way to "punish" a person but on the occasions I visited my brother Mike, as bizarre as this may sound, he had never looked so well. And was drug and alcohol free for the first time since he was a teenager. Seeing my brother in prison was in itself a sobering experience. Knowing that I could go home afterwards and he could not, really made me think.

A few other things struck me about Mike who along with his initial rhetoric 'I haven't met anyone in the prison who is a really bad person' was that he seemed quite happy and content.

From what prisoners told me, most seemed to have gone off the rails for one reason or another, drugs and alcohol being two of those reasons and the other reason, the big one, was that most of the inmates had suffered abuse of one kind or another when they were children. This was something I was to learn a great deal more about. It would be true to say that I could write a book about all the prisoners and all the prisons I visited over the next number of years. Men and women and all sorts of offences but one undeniable common denominator; most had suffered abuse in childhood. Not all, but most.

There are too many to name but Mark in HMP Manchester is someone who stands out. As I write, Mark has been behind bars for most of his adult life. He had the sort of dreadful upbringing that many of us would find hard to contemplate. It is the stuff of horror stories. But the result of Mark's awful past was a horrible murder he committed in a drug and alcohol-fuelled rage. And he is now paying the price for that crime. I have visited him for over 15 years and he, like the many other prisoners I have met, is not a bad man. And I would challenge anyone who thinks they would have led a different or exemplary life after what he went through as a child. Mark has never made excuses for his offending. Few of the prisoners I know ever did, either. They accept their crimes were wrong and they accept the consequences. All that most of them want is to be heard and understood. They don't expect forgiveness but they all seem to want to tell how their offending came about. If we don't get to grips with that, how on earth are we to protect future generations? As former Prime Minister Tony Blair famously said, we need to be, 'Tough on crime and tough on the causes of crime.' Sadly I still don't think we are tough on the causes of crime. And when you think about how much money it costs to keep a person in jail you would think we might have worked a bit harder on those causes. But I suppose it's easier to sweep these uncomfortable challenges once again under the carpet.

Another young man who sticks out in my memory is Joe (not his real name). He was also in HMP Manchester and I only visited him once but it was a deeply moving experience. When I entered the room to speak with him (one of the prison officers suggested I listen to Joe's story) he did not look me in the eye. I told him that I was a survivor of abuse and that, but for the grace of God, I could be sitting in his place. I told him I could have gone down a similar path. I could have ended up in prison. I said little else.

But what I endured as a child was nothing compared to Joe's early life. Beaten and abused by both parents from an early age he finally snapped and as a 10-year-old he set fire to his parents' home. No one died but Joe was taken into care. In care he was abused and in the foster homes he was subsequently placed he was again subjected to abuse. By the time he was a teenager he was on drugs and when he was finally flung onto the streets at sixteen he had nowhere to go and fell into the hands of predatory drug-controlling men. Thence to a life of crime. I remember asking him why he was in prison this time. He said he couldn't remember. He knew why. He had hit a policeman but had no memory of it. Joe was about 30 and had spent most of his adult life in and out of prison. I listened to him for what seemed like hours and I had to fight back the tears. Towards the end of the conversation Joe looked me straight in the eye. I hoped and prayed that the shame and guilt he had carried for so long was beginning to melt. There was little I could say to this young man, except that when he offended and was sent to prison the people who had hurt him in the past were winning. When I said that to him I think I saw a little light going on in his eyes, and he nodded.

We embraced and I left. A few weeks later I received a letter from Joe saying that our meeting had changed his life and he was never going to go back to prison again. I don't know if that was the end of the story but a couple of years later a prison outreach officer told me that Joe was free of offending and making a life for himself. And what had I done for him? Very little really. I listened and spoke a few words from the heart. Maybe that's what more of us could do. Just listen, hear and care. Speaking of prisoners, I'm reminded of an ex-convict I once met at a conference. He was known as Noel "Razor" Smith. I dread to think where he got that nickname but he said he had just served 'seven years for something I didn't do'. What didn't you do? Razor was asked. 'I didn't wear a fucking mask.'

I hate to use the tabloid description of "killer" but during my many years of work with survivors, I have met quite a few. Again, I reiterate that none of the people I met were ever "bad". They were people who never stood a chance. A barrister friend of mine once said that *most* murderers, once released, will never pose a threat to others. They have by and large killed the person they hated and wanted dead and they won't hurt another soul. Not that this applies to all killers, of course. Just like some child abusers, some murderers will probably have to be kept incarcerated for the rest of their lives. Mercifully the latter are few in number. I'm not so sure about the former.

An interesting individual I once met at my office was a young man called Christopher Hunniset. Chris had killed a man, a vicar, who he claimed had abused him. I personally had no difficulty in believing that this man was indeed an abuser but I seriously questioned the wisdom of young

Christopher taking the man's life. When one does such a thing it tends to lead to a life sentence in prison and whilst I can understand the utter rage that some victims feel we can never really take the law into our own hands. But, and it's a big but, when I knocked on the door of my abuser many years ago there was part of me who wanted to batter him and snuff out his life. And if I'm honest, the things that stopped me was not only my faith but also the prospect of having to see my children in a prison visitors room. In that circumstance the abusers have once again won and as my dear friend and fellow survivor Marion often says to me, 'Don't let the bastards win.'

Most abusers never face justice but don't be the one who takes the law into their own hands and end up behind bars. I suppose it also says something about our lack of faith in the criminal justice system that some feel it necessary to take that law into their own hands. I have a worrying tendency to admire someone who makes their own justice but I am not sure I would ever have the guts to emulate them. I often say that if someone hurt my children or grandchildren in the way I was hurt, they would certainly be visiting me in prison today because I would not let these creatures get away with it. I suppose I might take the law into my own hands if I wasn't sure that civil society would deal with them. And civil society and the criminal justice system often does not.

As well as visiting prisoners I have also been asked to speak to prison staff and I have done so a good few times. One of the first occasions was when I was visiting HMP Manchester and the governor asked me to speak to his prison officers. I couldn't speak to them all - far too many - but I had a slot when the officers who were on duty were urged to attend my talk. Many did and it was quite a terrifying experience. I did my usual thing of telling them a little about my background, the abuse I suffered as a child and how I set up NAPAC and how it led to being there with them today and visiting prisoners. Well, the stony-faced people sitting in front of me made me feel a little uncomfortable. Yes, most were in their uniforms and they all looked as though they were tired of hearing "sob stories" but then at the end of my talk their demeanour changed. They smiled, many came forward and said thank you and one chap approached me with tears in his eyes and said that he found my talk extremely helpful because his own daughter had suffered abuse. He also became a regular donor to NAPAC. This taught me that no matter how hard or intimidating a crowd might look you can never really judge them. It was the same after many of the talks I've given to police and other similar bodies.

I suppose we just have to remember that none of this is easy to hear. The abuse of children is something most people would prefer not to hear about. Not only is it painful to hear if you are a survivor but it is painful to hear if you are not.

I wrote to Lord Jeffrey Archer many years ago when he was in prison having been convicted of perjury and perverting the course of justice. I wrote to thank him for writing an honest assessment of what he saw around him when he was in prison. What he saw was many men who had suffered abuse in their youth or childhood and Archer was brave enough to admit that whilst he deserved to be there, many did not. Many did not have the opportunities that he had and many had suffered traumatic childhoods. I actually sent the letter to Lord Archer's home address and his wife kindly passed it on to her husband. The nice and somewhat unexpected ending to this story is that Lord

Archer instructed his agent to contact me and he made a substantial donation to the charity.

I visited many prisons over the years and the same theme came up again and again. Governor after governor told me that in their opinion most of their inmates were victims of childhood abuse. Not all, but most. I have the greatest admiration for those who work in the prison system. Many are working in conditions that can only be described as Victorian. They do a difficult job and the pay is pretty abysmal. NAPAC ran a number of support groups in prisons and although they were limited in number (actually getting into prison to run such things is a nightmare of bureaucracy), they were extremely successful. I remember one woman our team worked with in a prison in the North-West. She was seen as trouble and the staff had pretty much given up on her. Then NAPAC arrived and she was able to share what had happened to her and how she came to be there. The prison staff couldn't believe this turnaround. Once again, the power of giving someone the opportunity to talk is at work. To talk, to be heard and to have someone care. It's what most of us really want. It's called therapy.

Chapter 33

For more than two decades I have dedicated my life to making sure we survivors have a voice and there are people and an organisation that we can turn to. But more than that, to make sure that there are people and organisations who will simply listen to us. Victims and survivors have been silenced for too long.

When I started on this journey I would never have believed that there are countless individuals and organisations that either deny or downplay the phenomenon of the scourge of sexual, physical and/or psychological abuse during childhood. I've already alluded to certain establishment figures who brush it all off and use such terms as "malarkey" to describe the rape and abuse of children..

I am reminded of an incident on a train more than 10 years ago when I sat opposite a man who I instantly recognised. He was older than me and had also attended Wimbledon college. I won't name him but he had been a senior politician then. I plucked up the courage to speak to him and said we had been at the same school. We were in a railway carriage on our own and started to talk about our school days. Naturally enough he recalled several good stories about the school and its reputation for producing good rugby teams. I suddenly felt compelled to bring up not only the good things that happened at Wimbledon College (not that I could remember any!) but also the bad things and the many dark days. I told him about the bullying I suffered from some prominent members of the rugby team who were naturally much bigger than me. Then I brought up a few issues and named the teachers who some people knew were sexually abusing the boys, one of them being my former brother-in-law.

I could tell straight away that this person was uncomfortable, he clearly didn't want this brought up and out in the open and as a prominent public figure he certainly didn't want to be associated with any of it. Then to my absolute astonishment, after a few minutes he grinned and said, 'Ah yes, but it made men of us didn't it?'

I was stunned and at a loss for words. I wanted to scream, 'No it didn't, it ruined my life and it's still affecting me now!'

But I didn't. I didn't want a row with the man and I realised that he probably hadn't been targeted as a child and if he had then maybe he had dealt with it? He was not the first person of prominence I met who felt very uncomfortable about the subject of abuse and I get it when people say they have dealt with it and don't wish to revisit it. I really get it but I also know that the more people who speak out, the better.

So I said nothing.

When he left the carriage a couple of stops before me, he shook my hand and wished me well. I couldn't help thinking that he had probably been abused at the school, why else would he have said, 'It made men of us.'? I'll be charitable and assume he was talking about something else that made a 'man of him'.

I will never put myself in a position where I demand that a survivor confronts his or her past. I just wish more people who suffered child abuse would speak out, but like the politician on the train I respect anyone who deals with it in their own way. Bury it, move on, talk about it, share it with an individual, a group, or go public, if you feel really brave - some will say stupid - campaign against it! The choice is yours, but don't ever tell me it never happened in the first place and don't ever castigate a person who is unable to deal with it, or worse, tell them they could have stopped it.

Twenty-five years ago I had a meeting with a psychiatrist at a large teaching hospital in South London. I was honest and open, told her all about what had happened to me. She listened intently and I believed she was listening to me, understanding what I had gone through. Eventually her face took on a stern look and she wagged her finger in my face. 'Why didn't you stop it?' Unbelievable but true.

At that moment I asked myself the same question. I was in a terribly dark place at that time of my life and as I left the hospital that afternoon I wondered if I would have the strength to end it all.

The woman was a professional and she had confirmed what I had suspected for many years, that it was actually my fault because I didn't do anything to stop it.

I didn't end my life that day because I thought about my family and what it would do to them. I had two wonderful children and I wanted to see grow up, and I wanted to see their children grow up, but believe me I was very close to throwing myself under a train.

That psychiatrist didn't deserve her medical title, she was a disgrace to her profession and I often wonder how many of her survivor patients were affected by her attitude.

The simple truth is that I couldn't stop the abuse because my main abuser was an adult and I was a child. Likewise, at my school, I was a small boy who had been brainwashed by the Jesuits, and I could only speak when spoken to and my opinion was, like myself, worthless. At that time Catholicism had been drilled into me. Teachers were respected pillars of society, priests were next to God and they were not to be questioned.

I've met many Irish survivors where it seemed even worse. The power of the church was overwhelming in that country. Priests and bishops really were seen as conduits to God and were never to be questioned. What chance did children have there?

There are documentaries on YouTube and a movie and documentaries on the Magdalene Laundries that explains very well what happened to the boys and girls, particularly those who accused their priests of wrongdoing or abuse. Or worse still, fell pregnant out of wedlock. They were cast out of their communities, disowned by their families and sent to institutions like the Magdalene Laundries for years, and in some cases for the rest of their lives. Some were sectioned and sent to psychiatric institutions where the abuse continued.

Steve Coogan and Dame Judi Dench starred in an incredible powerful movie called *Philomena*. If you haven't seen that movie I would urge you to watch it. It's based on a true story about one woman who merely wanted to find the child that had been stolen from her. Unbelievably, the Catholic-run organisation that she had been incarcerated in went as far as to burn the records of her child who had been sold to an American couple 40 years previously.

The cruelty of such an act is beyond belief, but poor Philomena was not alone, there were thousands of "fallen women", as the Church called them, locked up in these institutions for decades, their lives ruined.

I haven't got space to cover all of these episodes here, but I would suggest a little research on the Tuam baby scandal in Galway, where babies of these "fallen women" who had allegedly been 'allowed to die', were dumped in septic tanks and mass graves. This went on for many decades. Their skeletons and bones were discovered in the 1970s by boys playing in the area. This was denied by the Bon Secours Sisters, the order of Catholic nuns who ran the Galway Council home for unmarried mothers. Catherine Corless, a local woman, completed a personal mission to collate the death certificates of the unnamed skeletons of the children who died at the Tuam home. There were 798 found.

However, it wasn't just happening in Ireland. As recently as 2014 a similar Scottish scandal has been uncovered at Smyllum Orphanage in Lanark. A witness who was at the orphanage in the 1960s told Scotland's Child Abuse Inquiry that there was a culture of evil among religious orders and that the nuns forced him to eat grass when he complained of being hungry. He told the inquiry, 'I don't believe I was looked after, the words "looked after" are meaningless to me.'

Another female witness told the inquiry, chaired by High Court Judge Lady Smith, that a nun walked in on her as she had been forced to perform a sex act on a priest. The nun attacked the small girl, threw her against a wall breaking her arm and warned her, 'Don't you dare tell anybody what happened, young lady, or I'll break your other arm.'

What chance did that small girl have to stop it, and yet the psychiatrist chided me for not putting a stop to it.

I learnt some years later, that this particular psychiatrist was a supporter of the False Memory Society. While you might find this difficult to believe, and I did at the time, there is actually an organisation who represents people who are falsely accused of sexual abuse. I understand that, because of the society that we live in, there will sometimes be false and malicious allegations against people for a whole manner of things, but we do have laws to protect individuals against that sort of thing. Perjury and perverting the course of justice are criminal offences. I refer again to Carl Beech and the 18 years he is serving for perverting the course of justice.

But I find it extraordinary that there is actually an organisation representing people who claim to have been falsely accused of sexual abuse. Surely they must understand that the law is there to protect them too? I don't know of any organisation in place that represents burglars falsely accused of burgling or shoplifters falsely accused of shoplifting, so why does such an organisation exist? Those who have abused children in the past and have been accused or even arrested must think all their Christmases have come at once when they realise that such an organisation is there to help them.

The organisation's website claims false memory is 'a condition in which a person's identity and interpersonal relationships are centred around a memory of traumatic experience which is objectively false but in which the person strongly believes. The accusers allege they have recently remembered childhood abuse, of which he or she had no previous memory.'

I remember being very angry when I read the last sentence. It took me decades to eventually confront my demons and I fear for the fact that the worst abuse I suffered has been blocked out. Everyone in the therapeutic community (including psychiatrists and psychologists) know that children block things from their mind when despicable things are done to them. It is a well-known coping mechanism. And, as everybody knows, certain events can trigger and bring into the present horrific episodes of abuse from the past. An internal trigger comes from within the person, it can be a memory that has been blocked, a physical sensation, or an emotion. It happens to soldiers returning from bloody conflicts. They hear a loud bang and it takes them back to the battlefield. Or it may be a *déjà vu* moment, an experience such as seeing the person who abused you for the first time since childhood. For me it was my father's death that prompted me to eventually confront the abuse and my abusers. It's hard to describe, but in a way I opened up my heart and mind after Dad's death, and over the course of several years after the event I recalled many of the things which George, in particular, did to me that I had buried for decades.

Were these "false memories"? Of course not and it is an affront to anyone who discloses such trauma to be told they are false memories. Yes, we know memory can be fallible in some ways but if your father raped you when you were a child you may well have buried that memory to protect yourself, but could you conjure up such a dreadful thing if it did not happen? So, instead of these false memory weirdo's insisting we have false memories why don't they just come out and say we are liars? Why anyone would want to lie about something so horrific is beyond me.

A lawyer's section on the organisation's website advises those accused of sexual abuse that 'you do have the right to remain silent when questioned' under caution and details three approaches to take when 'falsely accused.' Why you would remain silent if you were falsely accused I have no idea. If you have nothing to hide just tell the truth. The police are pretty good at knowing whether they are dealing with a liar or not so maybe that lawyer's advice is sound. If you are an abuser, best keep your mouth shut.

I don't think many people realise what courage and strength it takes to come forward and tell that you have been sexually abused as a child. It seems to be even harder for men. Furthermore, to actually come out and accuse a named person who has perpetrated that abuse is even more frightening, particularly when that person is in a position of power. We know that acts of sexual abuse are very rarely witnessed and usually involve just the perpetrator and the victim. Therefore, it may simply be a case of one person's word against another. And that is why it is sometimes helpful to the police to ask other potential victims to come forward. Abusers rarely only target one victim. So, if a High Court judge or a priest or an MP or even a policeman is accused of sexually assaulting someone it is very difficult to come forward because these people are seen as more powerful than the average Joe.

I dread to think how any survivor who has ever contemplated reporting sexual abuse would feel if they were directed to the website or found out about the claims of false memory syndrome. To me it is just another barrier, another excuse, another reason to question the claims of a survivor who dares to raise his or her head above the parapet.

Child abuse, which is at the heart of this publication, is a very difficult topic to address, particularly where there are accusations against people, some of whom may be relatives or friends. If you have not suffered abuse, and my fervent hope is that you have not, then it can be hard to accept that some people we know, like and love, sometimes do terrible things. And I can't think of anything worse than inflicting abuse on the most vulnerable people in society. But I fear that, given the wrong circumstances, we are all capable of doing bad things.

I also have to accept that sometimes people will not believe what someone they know is capable of, like people who claim false memory syndrome exists. I fear, in my opinion, it is more a case of denial or trying to wriggle off the hook.

A former prominent politician who I had a conversation with 25 years ago said to me, 'Peter, the abuse of children has always gone on.' His words displayed a sort of accepting weariness which troubled me. The politician was Tony Benn and he said I was very brave to take on this task of supporting survivors of these crimes and to therefore help protect children in the future. He pointed out that children don't get a vote and so rarely make it to the top of the political agenda. How true is that?

He also made some mention of child abuse going on in all levels of society. This was unlike another high profile MP who, after I debated the issue on television and while we walked out of the studio, said that the problem of child abuse was predominantly a working class, council estate problem.

I find it hard to believe how misinformed and ignorant some people can be, and it is particularly worrying when our elected representatives hold these views. This particular Member of Parliament was until recently a senior cabinet minister in the government of the UK.

I received more encouragement from Tony Benn, particularly in a letter he wrote to my late father, and I received many other replies from politicians who I had written to encouraging me in my quest. I've kept them all. But the letter to Dad was very special, indeed. Dad was a great admirer of Tony Benn, a fellow pipe-smoker, and if my memory serves me correctly they both served in the RAF during the Second World War. Their political views were also roughly the same. I was very sad when Tony Benn died. He was a rare individual who stuck to his principles and was not averse to answering his own phone should you choose to call his office on any particular evening, and I did that on a number of occasions towards the latter part of 1995. I still have the handwritten letter he wrote to Dad, encouraging him during his terminal illness and stating how proud he must be to have me as his son.

Sadly, that particular letter arrived the day after my dad died. Such is life. My father never knew of the things that happened to me as a child (the abuse I suffered) and I can only speculate what he would have done had I been able to tell him at the time. I'm certain he would have put an end to it but in common with most children, I kept silent. I fulfilled the abuser's wishes, for a while anyway.

After more than 30 years False Memory Syndrome has never been ratified by the American Psychological Association or any other mainstream psychological diagnostic system as an actual diagnosis.

Chapter 34

In my final year at NAPAC I made some more interesting contacts which I hoped would lead to some funding opportunities. Football had been in the news a great deal because of the offending by certain individuals attached to some of our biggest football clubs. One former coach, a man called Barry Bennell, had been a prolific abuser and had taken advantage of dozens of young boys who he was supposed to be coaching and looking after. Bennell went to prison but British football had taken quite a reputational battering. There was also a high profile case at Newcastle United. In 2008 George Ormond, a coach and kit man was jailed for 20 years after more than a dozen youth players spanning a 25-year-period came forward and gave graphic accounts of how Ormond groomed and sexually abused them. He was convicted of 35 charges of indecent assault.

Ormond was a classic sexual predator. He made himself approachable in the dressing room, he was a coach, a kit man and a minibus driver. Most of the youngsters thought the world of him, and with many of the boys speaking so highly of him, he was able to get away with it. I'm not sure if anybody stood up in court and sided with Ormond as a character witness but it wouldn't surprise me. It won't be the first time and it won't be the last. Even convicted paedophiles like Robin Peverett OBE had no shortage of people willing to stand up in court and say what a splendid fellow he was.

Judge Edward Bindloss said that Ormond had used his position to take advantage of impressionable young boys, some as young as 11. I salute the bravery of all those men who stood up in court and testified against Ormond, particularly Derek Bell, a former Newcastle United player. When his football career came to a premature end because of a knee injury, he was working in Newcastle City Council's housing department finding homes for refugee children in the late 1990s. One day he saw Ormond 'lurking' and decided it was time to put an end to the paedophile's despicable abuses. He secretly recorded a confession as he sat down and talked to the coach.

Bell waived his right to anonymity and accused Newcastle United of attempting a cover up.

What followed next came as no surprise to me, and probably no surprise to anybody who has been a victim of child abuse. This man left his council job after he was made to find new homes for paedophiles. Unbelievable but true. Already suffering from alcohol abuse, he had three divorces behind him and had attempted suicide. In 2009 he was convicted of violence against his wife and diagnosed with post-traumatic stress disorder and borderline personality disorder, all of which were undoubtedly a direct result of the childhood abuse he had suffered. Yet another example of a victim of these crimes who received no real support and very sadly became a hurting person who went on to hurt others.

As one middle-aged man said after the court case in which he testified against Ormond, 'We are victims of a broken and failed system'.

In January 2008 I met and chatted with John Barnes, the former England star who had played for a number of top division sides including Liverpool, Watford and Newcastle United. He told me that in his opinion he was sure that a lot of the lads he had played alongside had experienced abuse. And it turns out he was absolutely right.

So, being the opportunist I am, I contacted senior officials at Manchester City and Chelsea, two clubs linked to the abuse scandal. The lovely woman at Manchester City was very quick to respond and she kindly asked me to visit on a match day. And I did. It was amazing. I was given a VIP ticket and I cheekily asked if I could bring a colleague along. One of our team in Stockport is a massive City fan and she could hardly believe it when I said we were not only going to a big match but that we had VIP tickets.

We had a fantastic day, a fabulous pre-match lunch and sat with some directors of the club, as well as former players. I was sitting next to Mike Summerbee, a City and England legend, and a lovely man. Then we sat in the directors box, sipping champagne and watched City destroy the opposition. We followed this match up with another match day fixture, this time without the VIP element but the whole experience was wonderful.

Through the City connection I also met another former star player, Niall Quinn and one of my cousins from Seaham, near Sunderland, reminded me that both Niall Quinn and Mike Summerbee's son, Nicky, had played for Sunderland, Newcastle's biggest rivals! I had high hopes that these football clubs would support the work of NAPAC but other events got in the way.

In March 2021 Clive Sheldon KC released his report and recommendations into child protection in soccer and the scandals that prompted the report. It runs to about 770 pages and whilst I wouldn't necessarily recommend you read the whole thing it does give some indication of just how easy it was for corrupt football coaches to manipulate and abuse their charges and how this went on unchallenged for many years. Sheldon also points out that we should not conclude that our children are inherently unsafe in the football world. Certainly not. As I said on TV many years ago the majority of our children are safe but predators will always find ways of inveigling their way into the lives of children and young people. I spoke at some length to Clive Sheldon at the beginning of his assignment but I never thought it would take so many years to produce it.

The thing that depresses me most when I read these shocking reports is that I have been reading similar ones for nearly a quarter of a century and the conclusion I sadly come to is that things have not radically improved. Children are still not as safe as they should be. We have been having inquiries and investigations and recommendations for decades but we, as a society, are still not taking the protection of our children seriously enough. We've had child protection charities for well over a hundred years (and some of them are very well funded), but we still cannot say all our children are safe. The majority are, but a minority are not and that is unacceptable.

Chapter 35

Another phone call I received on holiday in Switzerland in the Summer of 2019 was from the chair of Trustees of NAPAC. It came within 24 hours of the journalist from the *Mail on Sunday* ringing me. The chair said, 'I have had an accurate report from the man at the *Mail on Sunday* newspaper.' I knew then that I was in deep trouble because that "report" was far from accurate.

But, as I should have done with the secretary to the Child Abuse Inquiry, I told the chair that everything the journalist was threatening to print was based on malicious lies and falsehoods, and that I would enjoy the last few days on holiday with Tricia and get back to him as soon as I arrived home.

My mother used to say, 'Don't be too hasty.' I can't quite remember what she was referring to but I know being hasty is one of my many faults and by resigning from the inquiry within minutes of taking their phone call, I knew I had acted irrationally.

To remind you, Tricia and I were having a break in Switzerland when the phone call came that was to ruin my life. The phone call was from a journalist from the *Mail on Sunday* and came less than a week after I had been interviewed for *Channel 4 News* about the scandal surrounding allegations of sexual abuse by a member of the British royal family. Was this a coincidence?

I should have simply put the phone down as soon as I realised the journalist was threatening to regurgitate the malicious lies of an allegation of rape against me 11 years earlier. I knew I hadn't done anything wrong, but being hasty I wanted to set the record straight with this man who was threatening to ruin me. He told me that they weren't sure whether to run the story or not, but it was clear from the outset that they would. Never let the truth get in the way of a good story! The *Mail on Sunday* was determined to shut me up.

I was aware of the reputation of this particular journalist and I had actually been on a TV programme with him (not in the same studio I might add) a few weeks earlier. And in that particular current affairs programme, *Victoria Derbyshire,* on the BBC, he and I were very much on different sides in a discussion about child abuse and false allegations. And now here he was regurgitating the false allegations that two women had made back in 2008.

I told him to go to the police who would verify that no crime had been committed, that I wasn't cautioned for any misdemeanour and that the woman had a history of this sort of thing. I told him about the emails that her and her husband had sent in 2014 and how I'd made a formal complaint at Bromley Police Station and as a result she had apologised and retracted her spurious claims. I suppose I appealed to his integrity as a journalist. Big mistake.

The *Mail on Sunday* printed the story a few days later. It was horrific, like a knife through the heart, and the journalist had twisted and manipulated everything I had said to him. As soon as I read the article I knew what an enormous mistake I had made in talking to him and actually believing that he would listen to me and print the truth.

However there were also some very worrying parts of the conversation with him that indicated he had somebody from NAPAC speaking to him about confidential information.

> The article said, *'After giving an interview at the BBC'* (I had given no such interview that morning), *'he joined the woman and her female friend for coffee before the group headed for lunch at a branch of Bella Italia, during which they consumed at least three bottles of wine. Before eating, Mr Saunders, a devout Christian who was appointed by Pope Francis as a member of a Pontifical Commission for the Protection of Minors in 2014, encouraged the group to join hands in prayer and thank God for good fellowship.*
>
> *Later, however, he went upstairs to use the lavatory where, he admitted, the sordid encounter took place in a cubicle. Mr Saunders insists that the episode was initiated by the woman and was entirely consensual, but she later made a complaint to police that she had been raped.'* (Along with her friend in a small toilet cubicle in a busy restaurant.)

Again, all of the above is true (though not the bit about the BBC interview), but it's all a clever play on words. The incident was without a doubt "sordid" but there was no mention of the fact that I had put a stop to it almost as soon as it had started.

> *'It is understood Mr Saunders was arrested and questioned by officers for more than three hours, during*

which he vehemently denied her allegation. Detectives sent a file to the

Crown Prosecution Service, which decided not to proceed due to "insufficient evidence"'.

Not true! I was held six months later in a police cell before being questioned by two detectives but it was not for three hours. Of course, what the journalist didn't say was that after a thorough investigation the police were satisfied I had committed no crime. But why would he? That's not much of a story.

'Describing the drunken encounter, Mr Saunders told the Mail on Sunday*, "She pretty much took me into a cubicle and she performed what they call a sex act on me. I was too drunk to stop it."'*

Again, he should have written, 'She pretty much took me into a cubicle and performed a sex act on me. I put a stop to it.'

'After lunch, the charity chief and the two women continued to drink in local pubs.'

Really? After I was alleged to have raped both of them anally and orally? No! We left the restaurant chatting and laughing but as we headed to a pub we became separated and I never saw them again.

'Mr Saunders admitted he "had little doubt she [the complainant] was an abuse survivor" and agreed research shows abuse victims are vulnerable, prone to mental health issues and, in some cases, seek to deal with trauma by behaving in a sexually inappropriate manner.'

And then, just to stick the knife in a little further, towards the end of the article, the journalist wrote:

'He expressed regret for paying the bill on NAPAC's credit card. "For the past ten years I have berated

myself for my stupidity," he said. "I was entrusted with a NAPAC debit card and on this occasion I abused it."'.

This infuriated me as much as anything in the entire article, because I recalled the journalist going on and on about the credit card bill during our phone call. Not only did he know I'd paid with the card but also exactly how much had been spent. Who gave him that information? I did abuse the card I was entrusted with that day, but only by a couple of bottles of wine. The rest was a legitimate lunch expense. I thought I was meeting with two women who would further the cause of NAPAC. How wrong I was.

I asked one of the Trustees from NAPAC (one with a lot of journalistic experience) whether I should respond to comment requests about the tripe that was now out there in the newspaper and on-line. I never got a response but I didn't spend much time responding to these other requests. Hence the story was mentioned in some other newspapers the day after it appeared in that bastion of truth, the *Mail on Sunday* and the *Mail Online*.

In my opinion I should have responded. What was encouraging was that colleagues from broadcast media got in touch with me to say they had no intention of running the story. They knew me and they knew it was nonsense. It was a non-story. That was certainly the case with the BBC and Sky News. Good on them both. They even sent messages urging me to enjoy my richly deserved holiday which my wife and I were still on.

Sad to say there was little to enjoy for the rest of the holiday as it became clear I had been well and truly stitched up. Once again, 'Watch your back, Pete' was ringing in my ears.

A few days later the chair of Trustees rang to say that with great regret I was being suspended from my job. No big deal there I suppose, given the attention by a national newspaper, but I felt confident that when I returned home everything could be sorted out. Surely everyone would see that this was absolute nonsense, that it was simply an attempt to shut me up.

I had been told in the past that there was quite a lot of jealously about NAPAC and about how much media time we used to get and I was practically always the spokesperson. In fact, when I stood aside as chief executive in 2015 it was so that I could concentrate on what I was good at, which was speaking up for survivors, appealing for greater child protection measures and the occasional bit of fundraising.

What became clear when I got home was that some people had turned on me and some had done so in quite a nasty way. I had emails and tweets forwarded to me by staff at NAPAC from unpleasant people (who didn't know me) but who obviously thought that the rubbish that was in the newspaper was true.

I couldn't believe how narrow-minded these people were and I couldn't believe the nastiness of some individuals. Talk about the hard of thinking! They couldn't see the wood for the trees. I had been accused of anally and orally raping two women in a small restaurant toilet and was then seen leaving the restaurant laughing and joking with the two accusers.

You could hardly make this stuff up.

Likewise, after their investigation the police acknowledged that no crime had taken place.

The thing that infuriated me more than that, however, was not only did one of those women proposition my teenage son, but they also accused him of drugging them. It was all beyond preposterous and as the days turned into a few weeks and I wasn't reinstated, the awful truth dawned on me that the charity wanted to get rid of me. And it might not come as a surprise to know that there were people now involved with the charity that didn't think survivors of abuse should be involved at all.

Crazy but true. What had sustained NAPAC all these years was the passion and hard work that was put into it, not just by me but by many other staff members and volunteers. Many of whom are survivors.

For the next three months I fought to save my job and it made me quite ill. What happened to me as a child was horrific but this was no less traumatic as I fought for my livelihood and my reputation. I was quickly told that the Home Office (the biggest financial backer of NAPAC, funding I had secured when Theresa May was home secretary and funding that was on-going) required action from the charity about the article and a similar sentiment was voiced from the Charity Commission. These two bodies obviously believed everything they read in that disgusting newspaper. Or did they? Who was pulling their strings?

One of the most distressing and, again, unbelievable things that happened during the weeks that followed, and before I became quite unwell with it all, was at one of the hearings I was summoned to by the Trustees of the charity. The utterances of a certain Jonathan King were quoted to me at this occasion. He attacked me publicly, saying that I was a hypocrite.

Jonathan King is a convicted paedophile. He was jailed for seven years in 2001 for abusing teenage boys and once claimed Jimmy Savile was innocent. I had plenty to say about his kind, and for the chair of Trustees to be quoting him to me in a meeting about my future was beyond the pale and hard to take. King even mentioned that my son worked in the media industry, as if that had any bearing on all this nonsense.

I suppose it was then that I realised I might not want to fight to keep my position. Who were these people who were now throwing such crap at me? It was most distressing. In the end I took a payment from the charity and walked away. My world had come caving in and it was hard to take.

For many months after this I remained in a state of depression and it was thanks to my amazing wife and some incredible friends that I kept it all together. At this point I want to mention my dear friend Jon Bentley (and his wonderful family). He is a cycling pal but he is so much more. He accompanied me to the meetings I had with the Trustees and I really don't know how I would have coped without him at my side. They say that when things are bad you find out who your friends are. You certainly do and I am so blessed to have more than my fair share of good friends and my cycling club friends at Big Foot Cycling Club in Bromley have been just that.

Many years ago, during the very earliest days of setting up NAPAC, I was interviewed on *Radio 5 Live*. On the same programme but in a separate studio a convicted paedophile was questioned about his offending. He said one of the greatest deterrents to child abusers was adult survivors speaking out. I then vowed I would always speak out, as long as I have breath in my body. Well, I was silenced as you have read, but not anymore. I don't claim this book you have kindly (some might say bravely) read to be a literary masterpiece but it is the truth, the whole truth and nothing but the truth. So help me …

A favourite saying of mine attributed to a certain book is, 'Then you will know the truth, and the truth will set you free.'

Chapter 36

I still maintain regular contact with my good friends at SNAP. Following their visit to the UK in 2010 to protest at the pope's UK visit, I remained in close contact with Barbara and the organisation. A few months later they invited me to join them at a training weekend in Orlando, Florida.

The choice of venue was clever. Hotel accommodation in the winter was cheap and the weather was beautiful. By all accounts all the SNAP members attending, being Americans, found it a convenient and relatively inexpensive place to get to.

The flight to America was barely a quarter full and I was thrilled to be going to a place that I thought I would never visit and to forge some great friendships with the members of SNAP. David Clohessy, one of the founders of the organisation, was particularly impressive, as was a lady called Barbara Dorris. Actually, they were all pretty impressive people.

David and I really hit it off and I was truly taken with his depth of knowledge about the clergy abuse scandal and his irrepressible way of handling the media. I learnt a great deal from David and like many of his SNAP compatriots, he has a great sense of humour, something which I think is essential when you work in the desperately tragic world of child abuse.

A few months later I was invited to their annual conference and was thrilled to be able to attend. It took place in Chicago, called the Windy City because of the strong winds that blow in from Lake Michigan on which its impressive skyline sits.

I attended the SNAP annual conference for the next six years and the venue alternated between Chicago and Washington DC. They were all very well organised and I made many friends. As well as the main conference speeches and presentations there were always some excellent breakout sessions which were more intimate and where you got to know people better.

One session I remember particularly well and with great sadness, was the one about men who had been abused as children by women, specifically Catholic nuns. I found this most disturbing, particularly as one of my sisters had been a nun and I had spent a fair bit of time at her convent when I was a young boy. Not that I witnessed anything that was vaguely abusive there.

But now we know the truth about what went on in so many Church (and nun) run institutions. Harrowing stories emerge to this very day about what was done to young girls and children in the "Industrial schools" of Ireland and in many other parts of the world. I understand when talking about child sexual abuse, why men come to mind. This is not always the case though, there are hundreds of well documented cases throughout history that have shown that there are women sex offenders too, but they do not fall into the nice stereotypes that male sex offenders do. The Lucy Faithfull Foundation (LFF), a child protection charity that deals with sex offenders, said its studies and results indicated that up to 20% of the UK's 320,000 suspected paedophiles are women. Frightening statistics.

If anyone questions the statement that women also abuse I would throw in just a few names: Myra Hindley, Rose West, Vanessa George, Angela Allen and Marie Black. The latter was jailed in 2015 for 23 offences including rape, conspiracy to rape and inciting a child to engage in sexual activity.

Most human beings do not respond well to the imposition of a law of celibacy and while some people may well be able to live a celibate life, Dr Richard Sipe's research would seem to indicate that for Catholic clergy at least, half of them don't manage it and there are thousands of priests who will wish that they could go back in time and rewrite history, have a quiet word with the popes of the Middle Ages and ask them to think again.

In the 11th century Pope Benedict VIII responded to the decline in priestly morality by issuing a rule prohibiting the children of priests from inheriting property. The Church was a thousand years old before it definitively took a stand in favour of celibacy. At the Second Council of the Lateran, held in 1139, the rule was approved forbidding priests to marry and reaffirmed the rule of celibacy. But it's not just the priests. Nuns, the brides of Christ, have been deprived by their church of leading and enjoying fulfilling, normal lives by taking a vow of poverty, chastity and obedience.

I am in my 66th year and my greatest life achievement is, without a doubt, my family, my children and grandchildren. I have experienced fatherhood and in later years the joys of becoming a grandfather. I've watched the sheer devotion and unconditional love a mother heaps upon her children. I'll use the phrase again, it's how we were all programmed, whether you believe in a deity or in Mother Nature it makes no difference. For an organisation to deprive a man or a woman of experiencing the joys of sex and the incredible satisfaction of parenthood defies any logic.

I attended a male survivor conference in New York and one of the breakout sessions was for survivors of clergy abuse. Practically every religious denomination was represented at that session. We, (the majority were Catholics) had suffered at the hands of priests but I remember another young man who had suffered at the hands of his rabbi and another who had been abused by the imam at his mosque. Men raised in other religious denominations told similar stories and the common denominator amongst all these men is that they had all lost their faith. I stress, faith in a higher power, as opposed to belief in a religious, man-made, institution. I have long since lost my faith in these institutions which have failed and continue to fail to protect our children from the evil of abuse. Or to support the adult survivors of that abuse.

It was at one of the SNAP conferences that I also first met Miguel Hurtado. At the age of sixteen, Miguel had joined the Scout Association of Montserrat on the recommendation of a friend of his mother's. Miguel, who had just begun to accept his homosexuality and who was dealing with it day by day, confided in the 60-year-old monk who had founded the scout group, a man loved and respected by the community.

Believing himself safe in Monserrat, Miguel confided in the priest who, under the pretext of helping him heal, sexually abused him. Miguel has written a book, *El Manual del Silencio, La historia de pederastia en la Iglesia que nadie quiso escuchar.* It translates to *The Manual of Silence, the history of paedophilia in the church that nobody wants to hear* and tells the story of his family and his path as a victim of sexual abuse in a society in which the Catholic Church still has immense power.

And what a history, what power, the church has in Spain. There aren't too many people outside of Spain who have heard of the Spanish missing children, it makes what happened in Ireland look like a drop in the ocean. The media has dubbed them the lost children of the Franco regime. As many as 300,000 babies are estimated to have been abducted from their mothers during the Franco era of 1939-75, and in the decades after his death.

The theft of new-borns began during the Spanish civil war. There wasn't one specific reason while babies were removed from their mothers, but it was generally seen as an ideological practice. Babies were taken away from left-wing or Marxist parents who were traditionally anti-Franco. They were also taken to benefit couples who were sympathetic to the Francoist regime and could not have children. It was claimed in some quarters that the kidnapping was state policy. A priest who did not wish to be named said it was all about indoctrinating them into the good Catholic, state model. Where have I heard that before?

The numbers of the Spanish missing children will always be disputed, but by 1943, only four years after the end of the Spanish Civil War, official figures tell us that 12,043 Republican children were in state custody. However, the number exploded during the 1950s, when poor families were targeted and classed as morally deficient. Many children were removed because the families were 'not good Catholics.' And yes, you've guessed it, the Catholic Church was directly involved and complicit in the process of removing the babies and the operation to rehome them.

Often the new mothers were told that their babies had died and the hospitals had taken care of the burials. They were sold for adoption. A well-run national agency involving a wide network of doctors, nurses, nuns, priests, cardinals and bishops sold the majority of the babies to America for as much as $10,000 each.

It was a lucrative trade and continued after Franco's death until 1987 when a new adoption law was implemented.

When I was interviewed for the Spanish Netflix documentary, *Examen de conciencia* (Examine your conscience) I said that the Catholic Church is the largest employer of child abusers on the planet.

I stand by that. Many of us have known for some time that the institutional church remains a fundamentally unsafe place, not only for children but for all people with a vulnerability. And saying what I said then will have undoubtedly added to the Church's desire to silence me.

Miguel's book was launched in 2019 just before the COVID-19 pandemic hit and therefore hasn't sold many copies but I'm pleased to say that he has become one of the main activists in the fight against abuse in the Catholic Church.

Barbara Blaine, founder of SNAP, died at just 61 years of age. I could hardly believe it when I heard. She was always so full of energy. She didn't smoke, drink or do any of the things that we are not supposed to and she kept very fit. She never seemed to slow down in her fight to get justice and to hold the Church to account.

She was undoubtedly the greatest and most effective thorn in the side of the Church. Whilst I would consider her to be one of Heaven's greatest acquisitions she is undoubtedly one of our greatest losses. She rang me just a few weeks before she died and left a message on my voicemail, thanking me for all I was doing and encouraged me to carry on. That was so typical of Barbara. And what was so painful was that I never rang her back, figuring I would get round to it when I was a little less busy.

Barbara Blaine's legacy lives on in a very real and powerful way. Not long before her untimely death she had mooted the idea of a different kind of organisation to tackle the Church and to hold it accountable. She gathered like-minded people from all over the world to do this, including me. She effectively sowed the seeds of an organisation, of which I am also proud to be one of the founders. As mentioned earlier, it is called ECA - Ending Clergy Abuse.

ECA was formally established in Geneva in the Summer of 2018. The thrust of the organisation is to hold the Church (or any other religious body) to account and to demand action to end the duplicity which exists around these crimes. Membership consists of people from all the continents.

On every occasion possible ECA would ensure it made its presence felt. We went to Ireland when the pope was visiting that country and we went to South America when he visited Chile and Peru. My time in those countries was amazing. I had visited South America before for a holiday - to Bolivia, Peru and the Galapagos Islands but I never thought I'd be flying so far to support survivors of abuse as they protested at a papal visit. It was a long flight to Chile, kindly paid for by Pete Townshend, and when I arrived I had to make my own way from the airport to the city. But it was an easy journey. I had been warned to avoid taxi drivers offering deals and I took a bus which was cheap and delivered me right to the centre of Santiago. From there I was able to walk to the hotel that ECA had booked for us all. Other ECA members flew in from Europe and North, South and Central America.

When I was in Chile I was privileged to meet the parishioners of Osorno mentioned earlier, who the pope had spoken so unkindly about. A bus full of them came up from Osorno, which lies many miles south of the capital. Nicer, more humble people you could not meet. People who had been so dedicated to their Church but who were now being let down so badly by the very institution they had followed and supported their whole lives.

Another thing that came to mind while I was in Chile was the tragic recent history of that beautiful country. How the elected democratic government had been overthrown by a fascist dictatorship led by General Pinochet and how many people had been murdered or disappeared during that tragic time. And I recall how the British Government gave succour to Pinochet in 1998, with surprise, surprise, support from the Vatican.

Strange how many murderous dictators tend to be church-going Catholics.

It should be noted that a great deal of controversy still hangs over the activities of the current pope when he was a senior cleric in his home country of Argentina. I often wonder why he didn't visit home during that South American trip, with Chile geographically so close.

The arrogance of some of these clerics is quite staggering, but sadly it is not uncommon. There are many who believe they are untouchable. One of the reasons we founded ECA was to ensure that clergy and the institutions that they represent are always held to account and brought to justice whenever possible.

I was still involved with ECA at the time of the *Mail on Sunday* story. I'd heard second-hand that one of the board members suggested that, as an organisation, they distance themselves from me. That was disappointing to hear, but I'm pleased to say my many friends within ECA have continued to stand by me. Who knows, in the future I may get involved again. I looked at their website just recently and I was glad to see that my photograph still appears several times in their gallery section, though sadly not in the section titled "Founders of ECA".

Chapter 37

'Those who do not move never feel their chains.'
Rosa Luxembourg.'

This chapter could have been either the shortest or the longest of the book. For your benefit I will make it the shortest.

As I have already shared with you, God has been a constant in my life. For many years I didn't question the existence of God. I didn't question my faith. I was raised in one of the biggest Catholic parishes in the country and being part of that community was as normal to me as going to school or riding my bike. As a child I never missed Sunday mass. My parents usually only socialised with other Catholics and my education from age five to 16 was entirely Catholic. Even my first cycling club was Catholic. For me it wasn't just church on Sundays, my way of life was guided by the indoctrination in all aspects of my life, as it was for the adults and other children around me. Little wonder I have found it hard to shake off those roots.

Talking to God throughout the day was second nature to me. I chatted away to him (not out loud I would hasten to add) as if he were in the room. I took great comfort from that. When on my bike I would ask him to keep me upright when the physical challenges of rubber tyres on greasy roads might have landed me on the tarmac. When I didn't crash it was because God had heard my prayer, when I did crash (and I've done that a good few times) I thanked God my injuries were not worse! He could do no wrong.

Having faith has brought me great comfort over the years. I didn't understand why my prayers went unanswered on so many occasions, but I trusted in God's almighty power and love and believed he had a plan for me. This extended to the tragedies in my life such as the death of my lovely niece. I prayed so hard that God would heal her from leukaemia, an illness she suffered from for five years. He didn't heal her and when she died I took comfort that she was in heaven and that we had been blessed with her company for 17 years. I questioned why God took her and those around me said, 'She is in Heaven', 'We will see her again' and 'She was too good for this world'. I accepted those answers and never really questioned whether God existed.

Also, when Dad died I believed the experience I had in his bedroom that day was of God or at least of a strong spiritual presence. That day I had a strong sense that God was telling me to do something about child abuse. It felt overwhelming and seemed to fill my very being. This may all sound quite strange but I felt compelled to speak out about what had happened to me as a child and that lead to me setting up NAPAC. I believed until recently that was God's plan for me. I didn't question that. For years I attributed all the good things that were happening to me and NAPAC to a benevolent God.

When things went wrong, I believed it was because of my badness. I attributed it to me falling out of favour with God. It took me back to my childhood and that indoctrination of the stain of original sin. It's probably why I worked so hard. There were many benefits from my hard work and my opportunist character meant I was able to achieve great things for the charity.

In recent years I have questioned my faith. Or should I say, I have questioned the bases of where that faith came from. I have also recognised what a malign influence religion has had in the world. On the question of child abuse the Roman Catholic Church as an institution, perhaps more than any other, actively harbours and protects those who hurt our little ones. What happened to the words of Jesus, whose simple message as far as I am aware was to 'Love one another.'? The abuse of a child is as far away from loving one another as you can get!

Faith without the institutions, spiritual meaning without organised rhetoric, worshipping free of charge is a nice concept, but one that most religious institutions will persuade you against. They prey on the individual's fear of death, of not knowing what happens after your life on earth. So, a few thousand years ago, someone suggests that there is a pleasant place high above the clouds where an individual can live forever, where he or she will meet up with old friends and members of the family long gone. And there are angels playing harps and there is no war and no conflict, and everybody lives happily ever after. Sounds heavenly!

In order to get to that heavenly place, you must toe the line and worship and pray and pay and obey an institution into which you were born. And you could argue our religion is merely an accident of birth, nothing more nothing less. Take a boy born in Islamabad, or a girl born in Southampton. Or to take it even further, the boy born to Protestant parents in Belfast, or the girl born to Catholic parents in Belfast. You are simply brought up to follow the religion of your parents, indoctrinated from a young age that your God is the only true God, and all the others are wrong.

Looking at the hard reality of the long history of religion and the malign influence it has had on the world I should have come to a conclusion a long time ago about the existence of God. But I say again, I am a slow learner. Plenty has been written about this long history and generally it does not make for very comfortable reading. In fact, it is almost impossible not to conclude that religion and people's desire to believe in something better, like a wonderful afterlife, is based on little more than a Bronze Age superstition and a great deal of taletelling and lying. And these tales go back way beyond the time of Christ. His story, the description of the life of a man called Jesus, had been written or recorded many times before he came along on Christmas Day two thousand years ago. The hieroglyphics of the ancient Egyptians had described an almost identical person called Horus, of who it is written that he was born of a virgin, had twelve disciples, walked on water, delivered a sermon on a mount, performed miracles and was executed beside two thieves, rose from the dead and ascended into Heaven, thousands of years before the birth of Christ.

Let's face it, even thousands of years ago there were people who wanted to control the world and what better way than to invent a belief that says someone is watching your every move? 24/7, 365 days a year and it applies to the entire population of the world and has done forever. As

I type these words, I am so conscious that some people reading them, particularly close friends and family who believe, will find what I say painful. I am not rejecting everything I used to believe but it may seem like that, or feel like an attack on them, which it absolutely isn't.

I am tempted to say that I envy that belief. Faith can be such a comfort and in times of strife particularly so. Maybe deep down I want to retain that faith. Call it an insurance policy! I was once told that when I gave my life to Jesus, nothing could separate us. Only time will tell if that is true.

If I had to sum up in a few short sentences why I now struggle to be a believer, it is not just because I have read and studied the history of these beliefs, it is because I have met many people with strong religious views across various faiths who have shown more hatred for their fellow man than any atheist I have met. If you are gay, you are going to Hell. If you don't follow the Ten Commandments, you are going to Hell. Had an abortion? You are going to Hell.

I was brought up to believe that if I did not go to Mass on a Sunday, I committed a mortal sin and I was going to Hell. I never quite got my head around how the Roman Catholic Church suddenly said it was no longer a mortal sin to miss Sunday Mass as long as you went on a Saturday evening. All of a sudden, some men decided they would re-order what was or was not a hell-bound mortal sin!

A bit like celibacy in their Church. I don't remember reading anything in the Bible about priests (whatever a priest is) not being able to marry. But a pope a few hundred years ago decided to change the rules around that. I wonder why. A little research will reveal the answer.

Some years ago I was attending a conference in New York. When I got into my hotel room, I switched on the TV and tuned into one of their many "God" channels. The preacher was actually saying that if you send him ten thousand dollars you will receive a 'miracle'. It was laughable, sad but laughable. Do people fall for this stuff? I suppose some do. It's bizarre that a God who knows everything, and can do absolutely everything (including miracles), always seems to need your money and the poorer people are, the more they seem to give. Religion is big business, there is little doubt about that and people of religion almost always have an answer as to why God does or does not do something in a particular situation. If someone dies, it's God's will. If someone lives, it's God's will. People all over the world suffer unimaginable pain and torment but it's all God's will. Even insurance companies wriggle out of paying up if the insured event is an "act of God". Well God must be mighty busy, that's all I can say.

If there really is a God, a truly loving God, why would there be so much suffering in the world? Why doesn't this benevolent man in the sky make us all good people? As Ricky Gervais once said, 'If there is a God why did he make me an atheist?' Apparently, God doesn't make mistakes! The obvious religious answer to this is that God gave us free will. See, there is an answer to everything! And countless books have been written about why God "allows" such suffering. But if I was God, I wouldn't want people to suffer.

I stress again that some of the most unpleasant, greedy, manipulative people I have met are people of faith and some of those people are almost gleeful when they pronounce that someone is going to Hell. But I've already been there. Having a man lie on top of you and abuse you when you are a child – that is Hell.

And doubtless some will say that Hell is where I will be heading. But I think I may be in good company because if it is only people of faith who go to Heaven, I think I would prefer the other place. I don't relish the thought of rubbing souls with the likes of Adolf Hitler, Mussolini, Jimmy Savile, Father Fernando Karadima, Father Marcial Maciel or General Franco, to name a few.

Let's be honest, more people have died in the name of religion than any other cause and we don't have to go back to the Crusades or the Inquisition. Look at the massacres of Bosnian men and children in 1995, and who on this planet doesn't know about the attack on the Twin Towers in New York in 2001 or the 7/7 bombings in London in 2005?

The recent Independent Inquiry into Child Sexual Abuse in England and Wales found that *every* religious institution that was examined was guilty of failing to protect our children. Worse still, all these institutions were found to have covered up these vile crimes and protected the perpetrators. Not very Godlike, you may conclude.

I don't think I need to say much more about this. Do I miss my faith? Of course I do. But I cannot have faith in something that is based on demonstrable lies. What a wonderful place the world would be if it was full of good people. Some might say that because the world is not full of good people we need a God to keep an eye on them. But if there is a God then he or she (or it) is clearly a very hands-off deity.

I feel I am in a place of mourning right now. I no longer have the faith that, at times, has sustained me over many years. But I do I reserve the right to pray if I want to. And I have no objection to anyone who wants to pray for me. I'm just not sure who might be listening. These days it's likely to be Google, Siri or Alexa who pick up the pleadings and try to make money out of them! I said this chapter would be short and I will stick to that promise. However, if you can bear it, I give below some more thoughts about why I have readjusted my faith and beliefs. I will describe some factual accounts of the atrocities that have been perpetrated by employees of the Catholic Church. Employees, who I would remind you, were all protected by the church of Rome.

There is the case of Mexican priest Father Marcial Maciel. He was honoured by Pope John Paul II and revered by many in the church as its greatest ever fundraiser. Late in his life Maciel was revealed to be a prolific abuser of children, an abuser of young women and it turned out he fathered as many as six children.

Chilean priest Father Fernando Karadima was another prolific abuser of young boys. For years this man was defended and protected by the church. Another man, another priest, who witnessed Karadima's crimes was promoted by Pope Francis to Bishop of Osorno. When the people of that city protested at this outrageous promotion, the pope called them 'dumb'. Karadima was eventually defrocked by the pope but only after a huge tide of publicity and public anger vented by his many victims.

I won't go into the whole issue of abuse and cover-ups in Boston, USA. I have mentioned it before. Suffice to say that the scale of those abuses in that city was on an horrific industrial scale. Remember *Spotlight*.

One of the reasons I suspect the pope has never returned to his native Argentina is because of the many church abuse scandals that have emerged in that country.

Indeed, there is scandal and abuse outrages emanating from places where the pope worked before he became pope. And many of his fellow countrymen and women have pleaded with 'their' pope to do something about it and surprise, surprise the pope has done nothing.

I would cite the case of the Colegio del Salvador where a Jesuit Brother, Cesar Fretes, was credibly accused of abusing more than 40 children. Fretes died in 2015 and whilst the Colegio acknowledged that he had been a prolific abuser they did nothing by way of compensating or helping his many victims. It also remains very unclear to what extent the current pope, when an archbishop in Argentina, cooperated or didn't cooperate with that country's former fascist government.

And I think back to a conversation I had with a nun nearly 30 years ago. Coming out of church, not long after my dad had died and just after I had revealed what had happened to me as a child, she asked me how I was feeling. I said I was not feeling good. She wanted to know why. I walked back to her convent with her and told her all about it. Her first words were, 'Have you prayed about forgiveness?' Not, 'Oh my God Peter, you poor man,' or even 'Gosh, we must report these abusers to the authorities.' No. I was given the responsibility of forgiving the men who had violated me and there didn't seem to be a flicker of care about what those perpetrators might be doing now. I think that sort of sums up why my faith has been so shaken. If there is a God then maybe I will have it out with him or her one day but in the meantime I will place my faith in the goodness of people and our ability to battle evil … and child abuse is most certainly evil.

Chapter 38

A few last thoughts. Reading this book will probably not have been easy. Reading graphic accounts of child abuse can be very traumatising. My footnote to that is to ask how the child (the little me) was feeling when these things happened. And even though they happened a long time ago they can still remain very fresh in our minds. And sometimes these horrific events emerge in our minds as though they have just happened. These are called flashbacks. And flashbacks can occur just about anytime and anywhere. I mentioned the man on the tube smelling of beer while he rubbed up against me. He's lucky I didn't punch him in the face. I came close. Luckily for him I got off the train instead. Ask any survivor.

Someone asked me what the purpose of this book is and what I hope the reader will take from it. Well, there are a few reasons I wrote it. Number one is that over the years many people said that I should. I think it is important that people know what child abuse really is. Know that attacks on children, whether they are physical, sexual, or psychological have profound, damaging and long-lasting effects. There are already some good books that describe this damage, the most powerful are written by adults who found ways to survive the trauma well enough to tell their stories. *Because It Didn't Stop When It Ended* (Gutenberg Press) is an example of one such book. My story goes beyond a personal experience of both familial and institutional abuse and I hope has provided an overview of this deep rooted social evil.

We should also appreciate that the costs to society of not tackling child abuse and neglect are truly astronomical. Many studies have looked at the social and economic costs of child abuse and these are staggering. I am also conscious that since I was effectively silenced, I never see or hear anyone, any survivors, speaking in the British media about the scourge of abuse. I never professed to represent all survivors, far from it, but I was given a regular platform from which to speak out and I see no one doing that now. You might conclude that the backlash is complete. Child abuse is back in the box. Swept under the carpet again. And this, after I spent years trying to drag it in to the open. It's one nasty disease that can thrive when the light of publicity is turned off. And that is my greatest fear - that child abuse, as Tony Benn once said to me, 'will always be with us'.

Speaking out was the least I could do, and I have done that for nearly three decades. I will leave it to you, the reader, to decide if I was treated fairly. Have I made mistakes? Yes, I have. Hands up who hasn't? Have I been downright stupid from time to time? Probably. Have I done my best? I hope so. Did I set up an amazing organisation to support survivors? Yes. No one can take that from me. And what have my rewards been? An attack from certain sections of the media and some pretty unpleasant individuals. Certainly, but as Pete Townshend said to me, 'When the *Mail on Sunday* attacks you, you know you are doing something right!'

I was privileged to receive a personal commendation from the Commissioner of the Metropolitan Police for my contribution to Operation Yewtree (the Savile scandal). I have a lovely picture of me receiving my commendation from Sir Bernard Hogan-Howe. I know that the organisation I started will have saved many lives over the years. That's good to know. I currently live on a pension that keeps me significantly below the poverty line. But and again, I stress it is a very big but, I have amazing friends and family all over the world and nothing is more dear to me than that.

I hope this book has not given the impression that it is only the Catholic Church that has so badly let children down. As the Independent Inquiry into Child Sexual Abuse stated in its report every religious institution it examined was just as guilty. And it is not just religious institutions. Institutions of all kinds have been guilty of allowing abuse to thrive.

As I have tried to make clear throughout my many years of working in this painful area of social tragedy, it all comes down to people, not institutions. They are made up of people and it's people who betray children. And when it comes to the greatest threat to children, that threat comes from within the family. The overwhelming majority of calls to the NAPAC Support Line were from people talking about abuse at the hands of a family member.

And that, dear reader, requires another book.

Printed in Great Britain
by Amazon

55391086R00179